Who Do You Think You Are... Michael Schumacher?

Who Do You Think You Are… Michael Schumacher?

IAN STAFFORD

EBURY PRESS

First published in Great Britain in 2005

10 9 8 7 6 5 4 3 2 1

First published by
Ebury Press
Random House, 20 Vauxhall Bridge Road, London SW1V 2SA

Random House Australia (Pty) Limited
20 Alfred Street, Milsons Point, Sydney, New South Wales 2061, Australia

Random House New Zealand Limited
18 Poland Road, Glenfield, Auckland 10, New Zealand

Random House South Africa (Pty) Limited
Endulini, 5A Jubilee Road, Parktown 2193, South Africa

The Random House Group Limited Reg. No. 954009

www.randomhouse.co.uk

A CIP catalogue record for this book is available from the British Library.

Cover Design by Two Associates
Text design and typesetting by Textype

ISBN 009190160X

Papers used by Ebury Press are natural, recyclable products made from wood grown in sustainable forests.

Printed and bound in Great Britain by Clays Ltd, St Ives plc

CONTENTS

PROLOGUE

An early May evening, seven years ago. I had just concluded an interview with Jacques Villeneuve, the Canadian Formula One driver, and was leaving the paddock at the Silverstone circuit in my Volkswagen Passat Estate.

In order to exit the site one had to first use a small part of the actual race track. This, I surmised, as I cruised around a bend, was cool. Really cool. But not as cool as what was about to take place.

Suddenly, right in front of me, was the unmistakable, red Ferrari sports car belonging to Michael Schumacher, the then double world champion. The German had completed a long day of testing and was meandering his way back to his overnight digs close by, no doubt consumed by his own thoughts of the session just gone and the session the following day.

Behind him the lights of a Volkswagen dazzled as the car fell into the Ferrari's slipstream. There might have been an empty crisp packet on the car's carpet, a half-drunk bottle of fizzy drink and an Action Man minus his left arm in the back, but the family estate had just transformed itself into a mean machine.

I had never daydreamed of this moment before, never given it any thought at all. But in a split-second a thirty-four-year-old man was suddenly consumed by an irresistible urge to seize a chance he would most probably never have again for the rest of his life.

Lurching my car rather dramatically out to the right I slammed my foot down on the gas and overtook the greatest racing driver the sport has ever known in a manoeuvre that, obviously, caught Schumacher cold.

Momentarily, as our cars drew level, we exchanged glances. Mine was somewhat triumphant whereas his, as he squinted in the blinding low sunlight of a summer's dusk, was a mixture of weary annoyance.

I wasn't surprised by this reaction at all. After all, I had just shown him how to overtake at Silverstone. It happened so quickly he had no time to reply to my impressive move. Resigned, he watched me turn right out of the circuit and head towards the A43.

That night, back at home, I felt rather pleased with myself. I felt rather good about it the next day, too, and the one after that. In fact, as the days turned into weeks, then months and now years, it still gives me puerile pleasure to think that I outsmarted the smartest driver on the Formula One grid.

My wife has a different view of this. 'Can you imagine how many times that poor man must be subjected to idiots like you overtaking him and then pretending you'd just beaten him in a race?' she reasoned.

Well, what does she know? Michael and I know the truth, and that's all that matters. And if he ever wants a rematch I'll be ready and waiting.

chapter one

TESTICLES

'Thud.'

Once my body had stopped jarring, and the vehicle I was wedged into had ceased to spin, I surveyed the scene. I was in a kart, a motorised contraption that looked a little like the kind of lawnmower people with huge gardens, fat wallets and obsessions with straight lines in grass tend to sit astride and steer on Sunday afternoons.

One moment I had been approaching a corner. The next I was sliding off the tarmac, initially front on but, once the spin kicked in, sideways and ultimately backwards before careering into a wall of strategically placed rubber tyres.

The circuit was completely mine. Nobody else would have been crazy enough to have driven in conditions which would have made a monsoon seem preferable.

My vision had been sufficiently impaired by a helpful

combination of torrential rain and condensation covering my visor; I was sitting in a small puddle of rainwater in my seat, and my waterproofs were anything but waterproof. I was, in short, cold, wet, half-blind and now, among the tyres and off the circuit, just crashed.

It was as far removed from the sight of Michael Schumacher spraying his champagne from the heat of the Australian Formula One Grand Prix winner's podium just the day before in Melbourne as one could possibly imagine. If he was at the very apex of the motor-racing pyramid, I found myself at the very base.

As I waited for all my bones to settle down and find their rightful homes I came to a weary conclusion. Not for the first time in my life, this was my wife's fault. Entirely hers.

If I'd been given five pounds for every time she had criticised my driving I would be a very wealthy man. Not even five pounds, now I think about it. Fifty pence would suffice. Fifty pence for every tut, every look, every loud exhalation of breath, and every purposefully conspicuous grip of the passenger seat, and I'd have Bill Gates and Roman Abramovich asking me for loans. Probably together.

A week or so before we had endured a scene familiar to every relationship just about anywhere in the world. I was at the wheel and my wife was complaining over the way I was choosing to drive. In the back seats I could see by looking in the mirror above me that both my children were exchanging glances and rolling their eyes as their parents ventured down a well-trodden path. I was driving too dangerously, my wife informed me, I'm reckless, and I'm way too fast. I enquired, seeing how she was such a fine driver herself, whether she'd like to take the wheel, then, adding that the journey would take an hour longer as a result and we'd no doubt get lost in the process.

Hah! We had ventured into an area which, as half of the planet's population will readily agree, provides man with the opportunity to play his joker. Be less than enamoured with my untidiness. Moan at my distinct lack of success when it comes to DIY. Complain about my attitude when I've had one beer too many. But never, ever, under any circumstances, criticise my driving.

Why? Well, I hardly feel an explanation is necessary. Man is better at driving than woman. That's a proven fact. Well, it's not, technically, but everybody knows this to be the case. We're more confident than women in a car. We're braver. We have a more natural affinity with the car. We have a bond, a togetherness, a fraternity. If it isn't a God-given right that the male half of the world's population are better drivers, then it should be. Man and car is like fish and water; birds and the air; fat, British tourists and sunburn. They just go together.

So, when it comes to my family everyone knows I am the number one driver. I know it. The kids know it. And I bet even my wife knows it. (Incidentally, I am a better navigator, too, another area in which fifty per cent of the human race also seems to have the upper hand, but let's not open up that can of worms here). Yet – and here's the irony of all this – she still believes she has the right to question my driving, not occasionally, but on virtually every journey we ever take. As far as I'm concerned, this is like Rolf Harris making suggestions to Michelangelo over the best use of his oils.

Actually, men do not believe that they are merely better drivers than any woman on any road anywhere in the world. They are convinced, too, that they are better drivers than any other man. Hence the constant gesticulations between passing men on a road as each takes the view that the other has made the error, is in the wrong and, obviously, is an inferior driver. I seem to get a particular type of hand movement offered to me by other male drivers all the time. Come to think about it, I get it whether I've done something wrong or not. Why else do only men become involved in road rage incidents, mad chases, and races on motorways?

The answer is that, alongside astronauts, engine drivers, World Cup-winning footballers and lumberjacks, men have always wanted to be racing drivers at some point in their lives. As a boy it is first on just about everyone's wish list. And, once you are sitting in a car, you can make some of it come true.

'Who do you think you are?' my wife enquired during our latest vehicular contretemps. 'Michael bloody Schumacher?' Now, to be fair to my wife, even she has heard of Michael 'bloody' Schumacher, on the basis that he is the best racing driver in the world by a major distance and, judging by the records he has set, in the history of the sport.

This, despite being uttered in the midst of an argument, struck an immediate chord. The first reason was personal and exclusive to me. That May evening seven years earlier at Silverstone was still as fresh in my mind as if it had just taken place. I still recalled exactly the pained expression on the German's face as I sped past, my unbelievably puerile joy, the misguided conviction that my overtaking manoeuvre had outsmarted the master, and the tremendous glee I have taken ever since in recounting the same, tired story to the same, tired friends.

So, yes, come to think about it. That was the answer to my wife's sarcastic question. I do think I'm Michael 'Bloody' Schumacher. Well, at least I did back then. I gave this notion some reflection as the predictable silence that follows every argument presented some valuable thinking time in the car.

When you boil it right down the main difference between Schumacher and me was the fact that he drove a much faster car than me, and had around thirty years more practice. Maybe, if I had started racing one day after being born, or when still a foetus, or whatever age it was when the German first started to race, I'd be as good as him now?

It's a hypothetical question that can never be answered. Schumacher will just have to accept, as an irrefutable fact, that he will never know if I would have been as good as him if presented with the same, level playing field.

Given that I couldn't possibly hope to emulate the great man, there was still no reason why I could not prove my worth as a motor racing driver. I kept my initial thoughts to myself, of course, as I fixed my eyes firmly on the road ahead and observed my children pinching each other in the back. If my wife was reading my mind just then she would have been well within her rights to have made a quick exit from the car, even if it was moving, and an equally rapid phone call to the nearest mental institution.

The second reason was not only universal but, as I analysed it more deeply, the overriding issue. I had just turned forty years of age. This, frankly, was not only unbelievable, but ridiculous. So ridiculous that I had kept on examining how this could possibly be the case. I didn't act forty. I didn't look forty, I convinced myself. For goodness sake, it was only a day or so ago that I was leaving university. Only five minutes earlier that I had turned thirty. How the hell could this have possibly happened?

I looked into the wing mirror again. I had a sixteen-year-old daughter. For Christ's sake! She was old enough to get married! When I first became a father, once I had overcome the terrible shock of disjointed nights, a wrecked social life and disgusting nappies, I thought it would be rather good to have a virtually grown-up daughter who would see her cool, still young, forty-year-old father as her soulmate and her companion, who would discuss music, and social issues, and boys with him, and who would actually want to have a drink with him in a bar with her friends.

That illusion had long since evaporated. What I failed to realise at twenty-four, but what I now understood at forty, was that the age difference mattered less than the fact that, whichever way we looked at it, she was my daughter, and I her father and that, because of this parameter, I was of a different generation. As a result, if I made a comment about music/fashion/boys/absolutely anything, it was always wide of the mark because . . . well because, how the hell would I know at the ripe old age of forty?

It was still silent in the car, save for the noise of the potted plants falling over in the back and scattering soil all over a paperback copy of the *Book of the Road*. Yes, I was almost ashamed to admit, we were, indeed, returning from the garden centre, like countless other families who live in the sprawling conurbation known as suburbia. After we had returned home I thought I might just wash the car, or clear out the garage and drive to the local refuse dump. Hey, the options are countless when you lead as wild a life as this.

But hold on a minute! This description had not been strictly fair, at least not in the recent past. I had been leading a double life. On the one hand there was suburban man, with his garden centre trips, parents' evenings at schools and dinner parties.

On the other hand there had been numerous journeys to exotic corners of the globe: to the Khyber Pass and the Rift Valley, to Copacabana Beach and Table Mountain. To Tokyo and Sydney, Bangkok and New York, Greenland and New Zealand. To practically everywhere!

Better still were the experiences. I had made a living writing about my sporting adventures in these far-flung lands. I had played football with the Brazilians, and rugby with the South Africans. I had run with the Kenyans, played squash with the Pakistanis and cricket with the Australians. I had boxed against American world champions, rowed with British Olympic gold medallists, played golf with Inuit in the high Arctic, and ridden elephants playing polo in Thailand. It wasn't quite Action Man, but it had been a pretty colourful last few years.

A friend of mine once admitted that when his company invited me to any kind of function he would always press the 'speaker' button on the telephone so that the whole office could hear my excuses. 'We used to have a sweepstake with a list of ridiculous excuses,' he admitted. Once I came up with the true fact that I would be in Finland competing in the world air guitar championships, live on stage, in front of thousands of music fans. 'One of us actually got that one right,' he added.

Right now, though, that office sweep would show items such as trips to the garden centre, the DIY warehouse, the dump, the supermarket and the video rental shop. Not exactly rock and roll.

Well, forty or not, there was no way on this earth that I was simply going to bow out of my well-extended youth, grow up and succumb to the onset of middle age. No way! For the past two years playing golf to the extent of meeting Tiger Woods had supposedly conditioned me for this but now, with my fortieth birthday party been and gone, and the hilariously funny greetings cards banging on about my 'old age' read and discarded, I was not going to lie down without one heck of a fight. The rot was beginning to set in. I had to stop it.

My mini-revolt was to complete the London Marathon, something I duly achieved in April 2004, albeit with post-race hamstrings so tight that getting in and out of my car proved a major operation, while the excruciating process of sitting on the loo made me yearn for constipation. But that was a one-off. Besides, I saw plenty of people in their sixties running alongside me, I was beaten to the finish line by a man wearing a telephone box, and I looked extremely old when I observed myself in the mirror of a post-race changing room.

My major revolt, however, would prove how turning forty had made no difference at all to the way I act, the way I am, and the way I will continue to be. Mid-life crisis? What crisis? What mid-life, for that matter?

This, ironically, had been precipitated by my wife's comments in the car and exacerbated by the fact that we were in the midst of living out the very kernel of suburban life.

She asked me if I thought I was Michael Schumacher. Michael Schumacher! Now why hadn't I done any motor racing before? Well, clearly I had been busy. There hadn't been much time to race cars, what with all the boxing and running and putting and rowing and everything. Besides, I had driven a car virtually every day of my life for the past twenty-two years.

Maybe there was more to it than this though. Maybe, deep down, I had shied away from it because, more so than all the other sports, its star components were not only inaccessible, but seemingly from another world. I had enjoyed a semi-jet-set life over the years. Nice hotels, a decent class of travel, a few posh dinners along the way, and some of the best seats in the house for most of the most prestigious sporting events on the planet. But my jet-set life was no frills compared to the supersonic standards of Formula One. While I drank Mumm champagne, they swigged Veuve Cliquot. And while I made small talk with PR girls, they swapped numbers with supermodels.

Could I, at forty, not only still carry off my version of a jet-set life, but lead the kind of lifestyle Formula One offers? Could I find a way into this inner sanctum? And, even if I could, would I then want to risk my life racing motor cars?

There were no bones about this final question whizzing around my head. There had been plenty of times when I had placed my body in danger. Fighting Roy Jones junior is an instant example of this. Playing rugby league for Wigan against St Helens is another. Completing the Cresta Run, fighting as a professional wrestler, fending off bouncers from Australian quick bowlers. None of these actually threatened death.

But motor racing. At high speed. With a naïve and inexperienced racing driver at the wheel. Quite clearly there were possibilities here.

The man who had just bought the potted plants would have dismissed this as a pie-in-the-sky notion, a great deal of hassle, and the creation of potential danger that was entirely unnecessary. The man who had been a reserve for the Springboks, twelfth man for Australia, and a human punchbag for Roy Jones, saw it as a challenge. At forty, a necessary challenge, too. Glamour and speed was, after all, an enticing cocktail to a man on the precipice of middle age.

As I pulled the car into the drive at home, lifted the boot up and filled my arms with a vast array of pansies and chrysanthemums, I realised the first strands of another journey had been born. I would attempt to become a racing driver of sorts, explore all kinds of motor racing in the process, travel the world in my quest, get to meet a who's who in the sport, learn the trade to the extent that no proverbial stone would be left unturned, and prove to anyone who cared to listen that I had what it took to become a racing driver, forty or not.

Then came the final goal. In truth it had been staring me in the face all the time. My wife, unwittingly, and to her subsequent horror, had presented me with the climax, indeed the only climax, to this high-octane adventure. I would meet the man himself. I would get to know him. And I would find a way, somehow or other, of proving to the greatest racing driver in the history of the world just how good a driver I really was.

The end result would be triumphant. If Michael 'Bloody' Schumacher was impressed by my racing skills, if Schumi, or just plain Michael, as everyone in the business seems to know him by, gave me the green light then nobody would ever again be in a position to pass any damning comment on my driving. Least of all my wife!

Maybe even more important than this was the fact that looming middle age would be no more than a figment of other people's imagination. If I could slot effortlessly into motor racing, with all its surrounding glamour and prestige, then even my daughter might take a different view of the so-called generation gap.

Within a week, after a couple of phone calls and the most economic of suggestions to my wife, I was sitting in a kart. My mind was still full of chequered flags as I lapped the circuit, my ears resounded with the deafening whines of passing racing cars, my nose smelling fuel and burning rubber. The grandstands were full, the scantily clad girls were parading themselves, the paparazzi were snapping away, the champagne was spraying, the . . .

'Thud.'

Ah, back to the cold, rather wet and slightly bone-jangling reality of the karting track. My kart made a kind of 'phut' noise; I moved my soggy buttocks over to a marginally drier side of my seat, turned the wheel, pushed my foot down on the accelerator, and headed off again on to the circuit.

It had been four years since I had last karted. My trip to Buckmore Park, just outside Chatham in Kent, was designed by the circuit to provide me with a one-hour refresher course. As far as I was concerned, though, this was the first, tentative step in my new, glamorous, fast-living and fast-driving life.

The circuit's owner, Bill Sisley, is Mr Karting UK, and there is nobody in British motor racing who has not come across Sisley at some point in their careers, normally early on when they begin their long apprenticeship in the karts.

Before I even sat in the kart I was made to sign a waiver. Signing waivers is not the norm for most people as they carry out their everyday lifestyles but I reckon I must have signed close to one hundred of them over the years during my various previous sporting guises. This one was no different from any other.

'I accept that I shall be solely responsible for any decision as to my fitness to participate and as to whether to drive or discontinue to drive any Kart or Vehicle at any time whilst it is in my possession or under my control,' it read. 'I understand that Buckmore Park Karting Ltd reserve the right to remove me from the circuit at any time if they consider my actions to be dangerous or detrimental to other users.'

In other words, if you smash yourself and your kart up, it's nobody else's fault but yours. Just to hammer the message home, beside the words on the form could be found a large triangle with an exclamation mark in bold, black ink and the words underneath: 'Warning: Motor Sport Can Be DANGEROUS.' It then added: 'Despite the organisers taking all reasonable precautions unavoidable accidents can happen. In respect of these you are present at your own risk.'

Right! Got the message, even if it wasn't the best psychological start to my season-long plan to become a racing driver.

Bill's son, Tom, a mean karter himself, kindly oversaw my sixty minutes in the rain, and reminded me constantly of the basics of motor racing. These include racing lines, which provide the smoothest ride and the shortest and quickest route; acceleration, on the straights and emerging from the bends; and braking, as late and normally as hard as possible. Even spinning off the circuit was a useful if slightly disconcerting exercise, because once you had experienced it you realised no major harm could be done to yourself nor your kart.

One hour later, although a little bruised and battered, I felt I had made a satisfactory start to my motor-racing career. Bill suggested I should enter their Grand Prix racing night, a series of heats and then a final over the course of a late spring evening.

This was just what I wanted to hear. After just one karting session I had already been entered into a series of races. I returned home, made a few telephone calls and discovered that in order to feature in single-seater motor racing I needed to acquire my official Association of Racing Drivers Schools (ARDS) driving licence, something obtainable after a course undertaken at the Drive School at Silverstone.

Ken Bowes at Silverstone Drive was more than willing to help when I contacted him, even if his opening gambit was not quite what I expected to hear. 'I have testicles,' he said, down the line.

He paused long enough for me to wonder whether this was a statement, an admission or a boast. 'Therefore I can drive,' he added, eventually. 'That's what all men assume, isn't it? Then they come to us and realise it's not as easy as they think. They come here with high expectations and assumptions, and sometimes they leave with their dreams shattered.'

This, quite clearly, was not what I wanted to hear. Besides, Ken was referring to other men, those men whom I overtake on the motorway, those men who are clearly inferior drivers to me, hence my expressions of contempt as I pass them by, and their hand movements in return.

I'd been to the Silverstone Drive School four years ago at the same time as my last karting experience and, over a couple of days, fared pretty well. On this basis Ken and I decided that I would require nothing more than a couple of days back there, plenty of time to reacquaint myself with single-seater racing cars, and to pass my ARDS test. He said he would get back to me to confirm the date.

In the meantime Michael Schumacher's career was, like mine, coming along nicely. In his famous, gleaming, red Ferrari, he had just added a win at the Malaysian Grand Prix to his earlier Australian triumph, and already most in the business were reckoning that the driver's title was decided, and it was merely a case of who would finish runner-up. Juan Pablo Montoya, the brooding Colombian who always refused to accept Schumacher's superiority, finished second in Sepang but of more interest was the young man who finished third.

For Jenson Button, after sixty-eight races, and more spotlight than most on a driver starting his fifth year in the sport, Malaysia witnessed his first ever podium finish, and also for his vastly improving team, British American Racing (BAR). In doing so he beat a Ferrari, a Renault and a McLaren, which was no mean feat, and a sign of what was to come. While all the hype and hoopla centred around Schumacher, this had been a significant achievement for the Briton, and a day he would remember for the rest of his career.

It also seemed to create a 'London buses' effect on Button. Having never recorded a podium in his F1 career before Malaysia, he would make subsequently a series of podium appearances as the Formula One season sped its way around the world and through the weeks of late spring and early summer. 'I'm incredibly happy for Jenson,' Schumacher announced afterwards, which was nice of him. Then again, it's easy to be 'incredibly happy' for someone you've just beaten.

He was incredibly happy for Jenson too after he won his third straight Grand Prix of the season in Bahrain at the inaugural race in the sand on a brand new, state-of-the-art racing circuit. Button grabbed a second third place, but already Schumacher was out of sight in the driver's championship.

A few thousand miles to the west I was preparing for race night at Buckmore Park. I had made the forty-minute journey from my home with my family's stifled laughter still ringing in my ears. I saw this night as first real proof of my motor-racing prowess. They saw it as more evidence of a man losing his grip and sliding down a vertical rock-face with a peak named youth.

I entered the changing room and nodded coolly to the assortment of men already in a state of undress. One or two were my age, even slightly older. The majority, though, were quite clearly younger. Some seemed to know each other. They joshed about work, their boss, a female colleague. They made bets and laid down challenges concerning the evening's racing. They seemed totally confident about themselves and of their ability. Tiny, nagging, gnawing doubts began to creep into my mind.

The only clothes which were mine were my special racing gloves, obtained a few years back when a company supplied them as a freebee. While most of the fifty-eight drivers arrived in full racing gear, I had to make do with overalls that made me look more like a local garage mechanic, plus an old helmet provided by the karting office, and a tatty pair of training shoes. Must buy myself some proper gear, I made a mental note, as I headed off to the race briefing in the centre's main building beside the track. Already I looked like a spare part. An old, spare part.

'Karting is a non-contact sport,' the race instructor began, using a Powerpoint presentation in a dimly lit, nondescript room. 'This means that under no circumstances should there be any barging, no undertaking of other drivers' racing lines, and no recklessness. Please be especially aware of the novices, too, and allow them a little more space.' That was good to hear, especially as I was deemed a novice due to my inexperience.

In my three heats I would be starting in fourth, eleventh and seventh on the grid out of fourteen. As I made my way over to my kart I gleaned that the group of drivers alongside me did this sort of thing virtually on a weekly basis. Things were looking worse.

As we sat in our karts on the circuit's grid and waited for the five green lights to flash to order us to start the race we revved our engines, a deafening crescendo of grunts and whines. Diesel slopped around in our see-through engine canisters perched behind us, fumes shot out of the most basic of exhaust pipes, and the last remnants of daylight were fast disappearing over the horizon.

Go! The green lights blazed, the engines whined again, and fourteen karts shot towards the first corner like a group of lemmings hurling themselves off a cliff. Within ten seconds of the start I realised the instructor's pre-race pleas had clearly fallen on deaf ears. Crash! I was buffeted to one side by a kart that cut inside me. Thump! I was knocked back into the centre of the circuit again by a kart overtaking me on the outside. Bang! I was forced off the track at the third corner by two karts having a personal dogfight. Bump! I found myself sandwiched between two faster drivers than me on the second lap. This was not karting as I knew it. This was high-speed dodgems!

The problem was that I was driving, not racing. I was far too polite, and not remotely aggressive enough. It was as if I were on a Sunday afternoon's drive in the country. The circuit had suddenly become dripping with testosterone, but very little was oozing from my pores.

And so the evening went on with me, bumped, bruised and battered, languishing in the latter stages of the race while the track became more treacherous by the minute as the evening dew began to settle and turn the tarmac into an ice rink. In three heats I recorded a tenth, eleventh and twelfth and, by my reckoning, the only people I managed to beat were mostly fellow novices. Out of fifty-eight karters that night, I ended up forty-eighth, and missed qualifying for both the 'A' and 'B' finals by a mile.

As those races began I sloped off into the night. By now it was cold and I was very wet and miserable. This was not quite how I had planned things. As motor-racing baptisms go, I had just drowned.

My wife and two children failed miserably to hide their smirks when I reported the news to them later that evening. 'Going well, then,' my wife commented, once I had tossed my keys on to the side, sat down at the kitchen table and owned up to a night of humiliation.

Other women married to forty-year-old men were adopting similar attitudes around the country as their husbands slapped on fake tan, joined health clubs, sported trendy new haircuts or started on radical diets. But very few of them would have announced that they were becoming racing drivers.

This minor setback would not deter me, however. Not even Schumacher senior started out winning every race. He must have lost a few in the early days. The best sportsmen in the world learn from their failures and emerge the better for them. This could be the best thing to happen to me. Soon I had employed a positive spin to the night's proceedings. Not bad for someone who hadn't karted for four years. Not bad at all. Just think what I could do once I'd grown used to racing.

In the time it took to reintroduce myself to karting and then flounder in the puddles, Schumacher won both the San Marino and Spanish Grands Prix to make it five wins in succession from the start of the 2004 season. In doing so he had equalled Nigel Mansell's achievement back in 1992. The race for the world title, and an incredible seventh championship for the iceman of motor racing, seemed to be all but mathematically over already.

I had taken to observing Schumacher at work, at least on the TV. Like Tiger Woods in his pomp, or Brian Lara or Roger Federer, his winning was seemingly effortless. Before, I'd flick over the channels, notice that Schumacher was about to win a Grand Prix, let it register in my mind for a few seconds, and switch over. Now I watched him with a very different view. Even if the main focus of the camera was on another car, I'd be watching Schumacher as he overtook the back runners and gobbled up the laps. He was a machine. Relentless, uncompromising and, on the face of it, utterly ruthless.

He was, very obviously, the best driver in the world.

In as wide a contrast imaginable I had just been made to look like a very average driver in a small corner of Kent by a gaggle of salesmen, accountants, dealers and bankers. My idea of showing Schumacher just how good a driver I was may have seemed far-fetched when it was conceived.

Right now it appeared impossible.

chapter two

BRAD AND GEORGE

The view out of the aircraft window was as exciting as it was spectacular. The French Alps stretched to the left as far as the eye could see, their snow-capped peaks gleaming in the early summer sun. Ahead, in the distance, shimmered the Mediterranean Sea, the Côte d'Azur and Nice, where I would be landing before making the half-hour taxi journey to the Principality of Monaco, the home of not just any Grand Prix, but the *Grand Prix* of the season.

Monaco made a natural choice as my first taste of the Formula One season because I not only wanted my racing appetite whetted, but also to drink from the goblet of glamour and all the other excessive trimmings that come with F1. There would be no better example of this than Monaco. In other forms of motor racing the sport is the show. But at Monaco, always staged on the weekend following Ascension Day, the show is the show, and anybody who was anybody wanted to play.

After the disappointment of Buckmore Park I had decided to go to the other extreme. A weekend at the Monaco Grand Prix was as exciting as it could get. Some may argue that Indianapolis or Le Mans is the greatest race in motor sport. Most would plump for Monaco, the jewel in the Formula One season. No racing driver in the world considered himself an achiever until he had raised the winner's trophy above his head at Monaco. From Fangio to Moss, Hill to Stewart, Lauda to Prost, Mansell, Senna and Schumacher. They had all won at Monaco, and had all considered it to be one of their greater feats.

Due to the popularity of the weekend's racing my hotel happened to be a five-minute walk from the airport. In Nice! A bog-standard airport hotel, it was far removed from the world I was about to enter a couple of bays along to the east.

Having dumped my bags on my bed and hurried out again to catch a taxi, I arrived in the Principality midway through the Friday morning. First on the agenda was a walk around the harbour to inspect the vast array of yachts that had claimed their prized berths, something everyone who does not live in Monaco tends to do. The tourists gaze and gawp at the boats, while the owners almost make a point of sunbathing or eating out on their decks in full view of the lesser people. Each are equally interested in how the other half behave.

The boats ranged from million-pound-plus 'tiddlers', such as former F1 star Eddie Irvine's *Anaconda*, which was parked as close to the race track as possible, to Roman Abramovich's 377-foot *Pelorus*, all £170 million worth, sporting a submarine among other toys. Looking at the Russian's 'yacht' – and it looked more like an ocean-going liner to me – it reminded me of John Paul Getty's quote: 'If you can count your money then you're not wealthy enough.' He must have been in Monaco when he came out with that!

Later that weekend the former Microsoft co-founder Paul Allen came to town to win the 'Who's Got the Biggest Yacht' prize. *Octopus*, a shade over 413 feet in length and worth close to £200 million, is the largest private yacht in the world. Among other 'necessities' it boasts a cinema, a music studio and two helipads. Elsewhere it also has a landing craft and a remote-controlled vehicle that transmits imagery from the sea. Paul Allen, it can be safely assumed, cannot count all his money, while Abramovich found himself in the unfamiliar position of runner-up.

The smells of fish and sun cream fought for premier place in my senses. The sea water slapped against the hulls of the assorted yachts, seagulls floated above, and as I placed the cheaper end of designer shades over my eyes, I reasoned that the Côte d'Azur was an infinitely better place to be in May than Kent.

On the 3.34 km street circuit that Friday afternoon, a tight, twisty, bumpy, relatively slow and totally unforgiving challenge, the drivers were adopting maximum concentration and consistency on what was their warm-up day. All the talk was about whether Schumacher could beat Mansell's record of five consecutive wins at the start of a Formula One season, and whether he could also match Senna's six Monaco titles. The high-pitched and unmistakable whine of Formula One cars echoed around the Monte Carlo harbours and the sun momentarily caught and flashed off the various coloured liveries of the cars as they shot around the water.

Away from the track the spotlight was very much on the Jaguar team. Their season had been disappointing in terms of Grand Prix points, and also uncertain with regard to their star driver, Australian Mark Webber, who seemed destined to join the BMW-Williams team for the following season. Yet when it came to publicity the team were the number one outfit.

At the centre of this was Nav Sidhu, the team's colourful

Director of Communications. I had known Nav for a number of years and liked him for his persistence, his ambition and his incredible enthusiasm. At the eighteen-mile stage of the London Marathon, for example, as my thighs felt like baobab trees and my bowels were threatening to explode, I received a text message on my mobile telephone, strapped to my waist in case of emergencies. It was from Nav and read: 'The finish line has your name written all over it. Go, motherfucker, go!' It was a typically over-the-top attempt at inspiration.

He was known in the business, however, for having pulled off a few stunts in his time – notably the previous year in Monte Carlo when he persuaded Arnold Schwarzennegger to be a guest of Jaguar's for the race – but this weekend Nav had pulled out all the stops.

On the Friday it was announced that Steinmetz, the Israeli diamond dealers, would be sponsoring Jaguar for the Monaco Grand Prix only. This meant that in the nose of each of the two Jaguar cars racing that weekend would be mounted a diamond. Insured for the small sum of £1 million, the diamonds encrusted into the cars would glint and glimmer their way around and through all the famous Monaco landmarks, from the tunnel to Casino Square, the Mirabeau and La Rascasse corners, and the Virage and Anthony Noghes straight, the latter named after the race's founder.

Now the sight of a diamond was hardly rare in a town such as Monte Carlo, but not even this playground of the playboy was used to seeing them being driven at 200 mph through the Monaco tunnel inserted into a car. Just to reinforce the message Nav had also employed the services of two models to sport yet more diamonds in the Jaguar pits together with Webber and the team's number two driver, Austrian Christian Klien. When the American model, Molly Simms, arrived, all long legs, high cheekbones and smouldering looks, it was noticeable how all the mechanics from the neighbouring pit-lane garages dropped their tools and crowded around the roped-off area surrounding the Jaguar garage.

Mix a beautiful girl with a gaggle of predominantly French and Italian mechanics, working for the likes of Renault and Ferrari, and the end result is mayhem. It got no better, either, when a second model, the equally stunning 'Natasha' from Brazil, turned up wearing a large rock of a diamond priced at £32 million.

The evening was spent divided between a BAR reception at the Amber Lounge, a favourite Monte Carlo nightclub haunt frequented by most of the drivers who lived in the Principality, and then on a yacht for the annual Monaco party held by the intriguingly named 'Doctor Chocolate', a successful businessman from the Black Country in England, in the company of the UK motor racing writers. One nightclub and one yacht on the first night. Yes, I was shifting seamlessly and willingly into the world of Formula One.

In the taxi, en route back to Nice and a little tipsy on all the champagne guzzled, I picked up a voicemail message on my mobile phone from home. Among various other snippets of news was the happy announcement that I'd forgotten to put a sack of rubbish in the dustbin. The local foxes had got to it, leaving a line of cartons, vegetable stalks and bones strewn across our drive.

Mornings in Monte Carlo, especially down at the harbour, are particularly beautiful. The water tends to glisten more first thing, while deckhands busily slip-slop their mops to wipe away the previous night's excesses. Some of the talk in the overnight Monaco media concerned Formula One tittle-tattle. Would David Coulthard be leaving McLaren and joining Jaguar; whether Webber would leave for BMW-Williams, or Toyota? Would Ralf Schumacher be joining Toyota? And just who was former world champion Jacques Villeneuve negotiating with? Most of the spotlight, however, fell on the sparkling Jaguar cars, and the sparkling Jaguar models.

If this was frustrating to the teams who had actually put in a much better practice performance than Jaguar, then there was more to come. Much more. Saturday saw the actual qualifying rounds to determine who would start the following day's Grand Prix on the grid – a grid more important than at any other race on the season's calendar because overtaking on the narrow, twisting Monaco circuit was nigh on impossible.

This, supposedly, was the second most important element of a Grand Prix weekend, save for the actual race, of course. Or at least it should have been. But Nav was about to pull off his greatest stunt yet. After eight months of negotiations he had persuaded studio bosses that the Hollywood movie, *Ocean's Twelve*, should be launched officially at Monaco with Jaguar, even though it was still in the middle of production, and would not be distributed until much later on in the year.

Here was the deal. All the Jaguar staff, drivers included, would for one race only ditch their usual green work clothing for a rather fetching black number with 'Ocean's Twelve' plastered all over the shirt and baseball caps, vying for exposure alongside Jaguar's usual heavyweight sponsors including HSBC, Lear, Red Bull, AT&T and Becks.

The Jaguar R5 cars, meanwhile, with their ten-cylinder, forty-valve Cosworth Racing CR-6 V10 engines, would also promote not only the film, with again 'Ocean's Twelve' written on both Webber's and Klien's, but also the cast list, hence the names Brad Pitt, George Clooney, Matt Damon, Catherine Zeta Jones, Don Cheadle and Julia Roberts also plastered over the famous green livery. The Jaguar motorhome, meanwhile, together with the sponsor's restaurant, and all-things Jaguar, had in addition the latest catchphrase to resound around Monaco in evidence: 'Twelve is the new Eleven.' Cute.

The pièce de résistance, however, was the utter chaos created just an hour before the start of qualifying by the sight of Pitt, Clooney, Damon and legendary Hollywood producer Jerry Weintraub strutting their way to the Jaguar garage. I had told Nav before even coming to Monaco that I wanted to experience the glitz and the glamour of Formula One. Now I was one of Jaguar's special guests. If I played my cards right I would be rubbing shoulders with some bona fide, A-list celebrities to whet my motor racing appetite, and you don't get more A-list than Pitt and Clooney.

Weintraub was one of the last of the old-school Hollywood moguls, the kind of guy who might have been a contender to discover a horse's head in his bed at his Hollywood Hills mansion. Weintraub could lay claim to being involved with the two biggest acts in the twentieth century, Frank Sinatra and Elvis Presley. The former he managed, and the latter he promoted, together with Led Zeppelin, Bob Dylan and the Beach Boys. He also discovered John Denver, so I guess we cannot thank him for everything. Having directed the hugely successful *Ocean's Eleven*, a remake of the original Rat Pack film of the same name, Weintraub was now at the helm of *Ocean's Twelve.*

The four Americans arrived on a motor boat at an innocuous jetty in the harbour. A small welcoming party, plus one rookie driver, stood looking down on the boat as it berthed. Within moments of Messrs Pitt and Clooney setting foot on dry land, they were mobbed by TV cameramen, reporters and photographers. Nav kept the party moving rapidly as we all made our way along the harbour, across the circuit, and into the pits lane. In trying to keep up with the rapidly moving party I resembled one of those silly walkers you see at the Olympics. It was a Saturday morning and, normally, I would have been in Sainsbury's arguing about whether we should buy one or two tubs of family ice cream.

As Pitt and Clooney walked and chewed gum furiously, the

crowds high up in the stands overlooking the circuit cheered and waved at the Hollywood stars. Down below a TV cameraman tripped over as he attempted to run backwards filming the actors, causing Clooney momentarily to stop and check to see if anything more than his pride was bruised.

Their destination was the Jaguar garage where, awaiting their arrival, was the most powerful figure in the sport. As the actors arrived so a mass of mechanics and onlookers divided like the Red Sea to create a natural channel leading to the throne. Mr Formula One had not come to meet Hollywood, you must understand. Hollywood had come to meet Mr Formula One.

Just who, exactly, Messrs Pitt and Clooney must have imagined, was the man whose show this was? What giant of a person could rule Formula One with such an iron fist? How impressive would a billionaire be when VIPs almost fell at his feet? It was a scene straight out of *The Wizard of Oz*.

'Hi, I'm Bernie Ecclestone.' A diminutive man in his seventies with a shock of white hair that made him resemble Andy Warhol emerged from the shadows with his hand held out in greeting. Looking up at both Pitt and Clooney, he added: 'Welcome to the Monaco Grand Prix.'

Throughout all this I stood next to Jackie Stewart, the former three times world Formula One champion who, in his professional capacity with Ford, was one of the dignitaries lined up to meet and greet the stars. It was like being an actor at a royal premier.

'It's a pleasure to meet you, Mr Stewart,' said a dutiful Pitt, in his blue jeans, white shirt and regulation shades, as he looked down on Stewart in his trademark green tartan cap and tartan trousers. 'Hi, good to see you,' added an affable Clooney, likewise dressed down in a loose-fitting T-shirt and jeans.

After gorgeous George had moved on, Stewart turned round and enquired: 'So, which one was George Clooney, then?' He was being serious. (A few feet away Clooney might well have asked: 'So, I've met the clown in the joke trousers, but where's Jackie Stewart.')

For some absurd reason I started to shake both Pitt and Clooney's hands and thanked them for coming along to the garage as if I was working for Jaguar. 'No, thank you,' replied the ever-so-smooth Clooney. 'No, thank you,' I echoed, struggling to think of anything else to say. Clooney stared at me for a second before recognising that this conversation had already reached its end. The pregnant pause could have lasted hours on this basis, had not Weintraub, who was clearly calling all the shots, uttered a loud command. 'C'mon boys, let's get outta here.'

There was just enough time for Brad to turn round and say to me: 'Good to see you.' Actually, when I say it was directed at me, it was, in truth, directed at the first person he laid his eyes on closest to him, which happened to be me. It was uttered with a bright, toothy smile that, so I am told, melts much of the world's female population. I was singularly underwhelmed by the whole experience.

I don't know quite what I expected. Can A-list Hollywood celebs flap their arms and fly, or reveal superhuman tendencies that us mortals lack? Do they appear significantly different to the rest of us? Or, once all the hype and spin is removed, are they just regular guys like you and me, who can act and have been able to capitalise on a few breaks that have come their way, and whose subsequent wealth means that their teeth are a little whiter, their skin a tad smoother, and their clothes that much more expensive? Maybe the public expectation level is too unfair.

I managed a slightly longer conversation with Damon as he was leaving which went something like this: 'So, Matt, your first time here at the Monaco Grand Prix?'

'Aha, and I'm really looking forward to the race,' Damon replied, with a big grin from beneath his baseball cap.

'Er, great. So you wouldn't fancy racing one of these beauties, then?' I added, pointing to a Jaguar R5 and rather pleased how I had shifted seamlessly into the vocabulary.

'Uh-uh, but I'm really looking forward to the race,' Damon repeated. He shook my hand and was ushered away.

So, I gathered, having revealed all my extraordinary powers of interviewing technique, he was really looking forward to the race, then. Messrs Pitt, Clooney, Damon and Weintraub returned to their Portofino retreat four hours away in Italy where they remained for the rest of the weekend. None would return to witness the Monaco Grand Prix.

Not that this concerned Nav nor the rest of the exuberant Jaguar team. Once again they had ensnared the paparazzi, leaving the rest of the pit-lane garages bereft of interest, and more than papered over the cracks of their poor performances on the track.

The *Ocean's Twelve* mob blew away every other celeb present in Monaco that weekend and, my word, there were a fair few. All you had to do was roam up and down the pit lane, if you possessed the kind of accreditation accorded to the teams or the media, or even along the harbour front, and you would be falling over them. I must have walked past Roman Abramovich countless times, the Russian multi-billionaire ambling along in his T-shirt, jeans and stubble, followed a few feet behind by four burly Russians who looked like they used to work for SMERSH.

This was rather fitting, seeing that Roger Moore was in town signing autographs and smiling to one and all. With all those walkie-talkied Russians around, it was comforting to know that the great raised eyebrow was monitoring the situation. So too was U2's Bono, supermodel Naomi Campbell, Indian cricket legend Sachin Tendulkar, former Formula One racing drivers Gerhard Berger, Thierry Boutsen, Jean Alesi, three times former champion Niki Lauda, and Lionel Ritchie, who was a guest of the Jordan team.

Ritchie, in particular, was rather overshadowed on qualifying day by Pitt, Clooney and co. At one point his small entourage in the paddock was suddenly engulfed by a much larger, fast-moving mob as the Hollywood contingent passed through. Later that day, after qualifying, he was still in the paddock when I heard some wag from the public sector behind the steel fencing shout out at the great permed one: 'Hello! Is it me your lookin' for?'

In the actual qualifying – and yes, there was still some interest in the sport side of all this – Renault's Jarno Trulli grabbed a first-ever pole position, Schumacher senior was fourth behind Fernando Alonso and second-placed Button. The top three drivers were then involved in a crash when the minibus carrying them to the obligatory post-qualifying press conference collided head on with the course-clearing car. It seems that driving F1 cars at 170 mph causes no alarm. It's only when you step into a minibus that the danger begins. No one was hurt, although Button sheepishly admitted afterwards that he had not been wearing his seat-belt. It set up what would be a uniquely exciting Grand Prix the following afternoon.

Before then, of course, came the second, compulsory yacht party of the weekend. This time it was Steinmetz, the diamond dealers, who hosted the event on their fancy yacht, another champagne-flowing event full of rich, middle-aged men and young, posh girls who, shall we say, were liberal with their affections. Just what was it about these millionaire men that these young, invariably pretty girls saw in them? The men looked more or less the same. Tanned, often over-tanned, faces, loud shirts and even louder expectations of the night to come. The girls were pretty, giggly and attentive enough to flatter the egos of anyone.

I wasn't quite sure whether I felt like an outsider looking in, or someone who had effortlessly switched lifestyles. I guessed it was the former on the basis that I was trying too hard to pretend that this was just another, run-of-the-mill night for someone like me. Besides, I had already phoned home just before to find out the night's football scores and the outcome of a TV detective series my wife and I had been watching. I reckoned that sealed it.

Fortified by countless glasses of champagne I began a conversation with Stelios Haji-Ioannou, the founder of easyJet, easy this, easy that, and easy everything. Nothing particularly unusual by this, you may think, except I attempted to speak Greek. Past experiences (calling people in Corfu *calamari* (squid) when attempting to say *kali mera* (good morning)) have taught me that this is a precarious route to take.

Stelios said something long and Greek to me in reply. His demeanour suggested it had been nice, but this could have been cleverly disguised by an intelligent man who had worked out after my first syllable that my Greek was very limited and my pronunciation disastrous.

To which I replied: 'Ha, ha, ha, thank you, good night, *efcharisto, kali nichte*.'

As luck would have it, that day I had met an old school friend of mine called Patrick Gosling. Pat had established himself as a leading motor-sports photographer. Better still, from my point of view, he had an extra room booked in a hotel overlooking the harbour in Monte Carlo which was empty. I needed no second invitation to move in for the weekend, thus forgoing my grotty airport hotel forty-five minutes away in Nice. Taking a wrong turning, however, on my stagger back to my new hotel I ended up in Casino Square. There, sitting on the steps of the Hotel de Paris, was a Scotsman in a kilt, looking as if he might have had a drink or two. On closer examination it turned out to be Rod Stewart. I walked on, back to my hotel and some much-longed-for sleep. Only in Monaco on Grand Prix weekend do you walk straight past a kilted, lonely Rod Stewart without batting an eyelid.

Sunday was race day, of course, which meant an early dash to the paddock before the whole area surrounding the track was closed off. Lionel Ritchie was there again, this time enjoying a little more of the attention now that the *Ocean's Twelve* lot had decided to stay in Portofino. So too was Roman Abramovich, involved in an interesting and rather revealing game.

There, as he ambled and strolled around, sometimes with his hands in his pockets, and once with his mobile telephone stuck to his ear ignoring his company, Abramovich surveyed the scene that is Formula One. He clearly liked what he saw, as did the two extra men added to his entourage of bodyguards. Bernie Ecclestone and Max Mosely, the President of the sport's governing body, the FIA (Federation Internationals Automobile), walked slightly behind the Russian, their pinstriped suits in contrast to the jeans and stubble look sported by one of the world's richest men.

Abramovich, as Chelsea Football Club can vouch, cannot part with his money quickly enough right now. For the past two years he has caroused around the West like a shopper on a supermarket trolley dash. Ecclestone and Mosely looked for all the world like a couple of traders close to securing a deal. For this even they seemed more than happy to play second fiddle at Monaco.

The atmosphere elsewhere in the paddock had noticeably become frenetic the closer the start of the race drew. Only a rapid leap to the right avoided a collision with some berk hurrying through on a motorised micro-scooter. As he disappeared into the horizon I realised it was Michael Schumacher. A collision with the great man less than an hour before the start of the Monaco Grand Prix would not have been the best of introductions.

The actual race turned out to be the most exciting and drama-filled so far in the season. So often better for its location than its substance, this time Monaco produced a show fitting its stage, with new names filling the podium places, high drama, incredible mistakes and angry outbursts from those many drivers who failed to finish the seventy-seven laps.

It was all played out in front of a hundred thousand spectators packed on to crowded rooftops and hotel terraces and balconies, boat decks, harbour walls and hillside vantage points. Brand new grandstands crammed in between the track and the sea, giant television screens were perched in various high-profile positions, and virtually everyone could see just about every second of action during the course of a couple of hours.

I spent the race alternating between a main grandstand constructed precariously close to the harbour and sea, the Jaguar hospitality suite, and the media centre that provided stunning views of much of the course. There was no doubt about it. I had been to a couple of Grands Prix before, but they had been at purpose-built circuits where you saw one glimpse of the cars as they whined past and were gone a split second later. But a street race – and especially around the sweeping bays, clifftops and hills of Monte Carlo – provided much more entertainment and action.

Trulli and Button were a split second apart at the end, the Italian adding a maiden Grand Prix win to his pole position, while Button was happy to notch up yet another podium placing. On this evidence a first Grand Prix win for the young Briton was imminent. Ferrari's Rubens Barrichello came third.

In typical Latin style Trulli made no attempt to hide his post-race emotions. First he leapt into the arms of his flamboyant team owner, Flavio Briatore, then he high-fived most of his mechanics, and then he knelt down and kissed his Renault. Up on the podium he received his winner's trophy from the late Prince Rainier, ever-present each year to dish out the awards, while Prince Albert and Princess Caroline looked on.

What, though, of Michael Schumacher? On course for his sixth, record-breaking win, the German emerged from the tunnel in the forty-sixth lap with only three wheels left on his car. Amid the semi-gloom of the tunnel, and away from the TV cameras, he appeared to be barged into the barrier by his fierce adversary, Juan Pablo Montoya, who was a lap behind the man leading the race at the time. Predictably, both blamed each other afterwards.

'Michael was full on the brakes for two and half seconds before we touched,' insisted the Colombian. 'I knew I was going to hit him. I moved to the right to get out of his way. But he moved to his right as well and there was nowhere for me to go.' Schumacher's response was cool and direct. 'The situation was that the race leader was knocked out by a back marker.' It was a first 'Did Not Finish' classification in nineteen races for Schumacher, not quite how he had planned his 200th Grand Prix to work out.

I felt Michael's disappointment too. Unlike most, I've never had a problem with total domination in sport. When someone is so clearly ahead of the game, I like to see them set new records and wonder if they will ever be beaten. Instead, at my first race of the season, I'd witnessed Schumacher's first loss. I wondered, idly, if my decision to write a book that planned to climax with the German and myself had anything to do with his Monagesque demise. This was the same kind of logic that sees fully grown men wear lucky hats because they believe it makes their favourite football team win. As if that has any influence on the outcome?

Afterwards, in the paddock, Montoya was subjected to boos, cat-calls and heckles from incensed Ferrari fans jammed up against some wire fencing as the Colombian walked back to the BMW–Williams motorhome. 'Faggot' was one of the nicer names attributed to him.

Elsewhere mayhem ruled on the winding roads. BAR's Takuma Sato's engine blew up in a giant plume of smoke during the third lap, previous Monaco winner Coulthard slowed down in the subsequent fog and was hit from behind by the Sauber of Giancarlo Fisichella. Coulthard's McLaren was written off, as was Fisichella's Sauber after it flipped spectacularly over Coulthard and into a barrier.

Coulthard demonstrated driver-speak afterwards by ever so

gently criticising everyone. 'Perhaps Fisichella was going a bit too fast,' he suggested. 'Sato's engineers must have had an idea from the telemetry that his engine was going to blow and should have called him in,' he added.

The safety car was required again after the forty-second lap when the Spaniard, Alonso, ran into the guard rail as he overtook Ralf Schumacher. Clearly blaming the German for forcing him off the racing line Alonso gesticulated angrily at him as he sat in his now dormant car and watched Schumacher junior race past.

Jaguar, meanwhile, had one of those forgettable weekends, at least on the track. Klien's Grand Prix lasted exactly one lap, while Webber went out after just fifteen. Both were changed into their black 'Ocean's Twelve' shirts and jeans and watching the remainder of the race from the Jaguar hospitality area with well over half the race still remaining.

As they did so the Jaguar boys were already dismantling the area and packing it away into huge juggernauts. That night they would be making the sixteen-hour journey to the Nurburgring in Germany in readiness for the following Sunday's European Grand Prix. Amid their ranks, however, there was great consternation.

In crashing out during the first lap young Klien had somehow managed to dislodge the £130,000 diamond in the car's nose. Of course, nobody realised this until the crumpled car was back in the garage, and nobody was willing to go crawling on their hands and their knees in the middle of the course while the Grand Prix was going on. Afterwards there was no sign of it at all, which meant that someone was suddenly £130,000 better off. Or was it just another clever marketing stunt?

'I guess that's the most expensive drive I'll ever have in my life,' the philosophical Austrian said later, slightly embarrassed by the whole episode.

As for me, a combination of all that noise, all that heat, and all that excitement, mixed with two nights of excess, was beginning to take its toll. I had found the Grand Prix exhilarating and spectacular. The setting was divine, and the drivers lived up to their rock star imagery by driving close and sometimes over the limit in their quest for yet more fame and fortune.

But I was just beginning to find the whole thing claustrophobic. And a little unreal. By early evening, I was beginning to yearn for a pot of tea at home.

A little nap in my hotel room and a shower soon transformed suburban man back into Monaco Man. Wearing what I regarded to be snappy clothes, and with a little too much aftershave splashed over my face, I made my way over to the Amber Lounge for what is, by common consent, the best post-race party of the year. Oh yes. This, I convinced myself, as an olive I was attempting to eat plopped off its stick and fell on to the floor, was very me. A long, thin, stiletto heel belonging to a long, thin model pierced the olive, which clung to the shoe as she waded through the masses air-kissing all and sundry.

Michael Schumacher appeared anything but depressed after his disappointing day, holding court at his own table with his wife, Corinna, and friends. By then I had joined Nav Sidhu and others from Jaguar at a table nearby, failing to come up with a single reason to introduce myself to the Schumacher party. There he was, just a few feet away, but it was clearly not the time to bluster my way into his conversation. A few feet along Barrichello was puffing away on a long cigar, Coulthard was shaking hands by the dozen, and Jenson Button was gliding in and out of tables with the biggest smile in the club, accompanied by his girlfriend, Louise.

Usually, on a Sunday night, I would have been falling asleep in front of the TV, having eaten too much of the roast dinner, and having made sure that all the necessary pre-week chores – washing the car, cleaning my shoes, putting out the rubbish – had been completed. Now I was in the midst of a celeb-fest at probably the most prestigious party in the world that day.

Jacques Villeneuve was there, fuelling more rumours of his intentions for the following season, and so too was Eddie Irvine, complaining of how his stubble was turning white, and admitting to the fact that he had given up trying to play the guitar despite the hour-long lesson I had given him four years previously during a day-trip to Italy. 'I like to leave my guitar perched up against the wall so that the girls see it and assume I play,' he explained. 'It seems to do the trick, so why bother actually playing it?' Same old Eddie logic, then.

Elsewhere, Flavio Briatore, in shades despite the fact that he was in a dark corner of the room, was with supermodel Naomi Campbell, all pout and pose, while U2's Bono was producing peace signs with his two fingers. The Premiership's Rio Ferdinand and James Beattie were trying to blend in to this international glitterati of stars (Ferdinand seeming to remember when and where the party was better than when dope-testers turned up to his Manchester United training ground), and Ross Kemp, TV's Grant Mitchell from *EastEnders*, was looking like, well, Grant Mitchell.

On reflection this should have been the best party I'd ever been to. In truth, I've held better ones myself at home in the garden with a marquee. I've certainly had more interesting conversations.

At the time, though, a forty-year-old man's head had been temporarily turned by Formula One drivers and supermodels, celebrities and champagne, yachts, Monaco and, of course, Brad and George. This was precisely why I was becoming a motor racing driver, of course. And already, after next to no time, I was bathing in all its glamour.

It was 4.00 am. I walked back to my hotel room, checked out and caught a taxi to my Nice hotel where I enjoyed precisely seventy-five minutes' sleep before the shrill tone of my wake-up call told me to get myself over to the airport. There was some kind of airport staff strike that morning, which meant a huge traffic jam a mile from the terminal, and the sight of one Englishman with three heavy bags trudging along the main road, the sweat developing on his brow as the tiredness and the hangover began to kick in.

I bet Brad and George didn't have this problem.

chapter three

A CLOWN IN OVERALLS

It took me two full days to recover from the weekend's excesses, the lack of sleep, the alcohol and the travel. When I was a student I could live my life like this, well, except for the fact that I didn't hang out on yachts and exclusive clubs quaffing champagne, but rather drank copious amounts of cheap beer from plastic glasses in various dingy student union bars. But at least I would be functioning just as well in the immediate aftermath. Not any more, though. Not now that I had reached forty!

Suddenly alcohol was in danger of becoming the enemy. Whereas the after-effects were once not a consideration because there were no after-effects, now the consequences of a night's excess had to be weighed up. Did the fun of the night before make the next day's gloom worth it? I found myself increasingly answering no to that question.

On the morning of the third day since my return from Monaco I woke with my head cleared and my mind active once more. This was just in time for a two-day trip up to the Silverstone Motor Sport Academy. This would be an important forty-eight hours. A very important time indeed. For, assuming everything went smoothly, at the end of these two days I would have passed the test that would recognise me, officially, as a fully-fledged racing driver.

The Association of Racing Drivers Schools (ARDS) test was the key to the door of every racing circuit in the British isles. Hold one of their certificates and you could do anything you wanted in a racing car. If I wanted to feature in any British motor racing, then I needed a piece of paper that every great driver, from Nigel Mansell to Damon Hill, and David Coulthard to Jenson Button all possessed.

The Academy's Ken Bowes recalled how I fared reasonably well when I was last visiting his school and came to the happy conclusion that, with my unquestionable talent as a driver, I wouldn't need more than a couple of days at most to refresh my memory of racing around a circuit before then taking the test. I decided not to mention my karting experience at Buckmore Park. With my taste for motor racing reinvigorated by Monaco I reckoned two days would be ample for a man of my obvious talents.

I was also required to undergo a medical examination by my local doctor, who had to fill in a form confirming that I was neither blind, nor deaf, had all my limbs, had no terminal disease, no history of heart problems, and no mental disorders. This was necessary for the School to send on to ARDS in order to get the go-ahead to receive my certificate and be put forward for a race that Saturday morning at Silverstone.

Ken sent me a package to be getting along with prior to my arrival, a blue book entitled the *MSA British Motor Sports Yearbook 2004*, with everything you needed to know about the rules and regulations and dos and don'ts of racing, plus a testosterone-packed video with a racing driver, Steve Deaks, telling you more or less the same, accompanied by some kind of heavy metal music designed, I guess, to sex up the imagery of racing. I was told to swot up on the various flag signals during racing, provided in the blue paperback, because this would form a large part of the written test.

Written test? Well, yes, apparently I not only had to pass a driving test, but also a twenty-minute written test at the school. The thought of the written test unnerved me far more than the driving test as I drove up the M1 motorway early on a Thursday morning towards Silverstone. The last time I'd sat down and undergone any form of written test was probably my last paper during my university finals. And that, as my wife pointed out, was a very long time ago.

Once you drive through the new, main entrance at the famous home of the British Grand Prix, you have to travel a good couple of miles around the outside perimeter of the circuit, past names even I'd heard of, such as Beckett's, Copse and Stowe corners, and then over a bridge across the circuit to reach the school. On arrival I was made to sign a waiver – again – and then told it might be an idea to visit the nearby Grand Prix Racewear store to purchase some racewear.

A short drive within the confines of the Silverstone circuit, Grand Prix Racewear provides crucial clothing for racing drivers which is unobtainable at general sports stores. This, in itself, was a reminder that motor racing is serious stuff. Whereas you can buy a new pair of trainers or running shorts from virtually anywhere, a motor racing driver requires fireproof clothing, for obvious reasons. I chose a red, all-in-one pair of driving overalls, with thick, white padding inside, as well as some red, felt boots, not dissimilar to those worm by wrestlers, and black, padded gloves. It didn't look too dissimilar to the Michael Schumacher look, I felt, as I tried it all on and preened myself in the mirror. It wasn't cheap.

But, as Steve Deaks said in the video, you should be buying the best quality racing clothes you can afford, just in case you and your car turn into a fireball. I was covered from neck to toe and felt a great deal happier about it too.

It was shortly after I had been driven to a far corner of the Driving School's grounds that things began to go a little wrong. Joining a group of men who were on a five-day course I was asked to drive a Formula First single-seater racing car around a cone-laden circuit, weaving in and out of a dual carriageway of cones, then performing twice a figure of eight around more cones, before speeding to the finish and slamming on the brakes.

The Formula First looks a little like a baby racing car just born from its Formula One mother. After my first few attempts the neat pattern of carefully laid out cones had been transformed into scattered chaos, with one of the cones still stuck to the underside of my Formula First.

Steve Warburton, my instructor, didn't mince his words. 'If you hit one more bloody cone I'm going to shove it right up your arse,' he announced, loud enough so that everyone else could hear. 'You got that?'

It seemed to do the trick. For the remainder of the exercise I managed to avoid mowing down any cones which, for their part, managed to avoid ending shoved up my arse. We then moved on to the South Circuit to drive Lotus Elise sports cars. The South Circuit is the southern half of the Grand Prix circuit, incorporating Beckett's Corner, Hangar Straight, Stowe and Club Corners, and finally Abbey Straight. Here I was joined by Chris Alford who, despite his fifty-eight years of age, turned out to be the current Formula Two European championship leader. At first I liked him as we poodled around the circuit and I followed his instructions as we approached and exited each corner. Then he asked me to pull over for a small debrief.

'You are a danger to yourself and to everyone else,' Chris

announced. 'You don't seem to possess any concentration, you can't do two things at once, and you have no vision.' He paused for a few seconds, stared at me and waited for a response.

I was in a state of shock and came back with a feeble: 'Apart from that, I'm not bad, though, am I?'

'You probably don't even know this,' Chris continued, 'but we nearly had three accidents out there. You're crossing your arms when you're taking the corners, you don't seem able to brake and change gear at the same time, and you're not going nowhere near fast enough.'

Actually I thought I was travelling at a pretty fast rate of knots but, seeing that Chris was leading the European F2 championships, I was hardly in a position to argue.

'You are going to need a great deal of track time,' he concluded.

We went back out on the circuit. My disposition, it was fair to say, was a great deal less cocky. My previous contentment and assurance had been shattered. Suddenly I was a bag of nerves, conscious of every slip from the tyres and crunching gear change. The more I tried to please my instructor the worst my driving became.

'No, no, no!' Chris screamed at me as the car spewed over a corner and onto some grass after I hit the previous corner too early, thus leaving it too prematurely as well which meant that the car could not straighten up enough. On another occasion Chris shouted: 'What are you doing?'

After a while it seemed to be going better, though. At one point Chris pointed out the end of Hangar Straight where we would turn into Stowe Corner. 'That's Michael Schumacher's favourite corner,' he said, referring to the crash the German had at Silverstone back in 1998 which saw him break a leg and ruled him out for most of the remaining races in the season.

'No chance of me making the same mistake as Schumacher,' I thought as I successfully negotiated the corner and headed off down the circuit.

Meanwhile Chris's outbursts began to peter out until he finally went silent. For a number of laps it was bliss. I drove, Chris stayed quiet, and I came to the conclusion that my instructor could not find any fault with my methods. Once again, my assumptions would prove to be way off the mark.

'Well,' Chris said, after he had asked me to return to base. 'I really hate having to do this, but I'm afraid I'm going to have to fail you on your ARDS test.'

I wasn't entirely sure I had heard him correctly. I felt a little nausea in my stomach, and my heart began to beat a little faster. 'What do you mean?' I asked him, after a few seconds.

Chris looked at me with an incredulous expression and then went on to explain that the reason why he had gone quiet for a number of laps was because I was taking my test. I recalled him saying that he would be doing this, but I wrongly assumed that it would follow another debriefing. Instead, unbeknown to me, I had just taken the test. And I had just failed.

I decided, like a child who had just seen his toy taken away from him, that I disliked Chris. I didn't like failing tests of any kind, least of all tests I did not even know I was taking, and especially when it came to my driving. I failed my first road driving test, too, when I was eighteen years old. Apparently, I had pulled out of a junction too impatiently, causing an oncoming car to slow down. I had failed to notice this at all, which probably proved my examiner's point. That was bad enough, but at least I was still a fresh-faced teenager. I had been driving for twenty-two years, for God's sake, by the time I took my ARDS test, so to be called a menace on the road and to have failed so abjectly was a lot harder to take.

Chris suddenly became all consoling. 'I really don't know what else was expected,' he said. 'After all, you haven't done any kind of motor racing for five years, and then it was just a few laps around the far easier Stowe circuit. Since then you've been driving on the road which, as you are discovering, is entirely different to the way you drive a racing car. You've turned up here, had a quick spin in a Formula First and a few laps around the South Circuit, and then you expect to pass an ARDS test. It was never going to happen.'

He had a point. I was still embarrassed but, clutching to Chris's straw, began to feel a mite happier. We drove back to the school reception area where I would discuss what to do next with the Chief Instructor, Mark Armstrong. We had been introduced to each other a couple of hours earlier but now a felt a great deal smaller.

'Do you know, seventeen people have been killed in the last three years alone in Britain in club motor racing,' he explained, without batting an eyelid. 'You never get to hear about it because the drivers are relatively ordinary members of the public and not famous racing drivers. But it's a fact, and a very damning fact indeed. That's why we take your teaching so very seriously, and that's why we won't pass you on the ARDS unless you deserve it.'

He agreed that my aspirations had been a little on the optimistic side, suggested I should have a one-day coaching session the following day, and then have another crack at the test at the end of it all. But the Saturday race at Silverstone was now out. 'Not enough time to get your application processed,' he added, when he saw my face drop.

I sloped off feeling exactly like I did after failing my maths 'O' level at the age of fifteen and realising I had to take the exam all over again.

Nick Harris, the Jaguar Formula One team's conditioning expert, agreed to meet me in the early evening. I had spent some time with him in Monaco and he promised to produce a fitness regime, seeing that I was attempting to become a motor-racing driver.

'Stamina, strength, reaction and agility,' he announced, as he looked me up and down. 'These are the core ingredients of a Formula One motor-racing driver. People completely underestimate how fit today's drivers need to be. I guess they've always needed to be, but it seems to me that fitness has become a far greater issue nowadays.'

One man has led the way in this department. 'Michael Schumacher has upped the ante and raised the bar when it comes to driver fitness,' Harris continued. 'There may be many reasons why he is considered to be the best current driver in the world, and maybe the best of all time, but it's no coincidence that he is also the fittest.'

Nick threw me a challenge. Before the end of the summer I would undergo a fitness test under his supervision. Then, once he had gleaned my strengths and weaknesses, he would set me a new mark to meet for when I met up with the two Jaguar F1 drivers, Mark Webber and Christian Klien, for a full-on fitness session.

'Your running should be okay, seeing that you've just completed the marathon, but get a lot of swimming and cycling under your belt,' he suggested. 'I'm going to expect one kilometre in the pool front crawl as a bare minimum.'

I nodded and tried to appear unconcerned by this. In truth my swimming had always been suspect. Sure, I could swim all day performing a type of breast-stroke, the type in which you don't get your hair wet nor your eyes stinging with chlorine by keeping your head constantly above water, but when it came to the crawl I was all over the place. And Nick expected me to produce an uninterrupted kilometre.

'No problem, Nick,' I lied.

He hadn't finished, though. 'I'm looking for some core stability, some upper body strength and a good, aerobic capacity, which is where the swimming comes in. What are you like at press-ups? I'll be wanting to see plenty of those. I'll be wanting 50k on a bike, and a run of 10,000 metres, although I might dissect this up into ten times 1000-metre runs at intervals.'

He was beginning to get carried away with himself as he mapped out my hideous physical schedule. This sounded as bad as any regime I had experienced before playing supposedly more physical sports such as rugby with the South African rugby union national team or rowing with Steve Redgrave and company.

'Whatever you say,' I added, weakly, as I regretted ever suggesting his help in the first place. Now that's what happens when you've had a few too many glasses of champagne on some fancy yacht in Monaco.

The night was spent in the Green Man, a local pub just a couple of miles south of the circuit, and a well-known local haunt for motor racing which is booked up to the hilt for the British Grand Prix months before the race takes place. There, over a pleasant meal and a couple of beers, I swotted up on all things relevant in readiness for the next day's written test.

This included trying to understand what was termed as the 'racing line', the quickest route around the circuit using every inch of the tarmac, and the full width, especially when approaching a corner. At the braking point the driver should then smoothly release the accelerator pedal and roll their foot onto the brake pedal. To avoid unbalancing the car the driver should adopt the 'heel and toe' technique, in which the engine is momentarily revved while the clutch is depressed, matching the car's engine speed to the speed of the road wheels when the lower gear was engaged, and in turn preventing wheel locking.

You still with me on this? I must admit my eyes were beginning to glaze over. Much of it I didn't really understand so, like the night before your physics exam at school, I learnt the various relevant passages in the book word for word believing that I could pass without necessarily knowing what any of it meant. This worked to an extent with my school exams. My grades in many of them suggested I had a good understanding of the subject. The truth was that 'understanding' lasted about forty-eight hours before all the information that had been stored up inside my head petered out. I was a fake, in essence, and wondered if the same was going to be said about my racing driving.

I returned to my studies. Learning the flags was a great deal easier for a petrol simpleton such as me.

A blue flag, for example, meant that a competitor was close behind you in a race. A blue flag waving meant that the competitor was about to overtake. A white flag denoted a slow-moving vehicle was on the track, such as an ambulance (a calming thought) or a safety car, a waved white flag that you were about to come across said slow-moving vehicle. And so the list continued.

Yellow flag – danger, no overtaking. Yellow flag waved – great danger. Red – serious incident, slow down, no overtaking. Yellow and red stripes – slippery surface ahead. Black and white striped – suspect behaviour. The dreaded black flag – driver must return to the pits and report to the clerk of the course for a rollicking. Etcetera, etcetera, ending with the famous chequered flag which, when waved, denoted the winner finishing the race.

I fell into a deep sleep trying to avoid dreaming of yellow, red and black flags, and instead imagining chequered flags fluttering in my general direction.

In the morning I felt better about myself. It was a new day, I was a good driver, and the previous day's horrors had been consigned to the past. I joined up with a one-day racing school group and drove more coned circuits in a Formula First, this time avoiding spreading the cones to all corners of the track and one of them ending up in a painful place.

Transferring to the small, Stowe circuit, we then lapped over and over again in the same, single-seaters, before being allowed to overtake those slower than yourself. Although one of the six cars overtook me, I was able to nudge past three cars myself. Now this was more like it. I was beginning to feel like a racing driver.

Steve Warburton summoned me into a room and announced that it was time for my written test. If I had been concerned beforehand, one glance at the questions soon made me realise that I had overdone the revision the night before. The questions were of the following degree of difficulty. If you damage your crash helmet to the extent that cracks appear in it, do you (a) ignore it? (b) put sticky plasters over them? (c) lend it to a colleague to use? or (d) buy a new helmet? It was akin to the type of quiz questions you see on early morning breakfast television in order to win a weekend in Paris: Is the capital of France (a) France, (b) London, (c) Mars, or (d) Paris? Twenty minutes later, having also interpreted all the flag questions, Steve re-entered the room, took my exam paper and marked it there and then.

'One hundred per cent,' he beamed. 'Congratulations. You've just passed your ARDS written test. Halfway there.'

Now that was much better. Even though this had nothing to do with actually driving a car I felt as if I had one hand already on my ARDS certificate. There was no time to lose, though. The remainder of the test – the driving part – had to happen immediately. Silverstone were bending over backwards to accommodate me, which made me feel both important and nervous. Muck it up again and I really would look like an imbecile.

Standing beside a Lotus Elise was not intimidating Chris, but Amanda Whittaker, a seemingly nice racing driver. 'Hi,' she said, with a huge, beaming, welcoming smile. Amanda, without stating the obvious, was a woman. I found myself surprised at my own reaction to this – which was one of illogical surprise. Okay, so she was a woman. And she was an instructor whom I needed to impress in order to gain my racing licence. This flew in the face of my whole argument expressed back in my own car with my wife.

Still, I reckoned, with absolutely no evidence save for her sex, Amanda would be a soft touch. Things were looking good.

There would be seven men taking the ARDS driving test, after I hooked up with another group who had been at the Drive School for the day specifically in order to secure their ARDS certificate. I noticed that I was the only one attired in proper racing gear. The others seemed to be in jeans, T-shirts and trainers. I looked at them slightly disdainfully. At least I looked the part, I thought.

I drove back out on to the southern section of the Grand Prix circuit and started to drive round, listening to every single instruction from Amanda. After fifteen minutes she asked me to exit the circuit and pull up in a lay-by.

'Well?' I asked, brightly. The bright demeanour was, in fact, a poor attempt at disguising my nerve. After my experience with Chris the day before, I wasn't sure whether I had driven well or not.

'Well,' Amanda replied, 'there's no way you are going to pass your test on this evidence. You have no consistency on the corners whatsoever. You need quite a bit more time yet on this circuit to grow used to the vision and the planning you need to tackle the circuit properly.'

I was utterly taken aback. This was the last thing I expected to hear. I was virtually speechless. I was embarrassed. I was humiliated. I had been transformed from a confident, been-there-seen-it-all, mature man, who had travelled the world and mixed it with the best in sport, into a spluttering mouse completely lost for words. And I was angry. How dare she talk to me like that!

'There really isn't any point you taking the test now,' Amanda continued. 'We may as well drive for two or three more laps and I can teach you a bit more.'

My initial annoyance turned to deflation. I decided I didn't like Amanda, after all. As I did not know when the next opportunity to take an ARDS test would be, and on this evidence it would not be in the near future, I reasoned that even if didn't believe I could pass it then and there, I may as well give it a crack. You never knew. I might surprise her. Amanda agreed, although I could tell in her eyes that she believed we would both be wasting our time.

I'll bloody show her, I thought, as I turned the steering wheel and sped out back on to the track. Amanda fell silent as the test began, and I felt the first trickle of sweat pour down the back of my neck. I didn't think it was going too badly at first. Perhaps I took one corner a touch wide, another apex a touch too soon, but in general I felt I was driving reasonably well. But I felt nervous. Far too nervous, and anything but relaxed. Then I misjudged exiting a particularly tight corner, attempted frantically to straighten up the car as I sped away, and ended up off the track and on some gravel.

I carried on with the lap, and completed a second lap, too, but I knew that I had failed. The visit to the gravel alone would have guaranteed this, although I'm sure there were plenty of other aspects which went against me. It was akin to smashing into the front of a car while performing the reversing around a corner manoeuvre during your driving test. When we returned to the others waiting their chance I climbed out of the Lotus without saying a word. It was pretty obvious.

Over the course of the next half an hour the other six drivers went out with their various instructors, and returned smiling. As I sat in a small room and stared out of the window at them, I watched as they shook hands with each other and high-fived. They were understandably pleased. They had all just passed their ARDS driving test and could, if they so wished, now enter races around the country. Only one out of the seven had failed. And that one was the driver sitting alone in a room, not only looking glum, but also the only member of the group togged up in all the fancy driver's overalls.

As I sat there I recalled emerging from the school gym having taken my maths 'O' Level for the fourth time at the age of eighteen alongside upper fourth boys attempting the subject a year early at fourteen. A few weeks later the school assembly was interrupted midway by the Head of Maths who announced, hamming up his shock in the process, how I had finally passed my exam.

This felt almost as bad. I certainly didn't want to hang around my celebrating colleagues. One by one they took turns in asking me how I had fared, assuming that I, like them, had passed. When I told them the news they all gave me a strange expression, clearly not quite understanding how anyone could have failed.

Steve Warburton sat down next to me. 'What the hell happened?' he asked.

I couldn't really tell him. I didn't understand myself. Maybe I wasn't a good driver, after all. Maybe I wasn't even an average driver. Maybe I was verging on being crap?

Steve broke the silence. 'I'm going to make it my personal mission to make sure you pass that bloody ARDS test,' he announced. 'We'll do it.'

Maybe, I thought, as I drove back down south to my home. But right then it was the last thing I wanted to do. Being told you are useless and a danger, and then being the dunce of the class, was not my idea of fun at all. You might have to put up with that kind of thing as a kid. But not when you are forty years old.

I felt depressed, and I felt angry about the whole situation. I had driven away from my home forty-eight hours earlier happy and confident that I would return as a success. Now, as I crept into the darkened house late at night and fumbled my way upstairs, I was quite clearly a failure. Feeling a great deal smaller, I slipped quietly into bed for what turned out to be a sleepless night. As I tossed and turned I thought about just how I was going to tell the rest of the family my news. And then, as I reviewed my time at

Silverstone, I concluded that trying to prove that I was, in my own way, Michael Schumacher, was one of the silliest, most ridiculous ideas I'd ever had.

chapter four

HEAD TO HEAD WITH MICHAEL SCHUMACHER

There is one thing worse than having your family thinly disguise their amusement at your own embarrassment. And that is when they start to feel sympathetic towards you. Give me their laughter and sarcastic comments any time. Listening to them say how they felt sorry for me, and perhaps this wasn't such a good idea after all, only darkened my mood.

Only I was allowed to start thinking that this was not such a great proposition. Only I could ever muse that perhaps my age was counting against me. Certainly nobody else was allowed to wonder whether I could no longer maintain a jet-set, high-octane lifestyle.

In contrast the man whose fault this was, Michael Schumacher, got back to winning ways after his Monaco setback by claiming his sixth Grand Prix in seven races since the start of the season at the European Grand Prix at the Nurburgring in Germany. A fortnight later he made it seven out of eight at the Canadian Grand Prix in Montreal, perhaps his best victory to date in the season because he started the race in sixth position on the grid. The win meant another record in the history of Formula One, this time with Schumacher becoming the first driver to win the same race, the Canadian Grand Prix, on seven different occasions. With team-mate Rubens Barrichello, Ferrari, the runner-up, were once again running away with both the drivers' and constructors' championships, although Jenson Button with yet another third place was hanging on to the Ferrari two by his fingernails.

Meanwhile, right down at the other end of the scale, I took a radical decision. I decided to take up a business opportunity Down Under, partly because it was good business, but also to escape from what was becoming an obsession for me. Ten days in New Zealand and Australia would be perfect to clear the confused mind and reach a decision concerning whether I would drop the project completely and return to normality.

For much of the twenty-two-hour journey to the furthest corner of the globe I sat and thought. Usually I would watch at least five movies and devour a book but this time I fought with myself. The easy and sensible option was to pull out. I had barely got started, after all, and who would ever know? At various times as we soared above the clouds and headed towards and then beyond the equator, I had all but decided to take this course of action. But something kept nagging me. It just wasn't the sort of thing I would do. Or at least, the person who used to be me.

The journey to the other side of the world is a long and soulless experience. The worst part for me is the aimless wandering around the terminal at Kuala Lumpur or Singapore, feeling sick with tiredness, and barely halfway to Auckland. Nearly a full day and night in the air, while the world carries on its confused way unabated. There then followed a desperate remainder of the day on arrival, and a losing battle against closing eyelids. There is no doubt that New Zealand's largest metropolis – the 'City of Sails' – is beautiful and well worth exploring, but all I could do that day was lie on my bed like a beached whale, before waking again at three in the morning and rejoicing at the beauty of jetlag.

Later that morning a Kiwi radio and television producer friend of mine, Greg Billings, phoned me in my hotel room to find out what I was up to. Greg produced the Murray Deaker radio and TV shows in New Zealand, cult sports programmes presented by the larger-than-life Deaker. They had been very kind about my previous books over the years, and were wondering what hare-brained idea I was pursuing.

When I explained my latest project, conveniently forgetting to mention my disastrous time at Silverstone, Billings said he had an idea and would email me back. Within an hour I was reading the kind of communiqué not even I usually receive. 'There's a guy over here, a local government official, who you could race against, maybe in a kart,' he wrote. So what, I thought, as I scanned the hotel's screen in front of me. Why on earth did I want to race against a government official? The next sentence provided the delicious answer. 'His name, by the way – and this is not a joke – is Michael Schumacher.'

I blinked a couple of times and read this last sentence over and over again. There is a bloke in New Zealand actually called Michael Schumacher! I asked Greg to look into it and, within twenty-four hours, not only had Schumacher (the Kiwi) agreed to a race, but we were exchanging emails.

'I'm rather embarrassed about stealing another man's glory but I'm happy to race you,' Michael wrote. 'I am the complete opposite of the other Michael Schumacher. I am employed as a public servant and the biggest risk I take is answering the wife back.'

I liked the sound of this guy. And I liked the idea of whupping Michael Schumacher in a kart race, too. If a public servant from Auckland beat me then that really would be it. I would can the whole idea and grow old gracefully. But if I could beat Michael Schumacher – and at this point any Michael Schumacher would do – then my comeback would begin, 12,000 miles away, on the other side of the planet.

Before Schumi and I could 'get it on' I decided to take the advice of a motor-racing writer friend of Greg's called Sandy Myhre and arrange a visit to see Chris Amon. I had not, to my shame, actually heard of Amon. Sandy explained how he was the surviving member of the great triumvirate of New Zealand motor racing – with former driver and engineer Bruce McLaren and former F1 world champion Denny Hulme. McLaren, whose team went on to become one of the most successful outfits in F1 racing, was killed in a sports car crash in 1970, while Hulme, the world champion in 1967, died of a heart attack in 1992.

Amon, whose biggest claim to fame was that he drove for the great Enzo Ferrari in 1967–69, was not only one of the best drivers in the late 1960s and early '70s, an era that included the likes of Graham Hill, Jack Brabham, Jim Clark and Jackie Stewart, but also the unluckiest. He never actually won a Formula One Grand Prix in the thirteen years he was involved in the sport, but was robbed on countless occasions by mechanical problems.

I've been on a good number of planes in my time travelling around the world, but I have never sat in a nineteen-seater propeller plane before in which the steward doubles up as the co-pilot. 'Welcome aboard this Air New Zealand flight to Taupo,' he announced, as we sat on the tarmac at Auckland Airport. 'My name is Tim, we'll be flying at 16,000 feet altitude, and the flight time is forty minutes. Enjoy the flight.' And with that he turned round, removed his cap, entered the cockpit, sat down next to the pilot and plonked a pair of headphones over his ears.

After a fairly bumpy journey, in which the drone of the propellers prevented any meaningful conversations, the modest plane descended rapidly into Taupo airport in the centre of New Zealand's North Island. As we drew close to the runway I observed the second largest lake in the southern hemisphere and all the glorious, geographical wonders that surrounded it. It was created, so the locals say, by a volcanic eruption so large that the sun went hazy over China. The area remains volcanic to this day, with Mount Ruapehu last erupting modestly in 1996. Skiers and snowboarders flock to the mountains on the southern side of the lake in the winter, while you can end your day by bathing in the plentiful hot springs.

My visit, though, was to relive the past with a sixty-one-year-old man who, so I discovered, had a wealth of both funny and poignant stories. Chris was kind enough to collect me from the tiny airport. He could not mistake me on the basis that I was the only person actually sitting inside the terminal building. Arriving at his holiday home that overlooks Lake Taupo, the first thing I noticed was the doormat at the front door. 'Bugger off', it read, in a welcoming kind of way. 'It could have been worse,' explained his English-born wife, Tish. 'There were all kinds of "offs" at the store where I bought it.'

Tess, their young Rottweiler, ran towards me. When a Rottweiler does this the first thing you do is brace yourself for the worst. Dog lovers – and the Amons certainly fit into that category – tend to ignore the fact that their darling 'Rotty' has just bitten off your finger, dismissing it as nothing more than Spot, Fido or Rover being pleased to see you. When Tess honed in on my crotch, which is what all dogs tend to do, no matter how big or small they or you may be, I would have settled for losing a finger. Instead she started to lick my hand before flopping on to her side and looking up with a doleful expression on her face. I stroked her, of course, pretending that I had never been concerned about the fate of my crotch.

Chris made us some tea and beckoned me over to the spacious

living room. A little mist hung over the lake, and a small boat chugged its way across the water, causing a slight ripple in the water. He opened a window, then settled down in an armchair, lit the first of what would be many cigarettes, and started to talk of an age, forty years ago, unrecognisable to today, both in motor sport and in life.

His ambition as a young, promising racing driver in New Zealand had been to feature merely in a few club races, then in a national series, then Australia and then, after all his previous hopes had been realised, maybe try out one year in Europe. It turned out to be thirteen.

Having caught the eye of European team bosses when he fared promisingly against some of the top names when they came down under for a few races after the Formula One season had ended, a nineteen-year-old Amon was asked by an F1 team boss, Reg Parnell, to come over and race for him in the driver's championship. 'I'd never taken a telephone call from anyone from England before,' Chris recalled. 'New Zealand in the mid-1960s was very unsophisticated. You couldn't get a meal in a restaurant after seven o'clock in the evening. I arrived in England very naive.'

After a couple of moderate seasons in F1 with the Parnell team Amon joined fellow Kiwi Bruce McLaren's fledgling operation of sports cars, entered the famous twenty-four-hour endurance race at Le Mans and, with McLaren alongside him, led until late into the day when the car broke down. The following year he and McLaren won. 'I entered Le Mans eleven times in total, and finished only once, when I won,' Chris recalled.

At the back end of 1966 he was in America when Keith Ballisat, Shell Oil's racing manager, informed him that Enzo Ferrari wanted to meet him at their Maranello headquarters in Northern Italy that Tuesday morning. 'You couldn't turn Enzo Ferrari down although, as it turned out, Ballisat had already booked the flights. He wasn't expecting a no from me.'

He, and Ferrari himself, later on got a yes from Amon who, after a test against the other three Ferrari drivers, found himself alongside the Italian, Lorenzo Baldini, at the 1967 Monaco Grand Prix. It was Amon's first F1 drive for Ferrari, and it would prove to be Baldini's last. 'Baldini hit the barricade at the chicane past the tunnel and his car burst into flames. It was a huge accident, Baldini had 90 per cent burns, but it still took him three days to die. The race carried on, there was no safety car, and I finished third, having passed Baldini's smouldering wreck each lap.'

Amon paused for a few seconds and looked out towards the lake. 'It was very traumatic. Lorenzo was a lovely guy. We'd won the twenty-four-hour race at Daytona together, and the 1000-kilometre at Monza. I came into the pits three laps after the accident because wreckage had punctured one of my tyres. All the Ferrari mechanics were ashen-faced. I remember their faces as if it were yesterday.'

Denny Hulme won the championship that year with Amon fourth, two triumphs from a country so small and unknown in motor-racing terms, but it was Baldini's fate that began a running theme in the conversation over the next half an hour or so. 1968, in terms of driver fatalities, was simply a disaster. 'You look at the grid at the first race of the season, and then look at the end,' Chris said. 'A fifth of the drivers had been killed.' It is a staggering statistic. The life expectancy of drivers in the late 1960s seemed to be not much better than Second World War Spitfire pilots. And this was supposed to be sport.

'We lost one driver a month for the first five months of the season. One of my former Ferrari colleagues, Ludovico Scarfiotti, Mike Spencer, Joe Schlesser' He stopped at the mention of the Frenchman, Schlesser, and screwed up his face. 'Had a horrific crash at the French Grand Prix at Rouen. Burnt to death. The worst thing was you could actually smell poor Joe burning.'

We both sat in silence for a while after this. At first I examined

Amon's face. He seemed to be a long way away from sitting at home in Taupo at this moment. Then I examined his words. I knew motor racing was dangerous. I knew, too, that it used to be more dangerous. But I'd never had a conversation with someone who had been in the thick of it and who could describe, in such horrendous, graphic detail, the raw, black reality of the sport in the Sixties. They clearly all possessed a death wish, something I most certainly did not.

And then there was Jim Clark. The Scot's death the same year was as momentous as that of Ayrton Senna in 1994, maybe even more so. And it hit Amon hard. 'It was a bloody stupid Formula Two race at Hockenheim,' he recalled, almost angrily. 'I knew Jimmy well. Very well. He stayed with me and my parents when he came over to New Zealand, and my parents stayed with his in the UK. Losing Jimmy was shattering. Up until then, despite all the other deaths, I always felt it would never happen to me. But after Jimmy crashed, I felt that if it could happen to him it could happen to any of us. We all felt the same.'

He would not be the last. 1970 proved to be another terrible year, a year that saw the deaths of English brewery heir Piers Courage, Austrian Jochen Rindt, who would posthumously become world champion that season, and Bruce McLaren, who crashed in a sports car at Goodwood. They would all affect Amon. 'I remember having dinner with Jochen,' he recollected. 'Jochen was very upset over the death of his good friend, Piers. He told me he'd had enough. This would be his last season. Then he goes and crashes in qualifying at Spa and kills himself. As for Bruce, that upset me as much as Jimmy. We'd fallen out a bit after I'd left the McLaren team for Ferrari, but I'm pleased to say we'd made up just before Bruce died. I'm so very glad we did.'

Chris decided to change the scenery at this point. We strolled down to a nearby marina to find his boat. He possessed another, smaller one in his garage, named 'EFF 2' but 'EFF 1', bobbing up and down in the marina, was his pride and joy. He and Tish sometimes chug out into the middle of Lake Taupo and spend the night there. 'Makes a nice change,' he explained, as we sat on EFF 1 and he continued his story.

As if the deaths of all his friends and colleagues were not debilitating enough, Amon also had to deal with an incredible run of bad luck. In fact, in his whole, thirteen-year Formula One career, he would claim five poll positions and six, eventual runner-up spots, but he would never actually win a race. Jackie Stewart, a reasonable judge, referred to him as the best driver never to have won a Grand Prix. Enzo Ferrari said he was the best test driver he'd ever seen. He was that highly thought of. But, like Napoleon and his ideal generals, he would have preferred to have been lucky, not talented.

'I ended up tenth in 1968 in the driver's championships, but that was because I couldn't seem to finish a race. I had poll at the Spanish Grand Prix, for example, led by thirty seconds in the race with three quarters of it completed, when my fuel pump broke. I led the Canadian GP by forty-five seconds when the gearbox went. We worked out that if I'd finished all the races I'd been leading that year I would have been world champion.'

Frustrated, he left Ferrari and joined March. 'It was the biggest mistake of my career,' Amon admits now. 'I was really stupid. Within a few months Ferrari had found a new engine and were the pick of the field.'

Chris would spend the next few years flitting from team to team, still devoid of any luck, before witnessing one accident too many that made him decide to call it a day. 'It involved Niki Lauda and happened during the first lap of the German GP at the Nurburgring in 1976,' he recalled. 'I got to within one hundred metres of the accident when I had to stop the car because the track was blocked. I sprinted down the track but by the time I'd got there Niki had been hauled out of his car and been laid down on the tarmac. I remember three things about that incident: first, that his car was totally on fire, second, that there was a complete lack of medical attention at the time, no safety marshals, and no way to extinguish the fire, and third, that I didn't think Niki stood any hope in hell of surviving. They would administer the last rites to him.'

Lauda survived and went on subsequently to become world champion twice more. Amon, though, had had enough. 'I got out of the car, didn't take part in the restart, and went home. At thirty-three I was young enough to start up another career, so I turned to farming and never raced F1 again.'

It was not all depressing for Amon. His fondest memories, save for his times with his fellow drivers, are reserved for Enzo Ferrari. 'He loved the fact that when you came to visit him you'd invariably pass famous film stars sitting outside his office waiting to see him. He also had an intense interest in his drivers' female relationships. Enzo became something of a father-figure to me.'

Amon laughed at this point as he stubbed out another cigarette. 'I'll always remember our lunches together. In the summer we'd go up into the hills. He had a chauffeur called Pepino who'd been with him for years and years, and also a poodle called Dick. Pepino and Dick would sit at one table, and the old man and I would be at another. Enzo would always have a few glasses of wine, and often a malt whisky too before insisting he drove us back to his office. I always felt I stood more chance of dying with Enzo at the wheel than ever during my F1 career. He'd hurtle down the hill back towards Maranello, with his horn blaring and donkeys and geese scattering in his wake. And I'll never forget the sight of Dick, the poodle, sliding from one end of the back seat to the other. He never let me drive his car. When I purchased a Mercedes Enzo asked me if he could drive it. I told him if I couldn't drive his car, then he certainly couldn't drive mine.'

We made our way back to Amon's house. The conversation still concentrated on old man Ferrari, but with a return to a familiar theme. 'He was badly affected by the death of Baldini,' Chris said. 'He'd lost a few others before then, too. It was noticeable that, after Baldini had died, he didn't want to use Italian drivers any more at Ferrari. He tended to shy away from them.'

Looking back Amon has come to terms with his ill luck as a driver, although it took time. 'Early on I was terribly frustrated with the deal I got in Formula One,' he admitted. 'The decision to leave Ferrari, for example, was one borne totally out of frustration. But now I remember the good times. And I look at what I have. A wife, my children, a dog (he said that because Tess had reappeared, once again honing in on my crotch), a lovely home here on the shores of Lake Taupo. I don't consider myself unlucky any more. I think I was remarkably lucky. After all, I'm still here, and I'm very grateful for that.

'I think often about Jochen, of Bruce, and of Jimmy. Especially Jimmy. They should all be in their sixties too, with children, maybe grandchildren, but they're all gone. Long gone. It's impossible to think of Jimmy Clark as an old man. It wasn't really his style. It's nice that my memories of him are of a young man. That image will never change because it is the last image.'

Chris Amon placed his hands on the wooden railing above the balcony and looked out across again over the lake as evening drew in. 'Even so, nice as that lasting image may be, I'd still rather be shaking the hand of a sixty-something Jimmy Clarke today, welcoming him into my home and reminiscing of the days when we were Formula One drivers. That would have been so very nice.'

As hospitable as the Amons had been, it had still been a depressing experience listening to Chris. In truth, as interesting and shocking as his story was, I was trying to sample motor racing myself and the last thing I needed, or rather wanted to hear, was a graphic description of the dangers involved.

On my return to my Auckland hotel I received a message confirming my race with Michael Schumacher for the following day. That was better. I took on an immediately more positive outlook on life. As depressed as I was about the huge loss of young, athletic lives in motor sport, the delicious anticipation of taking on someone called Michael Schumacher became the overpowering emotion.

Robert Lee at 'Karting Direct', a karting company based in the Auckland suburb of Penrose, had laid everything on for us, including karts with fitted seats relevant to our respective sizes, and track time booked at the nearby Mount Wellington karting circuit in Panmure. Mike, as he liked to be called, and his wife, Jill, had both turned up for the head-to-head, having decided to take a day off out of their respective jobs. 'Doesn't happen often that someone wants to race against me,' he explained.

Mike worked for Land Information New Zealand, a public servant who looked after the electoral database. 'I sit in an office all day, and like to play golf at the weekend,' he revealed. 'I'm the complete opposite to the other Michael Schumacher. I catch the bus to and from work, only drive at weekends, and have never been karting before in my life. To be honest, the idea of all that noise, the smell of petrol, the concrete, it's all rather off-putting.'

Things were looking up, I thought. I decided to take up the offer of a lift with Mike to the circuit, just to size up the opposition a little more. It was an interesting fifteen-minute journey. Most women – like my wife – criticise their partners for driving too fast. Jill admonished her husband for being too slow, and for driving 'like a granny'. Considering that her husband's name was Michael Schumacher this was an interesting twist, and one that filled me with even more confidence for the forthcoming race. I guess it was like living with a guy called Luciano Pavarotti who sung in the showers and was tone-deaf.

When Jill refrained from having a dig at Mike's driving,

Schumacher, who was in his mid-forties, explained what it was like going through life with a name like his. 'Actually it was fine until ten years ago when he emerged on the Formula One scene and started to win races,' he admitted. 'Then it became relentless. After all, I'm older than him. I was Michael Schumacher before he was. People would come up to me and would say – thinking every time they were being original – "Where's your Ferrari, then?" or "Well done at the French/German/British Grand Prix." I tried to buy a garden shed once and when I informed the guy of my name he said: "Right, and I'm Damon Hill." Renewing your driving licence takes five minutes. Not with me it doesn't. It took fifteen minutes because the person at the licensing centre had to show everyone my old licence.'

He was on a bit of a roll now. I sensed I had opened up the floodgates. 'I have a brother called James,' Mike continued. 'You want to know what everyone calls him at work?' I shook my head. 'Ralf.'

'It hasn't happened yet but I'm dreading the day when I get pulled over by a traffic cop. Can you just imagine his reaction when he asks me for my name and I tell him Michael Schumacher. He'll double my fine on the spot for being such a smart-arse.'

We sat in silence for a while, giving me time to conjure up this delicious image. 'Who do you think you are?' the officer, like my wife during our family outing a few months before, would undoubtedly ask. 'Michael Schumacher?' The subject matter would look up from his seat and reply: 'Well, er, yes, actually, I am.'

We arrived at the track on what was a bright and sunny southern hemisphere winter's afternoon. I would be driving a 'Top Kart' owned and used by the kart champion of North Island, one Dean O'Sullivan. He was there, too, waiting nervously to see what this rather weird Pom was intending to do with his beloved kart. Mike and I changed into driver's overalls. Mike, who was just beginning to realise what he had got himself into, seemed less than ecstatic when Sandy Myhre, the motor-sport-journalist, turned up to write about the big race for her weekly column. 'I'll never hear the last of this,' he wailed, as we posed for some photos. I shook his hand and announced: 'Let's get it on.' Suddenly Mike looked as if he wanted to be anywhere but here.

After a couple of warm-up laps we were ready for the start. On first evidence Schumacher did not appear too bad. A minor sense of concern flashed through my mind. Robert Lee would be the adjudicator. The race would be run over twenty laps, would begin and end with a chequered flag being waved, and a lap counter was evident at the start. Each lap would take around half a minute to complete.

Lee waved the chequered flag to start and I pressed my foot down hard on the gas, acting as if this were a matter of life and death.

I managed to get my nose in front at the first bend and sped away from Schumacher. As I headed round into the home straight to complete my first lap I noticed that my opponent had spun off the circuit at 'Hell's Corner'.

I could have continued at the same pace, but decided it would be no fun, nor very sporting. If I wanted to beat Michael Schumacher I wanted to beat him fair and square. I slowed right up to almost walking pace, so that by the time I drew level with him his kart was up and running again. The Scarlet Pimpernel would have thrown his opponent back his sword in a dual if it had been dropped on the floor. This was the karting equivalent, I reasoned happily to myself. I sped away again, deriving ridiculous and unbelievably childish pleasure out of showing a public servant from Auckland who had never karted before just what I could do.

Meanwhile Lee, O'Sullivan and Myhre, plus a bunch of

mechanics in their greasy overalls, stood with their arms folded and watched what could loosely be described as action. At Buckmore Park I must have looked very ordinary. At Mount Wellington my opponent was making me look good.

With two laps to go I lapped him. I'll repeat that. I lapped Michael Schumacher. Took him on the inside of the corner at the end of the main straight. A minute later it was all over. I crossed the line first, with Mike a few seconds behind me, before you include the extra lap he was behind. I shook both my gloved fists in the air just above the steering wheel, mainly because that's what the real Schumi does when he wins a Grand Prix, and careered around the circuit one more time on a victory lap. 'Well done,' my good-natured opponent said, when I finally clambered out of Dean's kart and shook his hand. 'Now can I go home?' He looked like my eleven-year-old son fishing the football out of the corner of the net while his father celebrated another goal in the garden.

Schumacher left, while I answered Sandy's post-race questions. 'Well, it wasn't as easy as it may have appeared,' I explained, as she scribbled down notes. 'But the thing about racing Schumacher is that you've got to take him out early, not give him a chance, show him who's boss.' And so this utter drivel continued for the next five minutes or so.

Life in my motor-racing career had suddenly turned for the better. Much better. I'd begun the long comeback from the ignominy of Silverstone. I'd won my first race in my quest to become a racing driver, and it was against, of all people, Michael Schumacher.

Deep down I knew this had hardly been an achievement at all. I had just defeated an older man who had never karted before, didn't like driving and hated the smell of petrol. It was ridiculous how cheaply my confidence had been boosted. Still, after the abject humiliation of Silverstone, I was a desperate man seeking desperate measures. This appeared to have done the trick, all on the far side of the world, where life, and indeed my own outlook, had turned decidedly upside-down.

chapter five

KINETICS AND KANGAROOS

You have to put your watch back by half an hour to cater for the differing time zones between Sydney, where I first entered Australia from New Zealand, and Adelaide, a two-hour flight away. It made me wonder whether this meant you had to turn your watch back ten minutes once you had journeyed a third of the way to Adelaide, in some hick of a town where the honky-tonk pianist never stopped playing, perhaps even twelve minutes once you reached the outer suburbs.

Although some business needed to be attended to in Australia my main purpose was now my quest once more. Buoyed by my questionable triumph against Michael Schumacher in Auckland, my old eagerness had returned. I felt that talking to a wide assortment of racing drivers could only enhance my education as a driver, as it did with Chris Amon, hence the meeting I had managed to arrange with a three-times Formula One world champion, a knight of the realm, and the only driver in history to have driven his own car to the world drivers' title.

Sir Jack Brabham agreed to meet me in the foyer of the Hilton Hotel, Adelaide. He was attending 'Classic Adelaide', one of Australia's most popular motor-sport events where cars from all ages gather to speed around the South Australian hills surrounding the small city.

I had been warned to be careful with Sir Jack. By all accounts his hearing was rather poor, although if he was growing bored with the conversation he would purposefully turn down his hearing aid and wink at a knowing acquaintance. At seventy-eight years of age he was clearly not as sprightly as he once was, but remained mentally as sharp as a pin.

Whatever he thought when he first met me he kept to himself, which was just as well, considering how it began in the most embarrassing of fashions. I was staring at an elderly gentleman wearing a blue blazer no more than a couple of feet away from me as I tapped in Sir Jack's number and called him on my mobile telephone. When Sir Jack answered I told him I was standing in the foyer waiting for him, as arranged. As I did so I turned round, all but bumped into the blazered gent, and realised that he was not only talking on his mobile, but saying exactly the same words I was hearing from my phone clasped to my ear.

'Ahem, you must be Sir Jack, then,' I said, trying to laugh the incident off. There wasn't much point trying to pass myself off as a motor-racing expert, not after this faux pas. Fortunately, Sir Jack was in a convivial mood and keen to talk. It turned out a wife – and wives were rapidly appearing to play a major part in everyone's stories – was the reason why he started racing in the first place.

'I was an engineer first, and a driver very much second,' he explained, once we had found a quiet corner and ordered some tea. 'I was building cars for other people to drive. One of them kept on having accidents, though, and eventually his wife put her foot down and stopped him from racing. We had money pumped into a car that was just sitting in the garage with no driver so I decided I'd give it a go. But if that wife hadn't stepped in, I'm sure I would never have started racing.' The rest, as they say . . .

Sir Jack would go on to become the world champion three times, in 1959, 1960 and 1966, but the most satisfying was the last occasion, when he clinched the title in a Brabham car.

'It was a very exciting stage in my career and, I guess, in Australian motor racing,' he admitted. 'The whole Brabham organisation was Australian orientated, you see, so it was very satisfying to pull it off, especially in the 1960s which I maintain will always be the golden era of Formula One.'

He would have raced Chris Amon a few times, although Brabham's most successful period was a little before Amon came on the scene. This means, nevertheless, that he would have witnessed similar traumatic scenes as the New Zealander.

'Well, it was certainly a very dangerous period,' he agreed. 'The circuits were too dangerous in those days. They had trees and telegraph poles lining the track. It was unbelievable, looking back. In my time in racing over thirty drivers were killed. It wasn't easy losing so many friends. The gloss was taken off winning the 1960 Belgian Grand Prix, for example, because two drivers lost their lives during the race. I think I survived for two reasons: luck, which I had a lot of, but also attitude. I drove within my means. I wanted to win races, but I wasn't prepared to take stupid risks. Ayrton Senna was a classic example of a driver who pushed himself too far. Michael Schumacher was beginning to get the better of him and he became desperate to win. Too desperate.'

The Brabham family's other claim to fame is that Sir Jack's three sons all followed their father into motor racing, with the middle one, David, driving Formula One. Although Damon Hill would later follow in his father, Graham's, footsteps, into the sport.' David Brabham became the first son of a world champion to make the Formula One grid. 'In 1989 David won the Formula Three championship in Europe, Gary the Formula 3000 championship and Geoffrey won the Inter Championships in America, all in the same year,' he announced, proudly.

But it wasn't all good. 'David drove in Formula One for one year only,' he explained. 'That was my fault. I placed him in a poor team, Syntec. I wanted to put him into Tyrrell but I was half a million pounds short. Geoffrey, being my eldest and therefore the first to enter racing, found it hard being my son. In Europe the attitude was "just because you're Sir Jack's son doesn't mean to say you will do as good". In America the attitude was very different. They wanted him to be successful. In America he was welcomed. In Europe he was not.'

Brabham certainly does not regret being born when he was. Today's Formula One is hard to recognise from the sport he once dominated. 'The circuits are safer and the cars are almost bulletproof, which is a good thing, but it's lost its sporting image. It's become big business, and the race is no longer between the drivers, but between the technicians. Whichever team wins the technological race wins the championship. In my day it was much more down to the drivers. The teams were all pretty even and the drivers could have recorded good times in any of the cars.'

That said, he was happy to accept that one of today's drivers was an exception. 'Schumacher stands out,' he said. 'There's no doubt in my mind that he's the best driver ever.' He took a sip from his teacup and looked straight into my eyes. That was a big statement. Sure, Schumacher's won more world titles than anyone else, more Grands Prix too, but he has the best car, and there are far more races these days than in the 1960s. Is Schumacher really better than the great Juan Fangio? Or Jimmy Clark? Or Jackie Stewart or Brabham himself? Or Senna, Niki Lauda, Alain Prost? I wasn't so sure myself. or maybe I just didn't want to hear this. Not if I was serious about somehow fixing a head to head with the man.

'Yes, that's my belief,' Brabham replied. 'Look, he's a natural driver. He can drive anything. If you'd placed him in any of the cars we drove during the 1960s I am certain he would have been world champion on many occasions. But what really makes him stand out in my opinion is what he's achieved with Ferrari. When he joined Ferrari, remember, the team were nowhere. He has taken them to the top. I wouldn't necessarily say single-handedly, but if you removed him from Ferrari they'd struggle. That's why he's the greatest.'

I refrained from telling him of my victory over Schumacher in Auckland. Somehow I didn't think Sir Jack would have been impressed. Besides, he had to go in a minute or two, and a lengthening queue of autograph hunters had suddenly appeared in the foyer waiting for him to finish with me. I noticed quite a few of the fans were in their thirties and under.

'Most people still seem to recognise me,' Brabham confirmed. 'Sometimes it's a bind, but mostly it is very satisfying that people still know of what I did. I receive a great deal of mail from all over the world, a lot from people who never saw me race but have just read about it. I'm very proud of that.'

And so he should be, even if I was standing two feet away from him and hadn't recognised him. Sir Jack's time was forty years ago, but he and his name have remained indelibly linked to motor sport ever since. Even I had heard of him, his team, and his sons. He may now appear to be just another old man, with a hearing aid clasped to his left ear, and a blazer around his shoulders, but Sir Jack Brabham remains one of the greatest names in Formula One, a competitor and, above all, a champion who achieved his goal in the full face of incredible danger.

I flew back to Sydney that night to receive the news from home that Buckmore Park had helpfully emailed me all the results from the night's karting a few weeks back. Now my poor series of results was there for all to see in black and white. My wife had appeared impressed that I had beaten Michael Schumacher in Auckland. 'Well, at least you can beat someone,' she said, cheerily. There's nothing like a back-handed compliment.

Despite all Sir Jack Brabham's global fame, in Australia there is another motor-racing figure far, far better-known, respected and followed than him. It is not Alan Jones, the only other Australian to ever win the Formula One world driver's championship in 1980. It is not Mark Webber either, the Aussie F1 driver for Jaguar whom I might be testing my questionable fitness against in a London gym. Every Australian, indeed every Antipodean I spoke to, all mentioned the same name. Peter Brock. The 'King of the Hill'.

I had not heard of the man, but when Sandy Myhre, the New Zealand motor-sport writer told me he had won nine Bathurst 1000s, he began to register. The Bathurst 1000, for touring cars with V8 engines, is the most prestigious race to win in Australian motor sport, bar none. Winning Bathurst is very big news down under. Certainly more so than winning an F1 race. And Brock had done it nine times, far more than any other Australian driver in the long history of the event. Along the way he had developed a huge and passionate fan base. 'Peter Brock is, quite simply, God' is a phrase I heard over and over again when talking to people in this part of the world. 'You've got to meet him.'

Paddy Dominguez, an old friend of mine now based in Sydney, was the clincher. 'I heard once that a man asked Brock to autograph his glass eye for him,' Paddy told me over a beer in Cafe Sydney, a restaurant and bar that overlooks Circular Quay in the very heart of the city. 'I don't know if it's true or not, but if it is it underlines how famous the man is down here.'

Sandy made the arrangements for me. I would catch the early morning flight to Melbourne where Peter's wife, Beverley, would collect me from the airport and take me back to their home. After a morning's chat Peter and I would travel back into Melbourne to attend a Melbourne Grand Prix lunch, where Peter would be speaking. All the bigwigs of the Grand Prix would be there, which made me, as Peter's official guest, slightly fraudulent. 'Peter and Beverley are very interesting people,' Sandy mentioned over the phone the night before. 'I've got a feeling you're going to find the day a bit different to what you are expecting.' She was talking riddles, but the very next day I would be discovering exactly what she meant.

Beverley was waiting for me at arrivals at Melbourne Airport. Although it was only 7.30 in the morning (I had been up since four) she was bright-eyed and raring to go. The Brocks lived thirty miles to the north-east of the city, right out in the country, in an area called Nutfield. They have a large farmhouse and 200 acres of land where their three dogs, Lil, Kia and Joss, like to roam about. The house, incidentally, is called 'Kiah Kerrabee' which, in aboriginal, means a beautiful place for people to join together and celebrate.

In the kitchen Peter arrived, having already been down the local gym. For a man of fifty-nine years of age he was in remarkably good shape. Lean, tanned, with a full head of hair, and looking good in a pair of jeans when most men his age do not, he exuded health and fitness. Bev offered me a cup of tea, which was when the fun and games began. 'Two sugars, please, Bev,' I asked.

'Two sugars? I'm surprised that a man as energetic and fit as you should be taking sugar,' Bev announced, shaking her head.

'Well, it's just about my only vice,' I replied. 'And it's not the biggest vice in the world, now, is it?'

Bev came over and asked me to hold my left arm up straight. She then placed her arm on top of mine, told me to push my arm upwards, and she would try and push mine down. Not surprisingly, she failed to do so. After all, I am a good ten to fifteen years younger than her, and I am male. No surprise there, then. I looked across at Peter, and gave him a quizzical look. He had a knowing expression on his smiling face.

'Okay, now hold out your right hand with your palm upwards,' Bev said. She had clearly not finished with me. She placed around a dozen granules of sugar in my hand. 'Now try and push my left arm up again.'

This time Bev pushed my left arm down to my side with ease. I declared that she had simply caught me out, that I wasn't ready, and that there had been some kind of trick. Bev suggested we should try it again. This time, with the sugar still in my right palm, I was ready. It made no difference. Bev pushed my arm down to my side and asked me if I still wanted sugar in my tea.

'What did she do?' I asked Peter, who was now laughing. 'What did she do?'

'I've seen her do this hundreds of times,' Peter said. 'It's kinetics, my friend. Bev had better explain.'

I turned round to Bev with a pleading expression. 'Kinetics, or kinesiology, is the impact of movement on your body,' she replied. 'The energy of the sugar weakens your body energy. That's why it is not good for you. You are not drinking tea when you have sugar in it. You are drinking a muscle-reducing liquid that is impacting on your body's well-being.'

As a compromise I asked for one sugar and stared at my cup of muscle-reducing liquid impacting on my body's well-being. Suddenly it didn't seem quite so appealing.

Peter grabbed his coat and his car keys and suggested we went for a drive around his land. 'You're gonna find this interesting, too,' he promised. We jumped into his old four-by-four and headed off into the countryside. Within minutes I saw something hopping at great speed in the distance. 'Peter, look, there's a kangaroo,' I shouted, with genuine excitement.

You have to understand that, being English, I find it exciting if I see a squirrel in the garden. I down tools if a fox scampers across the lawn. Catching a glimpse of something like a stoat is a real rarity. I don't think I've seen a hedgehog in twenty years. So to see something like a kangaroo in the wild and in its natural habitat, an animal only witnessed before in a zoo, was really something.

'Well, you haven't seen anything yet,' Peter promised. Sure enough, a little further on, we came across a bunch of roos, all hopping madly away from the approaching car. There must have been twenty there. 'The generic noun for a group of kangaroos is a "mob", by the way,' Brock informed me, helpfully. Around the next corner another mob was in full view. This time there were fifty, maybe more. 'This is ridiculous,' I said, as Peter clearly enjoyed my excitement. 'The place is teeming with them.'

And it was. The Brock land was a haven for wild bush kangaroos. We saw many more mobs over the course of the next twenty minutes. One came within ten feet of the car, with the leader, a big old buck, being the last to hop off, only after a defiant stand and a staring session with us first. 'They very rarely attack you,' Peter explained. 'But if they do they can deliver one hell of a kick.'

When God decided to invent animals and distribute them around the world he must have decided to make Australia the home of all his comic creatures. Hence Australia being the only country where hopping, pouched marsupials such as kangaroos and wallabies roam, where wombats burrow, koala bears climb and, strangest of all, the duck-billed platypus lives. 'We get a few of them, too,' Peter said.

There were other points of interest, too. The trees were filled with cockatoos and galahs, the latter members of the parrot family. 'The generic nouns for them are a screech,' Peter continued, sounding more like a safari ranger by the minute. He stopped the car for a second to collect a large mushroom growing wild. 'We'll cook it later,' he explained. On the way back we passed a billabong – a dried-out watering hole – a tree with a wedge-tailed eagles' nest perched high in its branches, and a spot which made him temporarily go all misty-eyed.

'That's where my last dog is buried,' he said. 'He went down a wombat hole and got nipped on the nose by a tiger snake. Took him twenty minutes to die.' This was not such good news, not for an Englishman who's never seen a snake in the wild in his life. I was sorry about his dog. I was more sorry about the prospect of coming across a tiger snake myself. 'You get tiger snakes here, then?' I asked.

'Oh yes, and other nasty snakes, too. Humans don't normally die from them, though. As long as you get to a hospital you'll survive. We have redback spiders here, too. You normally find them in the creeks. You don't want to be poisoned by them, either.'

I suggested we got back to the house. Not in a while, but right now. What with kicking kangas, biting tiger snakes and poisonous redbacks, the Victorian bush of north-east Melbourne district was suddenly not as appealing as I first thought.

It was on arriving back at the house, however, that the biggest surprise of the day fell. There, standing on the porch right next to the back door, was a kangaroo. She stared nonchalantly at us, without a care in the world. 'Peter,' I said, when I first glimpsed the animal. 'There's a bloody kangaroo on your doorstep.'

'Ah yes,' he said, smiling. 'That's Matilda. Or Tilly, as we sometimes call her.'

Peter explained that 'Tilly' came to their house once or twice a day, to sit outside on the porch, and to be sometimes fed. 'She can even open the door by jumping up and pushing down the handle. We've found her in the house before when we haven't been in. On a cold and wet day Bev and I argue about whether we should let her in or not. I always feel sorry for her. I reckon she's a bit of a reject. Anyway, I normally let her in. She's even been known to sit on our bed.'

Now my cat likes to sit on my bed back at home. But a wild,

bush kangaroo? Apart from anything else, breakfast in bed would be exceedingly difficult with a fully grown kangaroo bouncing up and down. The cornflakes would go flying. I was about to ask which side of the bed did Tilly prefer, and whether she was a one- or two-pillow kangaroo, but Peter interrupted my thoughts with a suggestion. 'Do you want to feed her?'

Bev had appeared by now as Peter gave me a biscuit. I half expected her to grab Tilly by one of her shortened arms, place some biscuit crumbs in her pouch, and stop her from bouncing by using that rare gift of kanga kinetics. Instead they stood back as I leant, albeit nervously, towards Tilly and watched as she grabbed the biscuit with her mouth. Somehow I hadn't imagined I would be feeding wild bush kangaroos with biscuits as I planned my day-trip to the Brocks.

It was time to leave for Melbourne and the Grand Prix lunch. Peter changed quickly into a suit, I thanked Bev for her hospitality and general entertainment and was about to leave when she announced, 'One more thing.'

Oh oh! Grabbing my arm again she closed her eyes, squeezed it hard, shook it up and down, and almost wrenched it from its shoulder socket, before finally releasing it. 'That's good,' she declared, with an approving nod of her head, as she walked back into the home. I sat in the car, turned to Peter and asked: 'What was all that about, then?' I was beginning to wonder whether Tilly had in fact been a previous visiting human whom Bev had turned into a bush kangaroo.

'It was an advanced form of kinetics,' he explained. 'It's something that I can't do, but Bev most certainly can. She measured your body's response to a question she asked of you. Are you healthy? Are you fit? You accepted the pattern she was placing in your arm. Your body responded favourably.' Right. So the upshot of all that was what, exactly? 'Oh, that you are indeed fit and healthy, and there's nothing to worry about.'

I sank down into my seat and breathed a huge sigh of relief. Being told by Bev that I was about to contract something horrible – like bush kangaroo fever – would not have been the best way of leaving the Brock household.

We headed off back into the countryside. Along the way I saw many road signs with fire warnings. They would be divided up into sections with an arrow pointing at either low, medium, high or extreme high. 'What comes after extreme high, Peter?' I asked. 'I suppose the answer to that is aaarrrgh,' he shouted. 'They probably can't spell it on the sign.'

A little further on we passed a field with a number of extremely large birds bent over pecking at the ground. 'Are those emus?' I asked my natural history expert cum racing driver friend. Actually I was pretty certain they were, but I just wanted to share my new-found knowledge of strange Australian creatures with Brock. He confirmed that they were. I then asked him a question he was unable to answer. 'So what's the generic noun, then, for a bunch of emus?'

Peter screwed up his face as he drove and thought long and hard. Eventually he had to concede he did not know. 'I can't believe I don't know the answer,' he said. It seemed to bother him genuinely. I consoled him with the little-known fact that the generic noun for a group of journalists was 'a fabrication', but still he seemed concerned. 'I'll have to find that out,' he promised.

It struck me, as the first sight of the downtown Melbourne skyscrapers came into view on the distant horizon, that while we had explored kinetics and kangaroos all day, we had not even ventured into the world of motor racing, which was the real reason why I had paid the Brocks a visit in the first place.

'I know it seems a bit stupid, Peter,' I ventured. 'But do you think there is any chance we can actually talk about motor racing, seeing that you are the nine-times Bathurst 1000 champion?' He laughed. 'Sure, sure. I'd almost forgotten myself, to be honest.'

In total he had raced Bathurst thirty times. His first win was way back in 1969, when he was twenty-five years old, and his last appearance had been in 1997, when he was fifty-two. 'Winning Bathurst is considered a big deal in this part of the world,' he explained. 'To win it nine times is the reason why everyone seems to know me. I can go to the most dead place in the outback and there will be someone there who can tell me exactly what I did on the tenth lap of the race in 1978, or the fifteenth lap in 1985. I've done a heap of other races, mainly in Australia, but winning Bathurst as many times as I did is what I'm best known for.'

His quickest time on the 6 km circuit is two minues, ten seconds, but he was best known for the way he tackled the various hill climbs found during the course. Bathurst, a three-hour drive due west of Sydney, is just beyond the Blue Mountains, hence its still hilly route, and Brock's moniker, 'King of the Hill'.

Did he ever feel the lure of Formula One? 'No, if I'm honest. Touring cars have always been the thing for me. I had a drive in an F1 car once.' He mimicked the noise of an F1 car at this point and pretended to change gear at the same time, with an exaggerated, jerking movement of his hand. 'It did nothing for me at all. I have no regrets when it comes to my motor-racing career.'

I asked him about the glass eye story Paddy had related back in Sydney. 'I've signed all kinds of things – G-strings, you name it – but never a glass eye before. This man came up to me and said, "You'd sign anything, wouldn't you?" I replied, "Er, yes, I suppose so." Then he took out his glass eye and handed it to me. Coming from a farming background I'm not squeamish, so I signed it and returned the eye. He placed it back in its socket. You could quite clearly see the name "Peter Brock" on the eye.' He paused for a second, shook his head and added: 'It truly is a strange world we live in.'

So when and why did Peter Brock change his ways? Beverley had told me during the drive from the airport in the early morning that in his younger days he was the archetypal racing driver, with no shortage of wine, women and song. 'That's true,' he conceded. 'But I've always been a bit weird, too. I've always been a bit different, a bit willing to explore new topics. It was in my late thirties, after I'd met Bev, that I started looking for other agendas in life. I'd like to say Bev suggested I should adopt a healthier lifestyle, but it was more like insisted. I won't use the word nag. Bev persevered with this, but I must have been open to it. So I started to exercise more, changed my diet completely, and changed my approach to life. I'm certainly a far more spiritual person now than I ever was before, and that's why I'm feeling still so fresh and energetic. Life is good.'

We were now in Melbourne, crossing the Yarra River, driving past the huddle of skyscrapers glinting in the sunlight, and heading into the southern section of the city. Drawing up to the Melbourne GP headquarters, just across from the Albert Park street circuit, a couple of unexpected things happened.

First, Brock received a call on his hands-free car phone. The voice on the other end of the line was asking him if he fancied having another crack at the Bathurst 1000, seven years after what was supposed to be his final appearance there. He had received offers before, but this was different. This time he would be provided with just about the best car in the race. Brock told the caller he was in principle interested, and would discuss it further with him at a later date. Ending the call, though, his eyes were lit up and sparkling. 'It's very tempting,' he said. 'I reckon I could do it, too. And it would be a great message to everyone that a fifty-nine-year-old can still win the very best races in motor sport.'

The second incident took place as we climbed out of his car and shut the doors. Peter's agent, who had been waiting outside Grand Prix house, introduced him to someone who was behind a new mobile telephone game called, provisionally, 'Peter Brock, King of the Hill'. Brock took a glimpse at a mobile as the man showed him how it worked, and looked suitably pleased. It wasn't quite being invited to lunch with Lara Croft, Tomb Raider, but it was the next best thing.

Inside we mingled and shook hands with various race sponsors before Ron Walker stood up, made an introductory speech about how wonderful it was that the city would be celebrating its tenth anniversary of the Grand Prix in 2005, and asked Brock to step up on to the stage. There then followed a totally unscripted fifteen minutes in which Peter schmoozed the assembled guests with his anecdotes of the past, his views of the Melbourne Grand Prix, of which he is a board member, and his belief that Michael Schumacher was the greatest driver ever. The enormity of what I was attempting to do thus increased in my mind. Brock's performance was impressively polished, although he struck a somewhat contrasting figure from the one stroking Tilly in his jeans just an hour previously.

Afterwards he introduced me to Walker, the man behind the Melbourne Grand Prix. Walker, in good shape for sixty-five, is six-feet-six-inches tall, a huge, imposing figure, with a huge, imposing character. A former mayor of Melbourne at just twenty, he managed to snatch the Australian GP from Adelaide, having shaken hands with Bernie Ecclestone.

That alone must have taken some doing, seeing that Ecclestone is five feet four inches, and Walker is fourteen inches taller. It must have been quite comical to watch. Either Walker would have gone down on his knees – which would have been in keeping with the hold Bernie has over Formula One – or Ecclestone would have deployed a stepladder. Either way, it must have appeared ridiculous.

Walker had also brought the first Bledisloe Cup game to the city, the annual Australia versus New Zealand rugby union double header, golf, in the form of the USA versus the southern hemisphere President's Cup, as well as the forthcoming 2006 Commonwealth Games. He was Chairman of the Melbourne GP Board, on the global F1 commission, a former Treasurer of the Australian Conservative Party for fifteen years, and the builder of the Crowne Casino in the city, the southern hemisphere's largest casino that, on any given day, has 30,000 visitors.

'Brocky is a superstar,' Walker leant over to inform me. 'He is very, very famous down here. Everybody in Australia knows him. If he entered politics he'd do very well. People love him, partly because he's a sporting hero, but also because he's never been a prima donna. Nothing is ever too much trouble for him.' I could vouch for that.

Yet even Ron was taken aback when Brock announced that Walker was standing in the company of a man who had just beaten Michael Schumacher.

'Really, Brocky?' he replied, before peppering him with questions. 'When did you do that, then? Where did it happen? What were you driving?' He had made the entirely understandable assumption that Brock had been talking about himself.

'No, no, Ron, it's not me, it's Ian,' he said, looking across at me and patting my back. 'And he lapped Schumacher, too.'

Before Walker could try and figure this out he was led away to talk to someone. On his return Brock threw him a second curve ball. 'By the way, Ron, do you know what the generic noun is for a bunch of emus?'

It wasn't a question he had been particularly expecting at a Melbourne Grand Prix sponsors' lunch, and clearly not one that he had previously given much thought to, either. 'Er, well, erm, let me think about that one Brocky,' he replied, his face as furrowed as the King of the Hill's. I turned round and asked a couple of other guys standing close by dressed in pinstriped business suits and holding glasses of wine in their hands. 'Do you know what a group of emus is called?' They took a couple of uneasy steps away from us and began talking to a new group of people.

En route to the airport Peter drove me around the Albert Park circuit that transforms itself from a series of car parks and roads surrounding a lake into a Grand Prix venue. It was barely recognisable, save for the black, rubber tyre marks on most of the curves and the long, flat building beside the grid where the pit lane and garages could be found. 'There's "Brocky's Hill",' he pointed out, referring to a steep, grassy patch beside one particular corner. 'That's what it is known as each year, for some reason. Don't really know why. After all, I've never driven Formula One.'

He parked the car outside the arrivals hall at Melbourne International Airport, shook my hand, and invited me back to visit him and Beverley whenever I was next travelling to Victoria.

It had been quite a day. I had probably not quite realised how so many motor-racing enthusiasts in Australia would have given anything to have been me that day.

Yet I got something else out of Peter, and indeed Beverley, than I had expected. Interesting, diverse, slightly eccentric even, but enormous fun to be with, Brock had introduced kinetics and kangaroos into my life, and that was something I had not planned for when I was first informed about the King of the Hill.

'Emus?' I said to him, as a parting question.

'I know, I know,' he replied, shaking his head and looking more frustrated than he really should have done. 'I'm going to find out if it's the last thing I ever do,' he vowed. And with that I walked to the check-in hall and a flight back home to resume my fledgling motor-racing career, while Peter Brock headed off back to Beverley and Tilly for more kinetics, and more arguments over whether three was one too many for their double bed.

chapter six

FAST, FURIOUS AND FLUKEY

The jet lag seemed to be getting worsc on my return to England, and much of the following week would be dominated by broken sleep. Someone told me it is because I am not as young as I used to be. Utter nonsense, I replied, wondering if in fact this was the case.

Despite this, it was good to be home, just to do the simple things after many nights of wining and dining abroad. I was back on a high again. The trip Down Under had done its trick, even though I had no idea I would end up racing someone called Michael Schumacher and feeding wild bush kangaroos.

I made a point of watching the French Grand Prix which my wife had recorded for me on TV the previous day. This was something I would never have previously asked her to do for me. If I'd missed a Grand Prix it wasn't a problem. Now I had to watch every single one.

Schumacher's win at Magny Cours was his ninth out of ten

starts in the season so far, his sixtieth for Ferrari, and his seventy-ninth overall. Now twenty-two points ahead in the driver's title race of his nearest rival, teammate Rubens Barrichello, he had amassed almost twice as many points as third-placed Jenson Button, who was continuing to score points on a remarkably consistent basis. As Barrichello was hardly going to be permitted to catch his team-mate up – officially or unofficially – the world championship was all but decided. Schumacher now stood just two short of his own record for the number of Grand Prix wins in one season, which stood at eleven. With still eight races to go, this record, too, would surely fall to the best ever in the sport, at least according to Brabham and Brock.

On the Tuesday night before the British Grand Prix a small slice of history would be made in the streets of central London. Eight F1 cars, driven by the likes of Button, David Coulthard, Juan Pablo Montoya, plus retired British icon Nigel Mansell and former Grand Prix driver turned television motor-racing commentator Martin Brundle, would scream their way up and down Regent Street in front of a quarter of a million spectators in order to promote the weekend's Grand Prix at Silverstone. It would be the first time the capital had ever heard the roar of F1 engines, and quite possibly the first step towards London's plans of staging an actual F1 race through its streets.

The day before, Brundle would be required to turn up at the Santa Pod drag-racing track in Northamptonshire. This was to test out the Jaguar R4 car he would be driving down Regent Street but, as he would no doubt be testing at speeds usually witnessed at Silverstone, they required someone else to 'cruise' the car at the kind of lesser rate needed for central London.

This was when Nav Sidhu, having just calmed down from the stress of organising Messrs Pitt, Clooney, Damon and company in Monaco, decided to put himself through the mental wrangle again. 'How would you like to drive a Formula One car?' his voice shrilled down the telephone line to me.

This was an unbelievable opportunity. I had raised the notion of driving an F1 car before with Nav but he had told me, if it were at all possible, it could cost as much as £50,000 to arrange. Now, out of the blue, he was giving me the chance to do something almost every man in the world would kill for. And it was free. 'You'll have to give me time to think about that,' I replied, before adding two seconds later: 'I've thought about it. Yes, please. I'm happy to be your guinea pig.'

Nav, after wincing at that last comment, said he would see if he could fix it up. Within a couple of hours this had been achieved, but his demeanour had noticeably changed. 'You do realise that this is the same car Brundle is using in Regent Street and, if you cock it up, the whole night will be off as far as Jaguar Racing is concerned, and Brundle, for that matter.'

'What's there to cock up?' I replied, with a fair degree of bravado.

A decidedly nervous sounding Nav explained that he would tell all on the Monday morning of the test. 'Let's just put it this way,' added the Head of Communications. 'My Managing Director, Dave Pitchforth, has told me to get my P45 ready.'

The night before my planned drive turned out to be an unmitigated disaster. I had enjoyed no more than two hours' sleep, courtesy of my daughter's middle-of-the-night flight to Germany on a school exchange trip. On my return to my bed I spent much of the remainder of the night envisaging various nightmare scenarios at Santa Pod, mostly ending with a crunched Formula One car.

I felt it better not to mention this to Nav when I arrived at Jaguar Racing headquarters in Milton Keynes. I felt so tired I was dizzy. Better keep that to myself, I decided.

Before the briefing could begin I first had to find the suitable gear. Carol Melville, in the Jaguar race office, quickly dismissed my cheap booties and overalls with a disdainful look, and handed me a pair of green Jaguar overalls covered from top to toe in sponsors' logos. Battling it out for positions on the suit were HSBC, Hangar-7, UGS PLM, DuPont, AT&T, Pioneer, Michelin, Becks, Castrol, Lear, Tom Tailor, Rolex, Puma, MSC Software, and 3I Systems. It is an incredible amount of sponsors, and yet more evidence of how F1 is more sponsor-driven than any other sport.

Carol and Nav raised doubts over whether I could actually squeeze into this new attire, seeing that it actually belonged to their number one driver, Mark Webber. 'Mark's got buttocks like peaches,' Carol commented. To their surprise, and mine, I achieved this, although the zipping-up process around my crotch required a slow and somewhat painful process. I had been on a protein diet since my return from Down Under after two weeks of dining out. Even though the less than healthy regime had caused me blinding headaches and hunger pains, it was worth it just to fit into Webber's clothes. My buttocks, unlike Webber's, used to look like pumpkins. Now they had been reduced to large grapefruits.

On our way back from the wardrobe we passed the advanced human performance module, an assimilator, complete with full Jaguar F1 bodywork, that puts prospective drivers through various kinds of driving challenges. It was, so I discovered later, a health and safety prerequisite which should have assessed my ability as a driver, especially in the art of multitasking. 'Anyone about to step into our car is supposed to go through this exercise,' Nav explained, puffing away on the first of a good number of cigarettes that day. 'And we're talking test drivers here, not members of the general public. But we just haven't got time with you, so it's in at the deep end. For you, and for me.'

Back in his office Nav laid his cards out on his table. 'Three years ago Mike Gascoigne, the Technical Director of Toyota, was given the chance to drive a Formula One car at the Goodwood

Festival of Speed. Now Mike had loads of single-seater experience as he sat on the start line at Goodwood facing nothing more than a straight line to drive along. He took his clutch out, gave the engine some welly, and careered, nose-first, into a large hay barrel. He was okay, but the car was, how shall we say it, fucked.'

He paused for a few seconds and observed my reaction. There was more. 'Eighteen months ago at Santa Pod, the very place you will be driving our car shortly, a BAR test driver called Darren Turner drove nose first into a concrete wall. So you see, my friend, considerably better drivers than you have gone horribly wrong in the precise exercise you are about to undertake.'

But why? How can you drive any car in a straight line and end up ploughing into the sides? Nav took a long, deep exhalation of his cigarette smoke and leant back in his chair. 'A road car has, say, 400 horsepower which is electronically fed to the rear wheels. The car's management system dictates the optimum power and optimum grip. In other words, a road car more or less does it all for you.

'In an F1 car you have double the power, and more. So, there's 900 horsepower all through the rear wheels on, in the case of Santa Pod, a dodgy surface. If we could choose one surface in the UK to undertake this test it would not be Santa Pod. It's not tarmac, it's concrete, and it's infrequently used which means the grip is negligible. At this eleventh-hour stage to test Brundle and, so it happens, you, it was the only place we could find. Let's put it this way. We could have lowered the risk, primarily to the car, but also to you, and that's not even before we accept the fact that you haven't undergone years and years of the physical regime F1 drivers have to put themselves through, especially on their back, neck and shoulder muscles.'

Nav paused again and shook his head. If his speech was hardly doing wonders to my confidence, it was shattering his. At this point he remembered a few other telling points. 'The sense of speed will be magnified because, unlike in a road car where you sit relatively high up, in an F1 car your backside is no more than a few inches off the ground. Then there's the engine. That's two thirds of the car. If Takumo Sato (the Japanese BAR driver and team-mate of Jenson Button) can overload his car at Magny Cours, then you can at Santa Pod. There is very narrow biting point on the clutch. If you overdo it you will overburn. If you do not enough you will not find the bite-point and stall. Everyone stalls. The more time you stall the higher the engine temperature increases. If you stall, say four or five times, than you won't be allowed to drive the car at all.'

We took the short drive from Milton Keynes to Santa Pod, found, rather hidden, in the Northamptonshire countryside. It prides itself on being, as the sign says at the entrance, 'the home of European Drag-Racing'. In reality I thought at first that Nav had taken a wrong turning and we had driven into someone's farmyard. Rather bizarrely, we were able to drive not only straight past the entrance, but also straight on to the actual track. Nobody was there to stop us as we zoomed under the sign endorsing Pukka Pies hanging over the start line and swaying in the wind. In F1 the likes of Vodafone and HSBC are key sponsors. In drag-racing, it seems, Pukka Pies are major players.

At the far end of the concrete straight Jaguar had set up shop. The full test team were out in force, waiting for Brundle to arrive and try out the R4. First, though, they had to make do with me. This would be the very same car that Mark Webber drove in only the previous year's world championships. Tony Burrows, the test-team manager, shook my hand. 'For every second you sit in our car I'm going to be holding Nav's gonads in my hands,' Tony announced. 'You see those concrete walls on either side of the narrow track? We wouldn't want you to go into them.'

And with good reason, too. First, there was the small matter of my safety, hence the compulsory fireproof long johns and vest to add to my green race-suit, boots, gloves, balaclava and helmet, and the unnerving sight of a fire engine, an ambulance and a doctor standing by. Secondly, there was the fact that if I happened to prang the car, or even damage the £75,000 clutch, then the following night's Regent Street extravaganza, and Brundle's evening, would be cancelled. And thirdly, with the car insured for £1.5 million, it could well prove to be a costly exercise. Very costly.

So, absolutely no pressure there, then, neither on me, nor the members of the Jaguar F1 test team, who stood and watched me ready to blast down the track with haunted expressions etched on every single face.

I shoe-horned my way into the car's cockpit. The first part of this exercise was simple enough. It was when I reached my hips that I had to use much of my strength to squeeze the rest of my torso in. Only when my shoulders had successfully crammed their way past the rim of the car could I sink comfortably into a sitting position, with my legs bent halfway down towards the nose of the car. Ian 'Shaky' Fraser – his hands shake so much he can barely hold a cup of tea or a pen – fiddled around with the car while poor Danny Slater had the dubious task of placing his hands between and under my legs to find the various seat belt straps. Once he had strapped me up I had barely room to breathe. On the plus side, though, there was no chance of my exiting the car. Stuart Ayling, the test-team engineer, then began his instructional brief.

This, not surprisingly, was a car like no other I had ever seen in my life. Your left foot was solely to brake, your right foot to accelerate. There were just two foot pedals. Your hands, in contrast, were required not only to steer, but also to use the clutch and press the neutral button. The clutch was not to be used after entering first gear, and you were to upshift and downshift using the handles on the side of the steering wheel. This, believe it or not, is just a fraction of what a driver has to do in a Grand Prix, for ninety minutes or so. Talk about multitasking!

Yet it was still an object of considerable beauty. Sleek, feminine, as feline as the Jaguar cat itself, and a deep, lush green, the car could glide at top speed, a contrasting cocktail of style and power. One could easily be lulled into forgetting just how dangerous a machine it was if placed in the wrong hands. Wrong hands such as mine.

Stuart's instructions were these. With the car started up and in neutral I was initially to enter first gear by pulling the clutch handle on the left or right bottom side of the wheel and clicking a handle on the upper right-hand side once. Then, having gently eased off the clutch, I could upshift gears as the car shot down the track by clicking the right-hand sided handle each time. I was expected not to exceed a speed of 120 mph, which would require nothing more than third gear, in the small amount of track we were using. At the end of the straight I would be unable to make a complete turn, even in full lock of the wheel, because Santa Pod was too narrow. A waiting team of engineers would be there to help turn and put me in the right direction for the return journey.

'Any questions?' Stuart asked, after all this.

'Yep, just wondering whether I use my left foot to change gears after first,' I replied, my brain rather sozzled by all this high-tech information.

As I asked this question I remembered that you use your hands, not your feet, to change gear, and laughed it off as a joke. I wasn't convinced Stuart and the team saw it that way, though.

Martin Brundle had just arrived on his motor cycle, fresh from commentating the day before at Magny Cours. This, you would think, might have been an exciting moment for me. After all Brundle had raced in a staggering 158 Grands Prix over a ten-year career in Formula One. The fact that the likes of Tyrrell, Williams, Brabham, Benetton, Ligier, McLaren and Jordan had all required his services said a lot about the man's ability, even if he never quite managed to pull off a GP win. Since retiring from the sport he had become one of the most respected and natural motor-racing broadcasters in the world.

Yet my own experiences with Brundle were different. And embarrassing. Back in 1986, when I had become a fledgling writer for a now defunct, Robert Maxwell-owned, general sports magazine, I found myself at Brands Hatch in the company of Brundle. The former venue of the British Grand Prix was staging some kind of racing driver's 'Superstars' day, where F1, rally and touring car drivers would take turns in each other's events. As my magazine was sponsoring Brundle's cars, it meant that their young, fresh-faced writer would join the driver in the rally stages of the day's events.

Brundle's instructions that day, once I had strapped myself in, were simple. 'See that switch there?' he asked. 'Turn it on when I shout. Okay?'

Seemed simple enough to me. 'What does the switch do, Martin?' I asked, thinking it would play a crucial part in our drive.

'It's the windscreen wipers,' he replied.

Midway through the lap the car failed to take a corner, instead ending up hanging off a grassy bank like the bus in the end scene of the original *The Italian Job*. It was noisy, we were both wearing helmets, and the wheels were spinning furiously around. An angry Brundle vented his frustrations. 'Shit,' he shouted, as he informed me later. All I could think of, in my state of frenzy having almost shot over a bank at a great rate of knots, was to fulfil my part of the bargain. Brundle had shouted, after all, so I flicked on the switch.

We both sat there for a few moments as the windscreen wipers began to move backwards and forwards across the face of the windscreen. Their help, at this precise moment as we were out of the competition and needing assistance away from the bank, was non-existent. Eventually Brundle turned to face me, pulled down his visor, and said simply this: 'You dickhead!' You couldn't really blame him.

Eighteen years on and a smiling Brundle shook my hand, told me how much he missed driving, and that commentating at least went some way to replacing the adrenalin buzz he felt each day he stepped into an F1 car. He had been looking forward to Santa Pod but first, together with the rest of the Jaguar Test Team, had to endure my cameo drive. 'Treat the car with respect,' he pleaded. 'It couldn't be more difficult for you today.' As he said this the first drops of rain began to splatter on to the track.

Despite my snug fit I would be able to escape from the cockpit within five seconds, or so I was told, by removing the detachable steering wheel. In fact the LEAR Corporation, in conjunction with the FIA (F1's world governing body), had developed the fully extractable safety seat which is now compulsory in the sport. This means that the driver can be removed from the cockpit still strapped in his seat.

It was a comforting thought as I observed the fire engine and ambulance but, as I sat in the cockpit and waited for the go ahead, I still wondered what possessed Nav to press the buttons and get me into this situation. After all, it had taken seven months to design this car, with in excess of 6500 components to build it. Around 80 per cent of the car was carbon composite, which has a similar stiffness to and higher strength than steel, but only 20 per cent of the density. Even the paint on the car was carefully managed, with less than two kilos in weight and using high-tech paints that actually contributed to the car's aerodynamic efficiency. The Cosworth engine had ten cylinders, with aluminium pistons and a steel crankshaft, with each piston rising and falling over 300 times per second.

And then you had the steering wheel. The various buttons and toggles or rotary switches enabled the driver to adjust a variety of parameters, including traction-control, engine and chassis maps, engine braking, radio transmission and one button even allows him to get a drink. The dashboard display is positioned on the wheel. It has an anti-glare screen. All in all, if I had not fully appreciated it before, I realised that I was sitting in nothing short of a modern-day miracle.

A very fast modern-day miracle, too, as I was about to discover. Tony Burrows tried his best to warn me of the rate of knots this machine can move. 'It can accelerate from 0 to 120 mph and back down to 0 mph again in five seconds,' he said, with a wary look. But these are just words and figures. The reality is altogether different.

It had taken the best part of half an hour to power up a modern F1 car. It wasn't just the Cosworth engine, but the oil pressure must be brought up to a level with a compressor that will allow the engine to turn over on its own, the gearbox needs warming, the electrical systems must be booted up and, naturally, the tyres must be heated using electric blankets. Then, of course, the whole process would be blown if I stalled, causing the whole start-up procedure to be repeated, and confirming the view of everyone present at Santa Pod that I really shouldn't have been sitting in the car in the first place.

Now it was time. I figured it wasn't probably the best moment to own up to the fact that I had not only recently failed my ARDS test at Silverstone, but had been told I was a danger to myself and everyone else around me.

The garage went deathly quiet at first until the revs were tested. From having been reasonably calm I suddenly felt the rate of my heartbeat jump to an alarming proportion. Easing the car out of the garage by holding the clutch down and changing into first gear, I began heading down the Santa Pod straight, changing gears with my right hand on the side of the wheel as I gathered speed.

Tony had placed some cones at the end of the straight. I first had to brake and then turn. So unsure was I of both the true power of the car and the strength of the brakes, that I broke far too early and ambled my way for the last quarter of the straight. This was disappointing, but at least I had not stalled, and I still had the return journey to make.

This time, I told myself, might be the last few seconds I ever spend driving an F1 car. I was to try and make the most of it, but still be able to recognise my limitations. Once the engineers had helped me turn and pointed me back in the direction of the Jaguar garage situated at the bottom of the straight, I was away. One touch of the throttle and I accelerated faster than I had ever done in my life in any kind of moving contraption.

It took me a fraction over twenty seconds to travel the mile-long distance along the Santa Pod track, changing gear quickly from neutral up to third, as I felt the downforce of the speed rock first my head back and then my body. I felt tears in my eyes, I felt breathless, and I felt deafened by the almost haunting wail of the engine, sounding for all the world like a weeping widow destroyed by her loss. Most of all, though, I lost sense of all gravity. My brain could not quite register what was happening around me. The concrete walls on either side shot past me as if my life had just been placed on fast forward. Like a dream I found myself a mile down the track before I had barely blinked.

I slowed up and swivelled the car around so that the engineers could reverse me back into the garage and to the waiting Brundle. I had managed, somehow, to deliver myself and the car in one piece. In the corner of my eye I could see Nav. His demeanour was similar to that an hour or two after he had bade Clooney, Pitt and Damon farewell in Monaco. He was in de-stress mode, slightly delirious, and beaming in an insane manner.

The relief in the garage was very evident, and almost matching the relief of their latest test driver. No prangs, no stalls, no engine blow-outs, no broken clutches equalled one successful day and, unless Brundle mucked things up, a successful evening the following night in London's Regent Street.

'Do you know, even Niki Lauda stalled this car when he tried it out a couple of years ago,' Tony told me, with an encouraging wink. 'So that makes you better than Lauda!'

Not stalling the first time you ever drive an F1 car really is quite an achievement, but I was damned if I knew what I was doing. Whatever I did – and don't ask me now – it worked. I got lucky. It was as plain as that.

Stuart Ayling studied the telemetry and confirmed that my top speed had reached 175 mph. Now that's the fastest I have ever driven a car, but I knew how much faster the car could have gone. It was as if I had just taken it out for a jog. I'd only got up to fourth gear, nowhere near the top gear of seventh, and I hadn't been even close to full throttle or come even close to the revs limiter. I felt a touch disappointed about this until Tony placed things in perspective. 'Quit while you're ahead,' he insisted. 'You've done better, frankly, than we all expected, you drove it responsibly and you drove it well. One other thing. You have joined just a handful of people to have actually driven an F1 car.'

Put like that I had nothing to complain about. Far from it. My confidence had been genuinely affected by what happened during my two ARDS tests at the Silverstone Drive School. It had been slightly repaired by my kart race win over 'Michael Schumacher' in New Zealand, but that was due more to my own ability to spin events in my own head than reality.

But this experience in an F1 car improved my stock greatly. Suddenly I felt good about myself again as a driver. Maybe the ARDS experiences were inexplicable blips. After all, I'd just driven an F1 car without stalling, and without any mishaps at all.

'Looks like your leaving party's cancelled for tonight then,' I said to Nav, as I thanked him for the rare opportunity he had presented to me.

He smiled. 'I can't tell you how happy I am to cancel my own party,' he replied. 'Looks like I've still got a job after all.'

chapter seven

TEDDY BEARS AND TEETH

The following night I stood on the second floor of the Jaeger department store overlooking a packed Regent Street and observed the eight F1 cars meander up and down one of London's most famous shopping thoroughfares. As a guest of Jaguar I felt very happy with life. There might have been one or two out of the two hundred or so guests inside Jaeger I failed to inform about my drive the previous day, but I doubt it. 'Go easy with my car, Martin,' I muttered as Brundle drove past, a remark that caused Stuart Dyble, the Vice President of Public Affairs at Jaguar Racing, to groan.

The actual event was more successful than anyone could have imagined. Guestimates ranged from 250,000 to 500,000 people cramming the streets of Central London to watch F1 cars star for the very first time in the capital. Whatever the figure was, it was one heck of a crowd. I could not work out why some of them had bothered. The hordes were eight, nine, maybe ten rows deep, but still those at the back were taking photos, holding their cameras high above everyone else in the hope of obtaining a snap.

Not only that but the cars were driving at no more than 40 or 50 mph, as fast as they were allowed to travel along what for them was a short piece of track that made up Regent Street. Maybe it was just the complete novelty of witnessing F1 cars in the centre of London. Perhaps it was a chance to see the likes of Jenson Button and Nigel Mansell. Or the stunning technology and engineering on show. Or maybe I just did not get it in the way that true petrolheads did.

The aftermath of it all made the week running up to the staging of the British Grand Prix at the much-maligned Silverstone interesting. Bernie Ecclestone, never a fan of the premier British motor-racing circuit, made it plain in various sections of the media that the events in Regent Street had whetted his appetite. London Mayor Ken Livingstone started dreaming of a London Grand Prix. And various drivers felt fit to defend Silverstone staunchly.

As the weekend drew nearer so the attention turned to Button-mania. Young Jenson, having recorded five podium places already in a quite breathtaking season, had become everyone's favourite to win his first ever Grand Prix. Silverstone would be the perfect venue to break his duck.

I had been afforded the opportunity to see what would transpire from a close angle. A very close angle indeed. BMW–Williams had invited me to join up with them for the weekend. This would not be as a casual observer, but as an addition to their sixty-five-strong workforce.

Peter Phillips, grandson to the Queen and a BMW–Williams sponsorship accounts manager, had already sent me two large packages full of Williams attire so that I could be dressed the same as the rest of the team. In the boxes I discovered two blue and white shirts covered in yet more sponsors' logos, as impressive and as blue chip as those that adorned the Jaguar cars: HP Invent, Fedex, Budweiser, Puma, Petrobas, Allianz and, most interesting of all, Niquitin CQ, the first and only non-smoking brand on a Grand Prix circuit.

The irony here is that for longer than most can remember Formula One has made much of its money out of tobacco sponsorship, with the likes of John Player, Marlborough, Benson & Hedges and Lucky Strike all being prominent in the sport. Now, with tobacco sponsorship being currently phased out of Formula One, at least in Europe, the Williams team have turned to the very antithesis, a product that helps you quit smoking. It was a clever and admirable idea, although one imagined it had less to do with being health-conscious, and more with simple business acumen. Tobacco companies had always found Formula One to be one of the few willing and remaining shop windows for their products and, accordingly, threw billions of dollars into the F1 pot. When it comes down to business – and this is what Formula One primarily is – then concerns about the world's health become secondary.

I dug deeper into the box and discovered more attire. Together with the shirts came two pairs of dark blue trousers, a fleece, a waterproof jacket, and a rather fetching pair of dark blue, Williams-logoed trainers. It must have cost them a bomb to have rustled up all this for me, especially when I noticed on the shirt breasts that they had stitched on 'Ian'. All the other teams have both Christian and surnames stitched on to their attire, but not at workforce-friendly Williams. It made me feel like an employee at Disney World, although by rights my shirt should have read 'Ian – London, England'.

Within five minutes of reporting for duty at the Williams garage on the Saturday morning I knew I would be in for an interesting time. Whenever in the past I have visited a pit garage in search of an interview with a driver I have noticed the same thing.

For all the high technology, the masses of money, the glamour, the team owners and the superstar drivers, the majority of the workforce in the pit garage are the most regular bunch of people you are ever likely to meet. Hard-working, and very professional, but also laconic, witty, down to earth, and tremendously good fun. The Williams garage was no different, although it just so happened that the man who took me under his wing more than anyone else was the craziest mechanic of all.

How, for example, is this for starters? Introducing himself as Darren Leadbeater he informed me that everyone called him 'Cracker'. This, I reasoned, may have had something to do with the successful Robbie Coltrane television series, in which the Scottish actor played a police psychologist. Wrong!

'Well,' Darren began, as if he were about to relate an everyday tale. 'I was telling all the boys here how I was cracking one off and the nickname seemed to stick.' He looked at my quizzical face for a while and then grew exasperated. 'Cracking one off,' he repeated. 'You know, masturbating.'

Of course. How stupid of me. And how shy and retiring of him to inform me. Once I had recovered from this way too graphic revelation I asked him what he did at Williams. Well, apart from that. 'I refuel Ralf Schumacher in sessions, and I'm in charge of the right rear tyre on both cars in the race as part of the pit crew. I'm also the team's entertainments officer. I organised a trip to Rio for the boys, for example, before the Brazilian GP in São Paulo, and various football tournaments between the F1 teams. In Canada we played against McLaren, BAR and a professional ladies team who beat us all.'

These were, to say the least, interesting times for Williams. Ralf Schumacher, waylaid for twelve weeks since a horrific crash at Indianapolis resulted in spinal injuries, had announced during the week that he would be driving for Toyota the next season. This news had been diluted by the shock in the team, still evident, of that 200-mph prang. 'When Ralf didn't respond to our frantic enquiries we feared the worst,' admitted one of the other mechanics. 'Fortunately, he was unconscious, nothing more.'

As Montoya had already revealed at the start of the year that he was off to McLaren at the end of the season, Williams needed to find two new drivers. Nothing had been decided, although Jaguar's Mark Webber seemed to be in the frame. Meanwhile Williams's test driver, Spaniard Marc Gene, was filling in for Schumacher junior, and recognised that this was his chance to convince his team bosses to look no further than him.

His chances would not have been improved with the knowledge that I had joined the team looking after his car for qualifying, even if at first this meant little more than polishing the bodywork. This I would do on Montoya's car as well, although I'm not sure whether I was also supposed to polish the Colombian's helmet, especially with Montoya's head still inside. Certainly he seemed a little surprised as I jerked his head around, wishing him good luck in the process.

By the time Gene accelerated out of the garage, down the pit lane and on to the circuit for first qualifying session, however, my responsibilities had increased dramatically. Now, together with mechanic Dan Robertson, I would be in charge of the pit board, and would be leaning out and over from the side of the track to provide information to the drivers using the board.

On the face of it this would appear a simple task, even for someone like me who has never spent a minute of his life beforehand under a car in mechanics' overalls. Yet one still has to acquire the Williams drivers' fastest laps, plus the best time of the session by the top driver, and how many laps your man has done, and has to do, and then stick various numbers on to the board, rather like a miniscule cricket scoreboard.

Of course, the temptation is to stick some messages on the board as well. 'You're too slow,' suggested Dan. Or: 'Is that the best you can do?' Actually, we came up with a few more, as well, which are best left to the day, but can you imagine how a driver would feel at 200 mph tearing across the grid if he read offensive messages flashing on a board held up high above the track and for the masses to read.

Even for first qualifying at 9.00 am on the Saturday morning the grandstands were full and noisy. Klaxons vied with sirens, and partisan groups of fans cheered for their specific heroes. Three drivers seemed to hog nearly all the support. The Michael Schumacher *tifosi* were out in full, of course, sporting the famous Ferrari logo of the prancing horse, as were Montoya's supporters, unravelling a Colombian national flag with the words 'Formula Juan' written in the centre, but Button, too, boasted thousands of Union Jack wavers with the letters 'JB' printed in bold.

It was in front of this lot that I leaned gingerly out from a gap in the steel fencing in front of the international media centre and pit lane, over the grid, and informed both Montoya and Gene how they were faring each time they zoomed past. Dan helped supply the relevant numbers to place on the board, and I prayed that I would not cock up a simple yet vital task such as this by dropping the board on to the circuit below.

With first qualifying over I returned to the garage and was introduced to Patrick Head, the team's director of engineering, who had been eyeing me up and down suspiciously for some time beforehand. 'I was just wondering who you were,' he said, with a chuckle. 'I thought I knew everyone who worked with us.'

It was a special anniversary for the Williams team that weekend, celebrating the twenty-fifth anniversary of their first ever Grand Prix win, the British GP at Silverstone in July 1979. Head, together with owner and founder Sir Frank Williams, had been there from the start, and in this time had seen the likes of Alain Prost, Nelson Piquet, Nigel Mansell, Damon Hill, Jacques Villeneuve, Alan Jones and Keke Rosberg all become world champions driving a Williams car.

Yet this year things had gone a little awry, with both Montoya and Schumacher languishing below drivers such as Michael Schumacher, Barrichello, Button, plus the two Renault drivers, Jarno Trulli and Fernando Alonso. 'We declared at the start of the season that we would be competitive and we clearly haven't been,' Head admitted. 'This isn't what we expect from us, and it's not what our fans, sponsors, partners and drivers expect, either. But we're not going to roll up in a ball. We'll keep on fighting.'

It didn't help that Montoya made it known that he was off even before the season before had been completed. 'He actually signed for McLaren a week after we finished first and second in the French Grand Prix,' Head said, with an obvious look of exasperation on his well-travelled face. 'I suppose it all comes down to money. We're not prepared to spend the money we have done in recent years any more.' I told him that, if it was any consolation, my services working with the Williams team that weekend were free. I'm not convinced the joke was fully appreciated.

Neither, as it would turn out, would be the amazing antics adopted by not only the Williams team, but virtually everyone else, as well, a little later in the day. Weather reports had suggested that rain would be hitting the Silverstone circuit at precisely 2.30 pm, midway through the final qualifying session. Under the latest change of qualifying rules, the second qualifying session would determine who would begin final qualifying, and who would finish it. The fastest in second qualifying would be the last to go in final thus, in theory, having the advantage of knowing exactly what times to beat, and using the better grip on the surface from all the cars beforehand. First in final qualifying meant poll position for the following day's Grand Prix.

The advancing bad weather, however, threw all this into confusion, mayhem and, ultimately, farce. I was still being employed as the pit-board operator, and so could observe the shenanigans from close quarters. Michael Schumacher began the procedure by spinning during the second session, thus knocking ten seconds off his earlier time. A huge cheer was heard from everyone bar the Ferrari supporters. The great man had just made an unbelievable mistake. Moments later Barrichello, incredibly, followed suit.

Both Ferrari drivers had spun their cars at high speed, which delayed their laps. These slower times meant that they would be going out in the first half-hour of final qualifying, avoiding the predicted rain at 2.30 and the resulting slower conditions caused by the wet conditions.

When Schumacher sneezes, the rest of Formula One contracts a cold. One by one, the drivers started to record slower times than their original marks set in the morning. There were exceptions. Button ended up as the fastest driver in the second session, thus meaning he would be last to lap in final qualifying.

David Coulthard, to whom I'd spoken in the Amber Lounge after the Monaco Grand Prix, was standing in his drivers' overalls with his arms crossed outside the McLaren–Mercedes garage, which happened to be next door to Williams. He wore a knowing look on his face. 'It's just a classic example of how the drivers and the teams find ways of getting around the rules,' he explained, with a shrug of his shoulders. 'I'm not sure the crowd understands what's going on, maybe not even the television commentators. But none of us want to be driving in a downpour.'

At 1.45 one of the mechanics phoned home to Birmingham to discover that it was raining, and that the rain was coming our way. Moments later the Williams team helicopter was sent up into the clouds to estimate when the rain would hit the circuit. They also referred to the Met Office, and used information derived from their portable weather station found alongside the 'prat perch', next to where I was holding out the pit-board sign. It was in there that the likes of team technical director Sam Michael would direct qualifying, using all the data at his fingertips, and be in constant communication with his drivers. The prat perch was also known as the 'Wendy House' by all and sundry at Williams. Strangely enough nobody in the team knew what the technical name for the facility was.

For a while Montoya enjoyed poll position, that is until Michael Schumacher, Barrichello, Coulthard and Alonso nudged ahead. At 2.33 pm a few spots of rain fell, but nothing more. Sam Michael kept holding his hand out into the air from the prat perch in the hope that it would become wet. But the rain, save for those few drops, never materialised.

Button ended up third, behind the poll position of Kimi Raikkonen and Barrichello. Montoya could only manage seventh, with Gene twelfth. 'Trying to predict the English weather is a pointless exercise,' muttered Frank Williams immediately afterwards.

Wheelchair-bound since a car crash in France in 1986, the team's owner had observed all this from inside the garage in front of a series of monitors. 'You need stable weather but we got random showers.'

Ever brutally honest, however, he refused to blame the weather for how his drivers had fared. 'It doesn't disguise the fact that we don't have a quick enough car and other teams produced better racing cars over the winter. We might get lucky with showers tomorrow but I'll just settle for some points.'

Williams, of course, was a fascinating figure, and not just because of a major disability that makes his achievements in the sport even more remarkable. On seven separate occasions his cars have created world champions, and in 111 Grands Prix up to this point his car had come home first, all from the most modest of beginnings from within the sport.

He had been involved in motor sport since he was a nineteen-year-old grocery salesman racing an Austin A30 when he met fellow racers Piers Courage, Jonathan Williams and Charlie Crichton-Stuart and shared a famously decadent flat with them in Pinner, north-west London.

By 1969 Frank Williams was in a position to go Grand Prix racing with a second-hand Brabham for his by then close friend, Courage. He had placed his own driving ambitions aside – 'I was too lazy and I couldn't afford more than half a dozen races in a year in any case, which is far too few to develop as a driver' – to wheel and deal in engines, cars and spare parts.

That year Williams and Courage stunned the established world of F1 by recording runner-up spots in both the Monaco and US Grands Prix. It was enough to persuade an ambitious Argentine entrepreneur called Alessandro de Tomaso to build an F1 car for Williams. It should have been the start of a beautiful, three-way relationship but, following a horrific crash at the 1970 Dutch Grand Prix, Courage was killed after his car overturned, caught fire and trapped him underneath and, for a time, his friend and partner was left a broken man, the more so when de Tomaso lost interest.

'I was very close to Piers and, of course, it was an emotional blow,' Williams recalled now. 'One was conscious of going to several funerals in those years. After a while I became determined not to be beaten and kept my head down and worked hard. I always believed it would come good.'

Come good it did, but only after the best part of a decade of struggle, a time when he famously had to operate from a phone box close to his factory after bills had remained unpaid. 'It was difficult but I was young and optimistic.'

He received his well-deserved break in 1976 when a Canadian oilman, Walter Wolf, teamed up with him long enough to pay off all the debts. This gave Williams the chance to get up and running and with his energy and the capture of a young Patrick Head, things were looking up. 'The arrival of Patrick in my life – aside from my wife – was the most significant event since I came on this planet. When I called him he was building a boat, not out of wood or aluminium, but concrete.'

Williams Grand Prix Engineering was born, albeit headquartered out of a former carpet warehouse in Didcot. Three further developments would transform the Williams fortune. Thanks to some clever marketing from old friend Crichton-Stuart he secured sponsorship from Saudi Arabia. Then he persuaded the experienced Australian, Alan Jones, to become his number one driver, with the experienced Swiss, Clay Regazzoni, joining a year later. Finally, just before the 1979 British Grand Prix at Silverstone, the team's engineers, including Ross Brawn who went on to become so influential with today's Ferrari, made a significant breakthrough in a wind tunnel. Now they finally had a fast car. Regazzoni claimed a first ever win for Williams at Silverstone and, the following year, Jones took their first world driver's title.

'Pretty significant days for the team, I grant you,' Williams reminisced. 'But I can barely remember them now. It's all such a long time ago. Besides, by then I was inured to disappointment.'

There would be only a very few disappointments for many years after that. Keke Rosberg and Nelson Piquet would deliver two more world titles in the 1980s, then Nigel Mansell, Alain Prost, Damon Hill and Jacques Villeneuve in the 1990s. But 1994 also saw the death of Ayrton Senna in a Williams car at Imola when the Brazilian crashed fatally at Tamburello. What actually killed him was a cruel slice of luck. A detached piece of suspension penetrated his helmet. An inch either side and Senna would have lived. To this day investigations continue in Italy, the reason for his death never quite rationalised, and for many years following the accident that made such a difference to future driver safety, cruel pressure was placed on Williams and his team.

'It was a terrible time, of course. It was only the third Grand

Prix of Ayrton's first season with us so I can't say I knew him well, but he was obviously a blessed racing driver. I would have loved to have seen his rivalry with Schumacher extend. Now we'll never know.'

Williams paused and drunk from a straw, his disability ravaging his body enough to prevent even a simple action with his hands. His own crash happened when his hire car was involved in an accident returning from testing at the Paul Ricard circuit. For a man formally super-fit and a regular half- and full-marathon runner, this would surely have been a massive blow but, typically, he dismisses it now as nothing more than a minor inconvenience.

'Yes, I'm disabled, but I'm wealthy and fortunate enough to have others who pick me up and take me everywhere. It could have been a lot worse. Look at the guy who played Superman. Christopher Reeve. He was barely living all those years. He couldn't do a thing. I'm an Olympic athlete compared to him. But his brain was still working and he achieved some fantastic feats. I don't feel at all sorry for myself. It's my tough shit, that's all.

'The only thing I regret about it is that I really lumbered Patrick in it for the year afterwards. Some people have called me brave. Well, that's bollocks. It's human nature, that's all. I didn't have an option.'

At this point he stood up, using a contraption that eased him from a sitting to a standing position. 'Oh, it makes all the difference standing up,' he exclaimed. 'It's good to get off my bum and it's great for the circulation.'

His team has not won a constructor's title and none of his drivers has won a world title since Villeneuve in 1997, a barren run by Williams's standards. 'It's not so much barren as embarrassing,' he put it. 'Disappointing and frustrating, too. This is why I don't dwell on the past. That's buried. It's the present what counts. Let's hope for a good day tomorrow. Maybe you can bring us luck.'

I woke early the next morning, genuinely excited that this was the day I would be adopting an important role for one of the most prestigious F1 teams at the British Grand Prix. It is always a good idea to get to the circuit as early as possible on race day to avoid the horrendous jams of traffic taking 100,000–150,000 people to Silverstone. Even though it was only 8.00 am, and my Northampton-based hotel was only eight miles away, it still took me forty-five minutes to make the journey to the media car park next door to the paddock.

Nevertheless, I made my appointment with Frank Dernie for breakfast in the Williams motor home. Dernie, the Special Projects Engineer, proved to be an interesting subject. Like Head and, of course, Frank Williams, he had been on board from just about the beginning. 'Actually, I was employee number 23, when I joined in 1978,' he informed me as we both tucked into our breakfasts.

'Initially I came in to look after the aerodynamic side of things. Subsequently I've been at Lotus, Ligier, Benetton and Arrows before becoming a consultant in 1997. I'm basically Patrick's old mate. Whenever something's broken I come in to fix it. I'm an engineer without portfolio.'

There then followed a fascinating half-hour of reminiscences and insights. On that glorious day back in 1979 when he, Head and Williams savoured their first ever win when Clay Regazzoni won at Silverstone, Dernie remembers his wife's actions clearly. 'She was asleep in the car with my young children,' he admitted. 'She had absolutely no interest in motor sport whatsoever. I had to wake her up to tell her the news.'

Mrs Dernie and, I dare say, a good number of other wives, too.

On how the sport has changed: 'When I started out there may have been 100,000 people interested in Britain. Now there are many millions. It used to be an engineering, mechanical sport. All we cared about were suspensions and gearboxes. Now it is glamour and business. People are more interested in who David Coulthard's girlfriend is now. It may have been an ego trip for engineers, but it's certainly an ego trip for businessmen now. I've been very critical of some of the technical changes that have taken place, but at least the safety has improved beyond sight. I used to expect at least one driver to be killed every season. Now I don't expect a driver ever to be killed.'

On the characteristics of a champion. 'There are certain ingredients the best drivers share. I was Michael Schumacher's race engineer when he won his first world title with Benetton in 1994. For a start, they have to be introverted. It is not possible to be an extrovert and a Formula One world champion. An extrovert can't concentrate well enough or long enough. Talent goes without saying, but intelligence is another necessary characteristic. They're the ones who remain calm, relaxed. I know of plenty of drivers who should have been world champions, and weren't.

'Away from the sport they can be the nicest people imaginable. At home with his wife, Roseanne, Nigel Mansell is just that. So too is Michael. Everyone used to think he was aloof and stand-offish, especially when it came to dealing with the media. The truth is he was scared shitless and found it difficult to look anyone in the eye. In the car, though, they are different animals. Michael is spectacularly ruthless and self-motivated. So too Nigel. He takes no prisoners. When he played tennis with his six-year-old daughter he always wanted to win. That's the nature of the beast.'

I didn't say anything, but when I play football, cricket, tennis, squash, marbles or hopping on one leg while counting blades of grass with one eye closed and my hands full of jelly, I always like to beat my eleven-year-old son, too.

Dernie's description of a top racing driver was particularly interesting. For a start, not many sports require introvert tendencies as a necessary ingredient, a contrasting element when one considers the lifestyle they lead out of the car. Most sports do not necessarily need intelligence, either. I've wasted many an hour talking to brain-dead sportsmen.

But the ruthlessness? Now that was a common factor. In all the top sportsmen I had met and indeed played with over the years this was always the one, common denominator. It didn't matter where they came from, what religious or political beliefs they held, or what sport they played. Put the likes of Steve Waugh and Roy Jones, Steve Redgrave and Jansher Khan, Tiger Woods or, it seemed, Michael Schumacher in the same room and they would immediately identify a common competitiveness and utter ruthlessness that set them apart as winners among winners.

Dernie's Frank Williams anecdote reinforced the character the man himself had presented to me the day before. 'I went to visit Frank with Nigel Mansell in hospital the day after his accident in France,' he recalled. 'We poked our heads around the corner of the door and stared at Frank. He looked, quite honestly, a total mess. There were tubes sticking into just about every part of his body. There was real concern for him at the time. And he looked up at us both and said: "Why the fuck aren't you testing?" That's when Nigel and I knew he'd pull through, regardless of any disability.'

Aptly, Dernie was called away for a meeting with Sir Frank within seconds of concluding that anecdote. I went outside into the paddock and stood with a gaggle of Williams mechanics for a spot of celebrity watching. A rumour had spread that Angelina Jolie was doing the rounds at the various F1 garages. This seemed to lure virtually everyone out into the paddock. The Jolie rumour turned out to be just that. Instead we had to make do with footballers Denis Bergkamp and Sammi Hypia, Sir Stirling Moss, impressionist Rory Bremner, Nigel Harman aka Dennis Watts from *EastEnders*, and a gaggle of politicians, headed by Deputy Prime Minister John Prescott and Defence Secretary Geoff Hoon, who happily toured the paddock on a jolly while our troops continued to be maimed and killed in Iraq. Maybe the fruitless search for weapons of mass destruction was continuing at Silverstone. . .

Cracker produced a hideous set of false teeth, some black, others yellow, and nearly all crooked, placed them into his mouth and stared straight at John Prescott. The Deputy PM took one look at him, dropped his rather large jaw and moved swiftly on. Before I could ask what that was all about, another mechanic produced a new set of clothes for me. In order to work in the garage during the actual Grand Prix I needed to wear fireproof overalls, shoes, long johns, gloves, a balaclava and a helmet. I was told to wear them immediately, only to discover that the team had played a small joke on me. Everyone else would be wearing similar attire, but not for at least a couple of hours. It caused much mirth to see me traipsing around like an astronaut.

The false teeth made a second appearance, but this time on the grid moments before the start of the race. I was not really supposed to be out there at all, but Cracker told me to stick with him as we wheeled out a trolley full of gear and stood beside Gene's car in position twelve on the grid as final checks were made on both driver and car. A second pair of false teeth appeared as one of Cracker's assistants posed with him for photos, before then carrying out all the necessary, last-minute work still donning the teeth.

You could sense the growing tension on the grid. The cars revved their engines, the drivers sat motionless inside their cockpits, their hearts no doubt pumping with adrenalin, and the race engineers and technical directors barked out their final orders.

Walking amid them were Zara Philips, Peter's sister, and her boyfriend, Mike Tindall, who always seems to crop up in my books. Before I was about to play in a pro-am golf tournament alongside Bernhard Langer, Tindall, the World Cup-winning rugby star, had informed me that if I hooked my opening drive in front of all those hundreds of spectators and Langer, he would 'piss himself laughing'. This time he just stared at me in horror and said: 'Bloody hell, if you've got anything to do with this it's going to be a bloody disaster.' Mike Tindall. Another appearance of Hitchcockian proportions.

With just a few minutes remaining before the start we all had to leave the premises. As I wheeled the trolley back to the garage with Cracker I noticed a rather battered old teddy bear strapped to the front. Before I had time to ask Cracker what this was all about he had stooped down, grabbed the bear by a paw, and started waving to the mechanics in the other team garages. 'Teddy says bye-bye,' Cracker shouted, in a *Watch with Mother* kind of voice. The mechanics from the other garages waved back and shouted: 'Bye bye Teddy, bye bye.' I looked blankly at Cracker, trying to place this moment of madness amid the high-octane tension of the British Grand Prix now just seconds away. 'It's become a regular feature at every race,' he said, believing that this was a full enough explanation. It wasn't really but, seeing that I had just been standing on a Formula One grid next to a car and a driver about to race in the British Grand Prix, in the company of a madman wearing false teeth and waving a teddy bear's paw at anyone who cared to look, it would do.

During the race, however, the insanity became anything but. Gene first appeared in the pits after just nine laps for some refuelling. The whole procedure took six seconds. Twenty-one mechanics, all in their fireproof clothes from head to feet, crowded around the car and worked in perfect synchronisation. Everyone knew exactly what they were doing, and revealed tremendous teamwork within a potentially dangerous environment. Montoya came in next and left, this time after eight seconds, having required a touch more fuel. Afterwards high-fives were exchanged among the twenty-one mechanics, before they all sat down to watch the rest of the Grand Prix unfold on a large television screen inside the Williams garage. Both drivers would make second pit stops later on in a race that failed to live up to expectations.

Jarno Trulli stepped calmly out of his Renault after a spectacular crash, and Montoya was instructed by Sam Michael to 'try your best to get past Fisichella', but in the end the British Grand Prix finished as ten others had beforehand that season. Michael Schumacher won again, with Raikkonen second and Button third. A fifth place for Montoya was received enthusiastically by the Williams team, although Gene's twelfth probably meant the end of his chances of taking over from either Ralf Schumacher or Montoya next season in the car.

As soon as the post-race presentations began Williams began to pack. 'Now you'll see what we're best at,' shouted one of the mechanics, as he and I removed some bodywork from the spare, or 'T' car. 'Pack up and get the fuck out of here.' They had no time, nor inclination, to watch Michael Schumacher spraying so much champagne from the winners' podium over the cheering crowd and Ferrari mechanics that the place soon reeked of alcohol.

Within a couple of hours the Williams team were ready to move on. Both drivers had given their versions of the day's events to Frank Williams, standing up again in his motor home and looking like an emperor receiving a briefing after a battle from his generals.

Back in the garage Cracker made an impromptu announcement. 'I'm going home now to rediscover my life,' he said. 'Six Grands Prix in eight weeks. Horrible. Bloody horrible.' And with that he went off into the early evening, complete with false teeth and teddy.

Bye-bye Cracker. Bye-bye.

chapter eight

THE PRANCING HORSE

The morning after the night before. It is early on a Monday and red painted shutters which keep out the summer sun are closed on an otherwise white house that once belonged to Enzo Ferrari, and is now being used, at least for the night, by Rubens Barrichello.

The Brazilian arrived at the Ferrari test circuit at Fiorano, just a five-minute drive from the team's Maranello headquarters in Italy, late the night before, having flown from the Belgian Grand Prix. Barrichello had just notched up third place at Spa, one behind runner-up Michael Schumacher who, in the process, had officially wrapped up his seventh world driver's title.

Spa, ironically, is Schumacher's favourite racing circuit of all but, in an uncharacteristic show of conservatism, he held back to avoid any unnecessary risks to allow McLaren's Kimi Raikkonen to win the race. He knew that simply finishing ahead of Barrichello would confirm his status. Thus the German's record read fourteen races in 2004 to date, twelve wins, one no finish (after his altercation with Montoya in the Monaco tunnel) and now, the humiliating failure of finishing second to Raikkonen at Spa. Raikkonen joined Jarno Trulli as the only other driver who had experienced a victory all season in a Grand Prix.

Barrichello emerged from Ferrari's house yawning. He had enjoyed a good season, no doubt, had played a significant role in helping Ferrari claim their sixth, successive world constructor's title, and needed one more good performance to guarantee the runner-up's spot in the drivers' table. Still, being the competitive animal that he is, his view on this was pretty harsh on himself. 'Oh yes, I have a very good chance of becoming first loser,' he announced, with a slight grimace.

You would think the last thing he needed right then was to spend time with me and, indeed, drive me around the Fiorano circuit in a super-charged Ferrari Challenge Stradale, but he had agreed to do so, and Rubens, ever the polished pro, would stick to his word. Besides, once he had woken up, stretched a little and squinted up at the already beating Italian sun, his naturally happy, Brazilian persona reappeared.

My Formula One education was gathering pace. I was a little nervous to take the next step as a driver, happy to bask in the 'glory' of beating Michael Schumacher in Auckland and then successfully driving an F1 car without stalling or crashing, but in all other departments I was ticking all the boxes. Fresh from my British Grand Prix experience, I was now not only going to meet Barrichello, and be driven by him, but also spend a day at Ferrari, the Mecca of motor racing.

Aled Rees at Vodafone, one of Ferrari's main sponsors, was also at Fiorano, having helped arrange the day for me. In obtaining some research on me from the Internet for Ferrari's benefit he came across some interesting facts. Above and below my name you can find information concerning my other publications, but what really caught Aled's eye – and, as a result, everyone else at Ferrari – were the words 'Penis enlargement pills' and 'Penis pills – the experts talk'. This seemed to cause great consternation at Ferrari, and a fair deal of mirth, too, as virtually everyone made a point of asking me if I happened to have any pills on me, and whether they had worked for me.

I mentioned this to Rubens who, until I had fully explained the joke, was wondering why a person he had met just five minutes earlier was offering one of the best Formula One drivers in the world the chance to buy some penis enlargement pills. It had been my way to break the ice with the Brazilian. Fortunately, it worked. 'I don't need any myself,' he informed me. (Incidentally, according to the one page from the net Aled presented me with, there is an Ian Stafford at the Foreign Office, an Ian Stafford who is an expert on rats, an Ian Stafford who played American Football for Tampa Bay and, of course, the penis expert.)

Before Rubens and I would take a drive I was shown around both Maranello, where the factory is, and Fiorano, where the track and Enzo Ferrari's house is found. Indeed Enzo – he of the liquid lunches and hazardous post-lunch drives down the hill with Chris Amon, Pepito and a sliding Dick the Poodle – has a quote of his emblazoned on one of the walls at Fiorano. 'If I had to say that when I started I thought of making more than just one car I would be lying,' it reads, with a black and white photo of a young, smiling Ferrari behind the wheel of one of his cars.

Everywhere you looked you saw 'Il Cavallino Rampante', the famous black Prancing Horse emblem of Ferrari. On the walls, on the doors, on the tables and, of course, on the cars. Everywhere. This, tied in with Ferrari's unmistakable shade of red, 'Chiaro Rosso', adds to the charisma that seems to outshine every other team in Formula One. It goes a long way to explaining why any driver finds it impossible to turn down the opportunity of driving for Scuderia Ferrari.

On this day, old man Ferrari, who passed away in 1988 at the ripe age of ninety, would have been especially happy. There had been celebrations the evening before both in Kerpen, Schumacher's home town in Germany, and in Maranello where, in typical Italian fashion, the locals had honked their car horns long into the night. As Enzo lived the last few years of his life almost wholly in the house in the centre of the Fiorano grounds, liking to be as close to his team, his drivers and all happenings as possible, he would have been in the thick of the reaction to yet another Ferrari success.

Normally the racing cars would be safely ensconced back in their rightful spaces at the Maranello garage by now after a Grand Prix, but partying in Spa as a result of Schumacher's success meant a delay in their return. Instead, one had to make do with the sight of a large photograph hanging from the garage wall of Schumacher, Barrichello and team technical director Ross Brawn on the winner's podium in Sepang after the 2000 Malaysian Grand Prix, all donning ridiculous red wigs while enjoying the acclaim of the cheering masses. As this was the team's first title for a driver since 1979, they felt it suitable to produce the wigs, not just for the drivers and Brawn, but for the whole, 900-strong workforce. David Coulthard, on the podium in second place, and dressed relatively conservatively in just his McLaren race-suit, looked suitably bemused.

I was taken into a large hall which, like a church, had a reverend silence about it. Here Ferrari housed many of their past Formula One cars, with the drivers' names plastered clearly over them. There were plenty of Michael Schumachers' from the past seven years, but there, also, stood cars once driven by Gilles Villeneuve, Niki Lauda, Alain Prost, Nigel Mansell and Gerhard Berger, the latter now stuck to a wall like a spider clinging to its web after what could only have been a particularly reckless spell of driving.

Ross Brawn suddenly appeared, all smiles after his part in

Ferrari and Schumacher's success at Spa. Beneath the happy exterior, though, was relief after the jolt he, Schumacher and the team received the season before when it needed Schumacher's single point at the final Grand Prix of the 2003 season in Japan to secure the title from a threatening Raikkonen in the McLaren.

'Michael's had his best ever season,' he told me, as we sipped cappuccino in an air-conditioned room at Fiorano. 'In previous seasons he's had bad races and still won, but this year he's not produced one bad race. I don't think Michael chases records but last year he knew if he won the title he would win his sixth, record-breaking title. I think beating Fangio's record was there in the back of his mind. This year he's been far more relaxed.

'I think the foundations to this year's success was what happened towards the end of last season, especially that close scrape in Japan. I mean, it took Rubens winning the Grand Prix, relegating Kimmi Raikkonen to second, and Michael just hanging on to that eighth place, and the single point as a result, to win it for us. Because the other cars were using Michelin tyres which were better in wet conditions, we were a rain shower away from losing our title. I think that shook Michael up a bit. We never really spoke about it afterwards. We didn't need to say anything. It's an unspoken deal. Michael went away and clearly decided he would not allow it to be as close again.'

Schumacher was not the only reason for Ferrari's unprecedented success. 'We had a very, very good car. Last year's car was a compromise because they changed various regulations to do with the car's make-up, but this time we knew the regulations and prepared a proper car. The way we've dominated the sport this season is not just a reflection on us, but also on our competitors. It's got to the point where we're being criticised for winning so much. What are we supposed to do? The sport needs competition, and so do we, but if you want to be critical, criticise the other teams for not giving us a tougher fight.'

Nevertheless, it helps having Schumacher on board as Brawn, who has known him since his days working at Benetton in the early 1990s, testifies. 'It goes without saying that you need to have a huge amount of natural talent and incredible ability in a car, but what makes Michael so different from the rest is his intelligence and application outside the car. He's still the fittest driver out there, even though most of the others are now younger than him.

'The proof of this is how he is having just finished a Grand Prix. There is not a bead of sweat on him. After a race we can talk just like you and I are now. You would never have known he's spent the past hour and a half driving at speeds averaging over 150 mph in a race against nineteen other drivers. When you talk to him over the radio, like I did yesterday at Spa, he is always calm. In Spa he wanted to know about the weather forecast, where Rubens was, what the running order of the race was. Normally, when you talk to a driver over the radio he is panting and barely able to have an intelligible conversation. But Michael is not normal.'

Rubens walked past and waved at us both. This reminded Brawn that his other driver wasn't too bad, either. 'Talking of panting over the radio, Rubens used to be like that when he was what I'd class a normal driver, but he's seen what Michael can do and stepped up the mark.'

I mentioned Barrichello's apparent dissatisfaction at the prospect of finishing runner-up to Schumacher – again – in the world driver's title. 'Well, in my view, Rubens has the toughest job in Formula One,' Brawn suggested. 'He has to beat the best driver in the sport, quite possibly now of all time, in the same equipment. There have been a lot of world champions who have been the best drivers and not had the best equipment. There's been a lot of world champions who have not been the best drivers but had the best equipment. But Michael is the best driver and now has the best equipment too. That makes it a formidable task for

Rubens. I feel sorry for him, actually. Rubens would most probably have been world champion by now, if it wasn't for Michael.'

It's an interesting thought, and one that led me temporarily to imagine the sight of a Brazilian motor-racing driver sneaking into the Ferrari garage at night to stick pins into Schumacher's tyres or tamper with the gearbox. That's the thing about Formula One. It's supposed to be a team sport, with Ferrari united as one in joy when they win the constructor's championships or, as of the night before in Spa, they win the driver's title. Well, try telling that to Rubens, especially when he's been instructed in the past to ensure Michael grabs the points.

'It's a really important aspect of our job,' Brawn conceded. 'We're involved in a major team sport here, but yet within it we have two guys on the same team trying to beat each other. Occasionally we've made decisions where Michael's benefited from a fifty–fifty call. Rubens hasn't been happy about it, and quite right, too, but it's been in the best interests of the team if it helps Michael, who is in a far better position than Rubens in the race for the title, to score the points. It happens two or three times a year, depending on the circumstances of the driver's championship.

'Despite this I'm pleased to say our drivers seem to get on. (Certainly, judging by the way Rubens was puffing on a cigar and laughing with Michael in the Amber Lounge after the Monaco Grand Prix, this appears to be the case.) We've managed to keep our two drivers talking to each other. That's no mean feat. It doesn't happen often. We have rules of engagement which we expect them to respect, and they do. The worst thing for a team is to have two drivers at war with each other. Some people think it provides extra motivation. It doesn't.'

Being the down-to-earth Mancunian that he is Brawn was none too concerned with the aura and tradition of Ferrari when he was asked to leave Benetton and join the team at Maranello. All that mattered to him was whether Ferrari could do the business now. 'Sure, they had the name and the history but I wanted to know if they had the resources. Michael had joined from Benetton the year before, and it was he who told me I should come over. I wanted to know that I could organise the team without any interference. When I was happy that those questions had been answered I joined up. The first day I saw Maranello and the set-up was my first day at work.'

Of course, since those days Brawn has come to appreciate the allure of Ferrari, especially the *tifosi*, the fanatical Ferrari support that tends to dominate every crowd at every Grand Prix. 'I've never seen anything like it. Their passion is a huge strength to us. I've had abuse from hotel porters if we've had a poor Grand Prix, but that's because there are three religions in Italy, and two of them are football and motor racing. But you have to remember, for all the positives of such a support, it doesn't actually make the car go faster.'

Schumacher does, though, and looks likely to be doing so for quite a while yet. 'Expect Michael to be even hungrier next season,' Brawn reports. 'He's really enjoyed himself this season. (So would you if you'd won twelve out of fourteen races at this point.) He knows if he's dominated a race then it's down largely to a great technical job. If it's a tight win, then he knows he's probably made the difference. Either way he doesn't care. Just as long as he wins. I'll know when he's lost his hunger because the barometer is how hard a time he gives me. At the moment he's ringing me every other moment wanting to know if we've done this or that, when something will be ready, or if I'm going to do something else. He's always chasing me.'

Brawn chuckles to himself and then agrees to share the thought. 'The other night we played football,' he began. 'The Ferrari team often get together to do this. Anyway, after the game Michael looked downcast. I asked him if there was a problem. He told me he hadn't scored a goal that night. Then he suggested we played a second game. I realised later he only did this so that he could score a goal. That's Michael. He wants to win everything.'

Slowly a picture of the man was developing. An arch competitor who is his own biggest critic and who lives, seemingly, for his sport and few of the trappings that go with it. Maybe that last point was the key. There were no compromises with Schumacher. His output needed to be 100 per cent, with no distractions. He seemed a formidable proposition to the other drivers. He seemed untouchable to me.

It was time to sample some racing, at close quarters, on the Fiorano test track. Built in 1972 on a plot of land adjoining the factory, the original track still exists today, although a chicane was added which increased its overall length to 2976 metres. Its main use is to test both racing and road cars, the latter straight off the manufacturing line. Before Rubens and I could 'get it on' I was first to be driven around the circuit at high speeds by Ferrari's main test driver, Andrea Bertolini, an engaging young Italian from nearby Sassuolo with a bright, beaming smile. He was going to take me around at high speed in a Ferrari 575 M, a modified version of the 550 Maranello. It would be, so Aled Rees explained, the hors d'oeuvre, before I joined Barrichello in a 360 Challenge Stradale, a car and a driver which would make the 550 and Bertolini seem like a milkman doing his early morning round.

Before being allowed to step in to either car a waiver – yes, another one – was thrust into my hand. Like the many others beforehand Ferrari's version was worded differently but more or less meant the same thing: die or be seriously injured, and it's down to you, pal.

Ferrari handed me a red race-suit and a helmet. Both, I was told, I could keep, which was both really nice of them, and also annoying, bearing in mind I had forked out nearly £300 on a race-suit a couple of months earlier before my humbling experience attempting to pass my ARDS test at the Silverstone Drive School. I was now the proud possessor of two race-suits, and no racing car.

Shaking hands with Andrea, I squeezed myself into the passenger seat to his right and made a quick appraisal. I was about to place my life in the hands of a young Italian driver, in a souped-up Ferrari, on a test track in Italy. Hmmm. The last time I'd been given a lift by an Italian in his home country was three years previously when, during a week's training with Everton Football Club in Tuscany, myself and three Premiership footballers hitch-hiked a lift back to our hotel after a slightly drunken evening out at a local night club. The driver, a massive football fan (well, he was Italian) was so excited about having four footballers in his car – he did not know I was an imposter – that he veered and wandered from side to side of the hairpin bend-riddled mountain road. Craig Short, the big, central defender who went on to play for Blackburn, was almost sobbing at the end, and Terry Phelan, the Republic of Ireland international, started to pray.

When Andrea informed me as we sped off on to the track that he supported Juventus I thought of my former colleagues at Everton. But only for a second or two. After that it was a case of hanging on to my seat, pretending to enjoy myself, appearing completely unfazed by the fact that we were circumnavigating a small circuit with chicanes and bends at a ridiculous speed, and worrying myself over the first signs of nausea from the pit of my stomach.

The spin with Andrea took only a few minutes, but in that short amount of time my new Italian chum managed to get across much of his life story. He started racing karts at eleven. I told him I raced karts, too, and we smiled at each other. Two points here. The statement that I race karts is true. The fact that I didn't make the top fifty at Buckmore Park is a moot point. Also, as I was the passenger, I was happy to smile at Andrea, but not so happy to see Andrea smiling at me, rather than looking ahead over the wheel. At just eighteen years of age Andrea was invited to test a Ferrari F355 Challenge at Fiorano, a performance that caught the eye of the then head test-driver of the House of Maranello, Dario Benuzzi. As a result of this he became the youngest test driver in Ferrari's long history, and has since been notching up all kinds of wins in Italy and elsewhere. 'But my dream is to be like Rubens,' he said, jerking his head towards the Brazilian who was standing in the garage watching the proceedings. 'Formula One is my goal, my dream, and I believe I will have my day.'

I thanked Andrea for the experience, stepped out of the car, and was instructed to step immediately back into the nearby Challenge Stradale. I was rather hoping, seeing that the nausea was causing stomach cramps, that I might have at least a few minutes' respite. I could not say this, however. After all, apart from my expertise in the penis enlargement department, Ferrari had also formed the opinion from my previous sporting escapades that jumping in and out of stupidly fast cars was small beer for a man such as myself.

Slightly more disconcertingly, Rubens was already in the driver's seat and eager to play. 'This time we will go fast,' he announced, slapping me on my knee as I smiled wanly and replied: 'Yeah, great, let's do it.' As if the last time had not been fast enough.

As we shot down the first straight he started to laugh. 'You know, I once did this with Sylvana, my wife,' he explained. 'Only once. She screamed for the whole time. Never again. Yet she doesn't like it when I'm the passenger and she's driving. She thinks I talk too much, and she thinks I criticise her driving.'

That is an interesting twist on my own premise for experiencing this whole adventure. After all, the norm is for the male in the relationship to be irritated by the back-seat driving of the female.

Just how irritating is it, I mused, as we hurtled around the test track, to have someone like Rubens Barrichello criticising you? After all, you can hardly bounce back with a 'Well, what do you know,' can you, considering he is the second best-placed racing driver in the world?

'Mind you,' Rubens shouted across the noise of the engine fuzzed by our helmets, 'my mother took me out for a drive when I was sixteen and I told her never again, too. Certainly, from the age of eighteen, I have never allowed my mother to drive me.'

The pit of my stomach was beginning to cramp up badly. Rubens suggested we should circumnavigate the track for longer than was planned. Oh joy! Now my overriding concern was whether I would be able to prevent myself from throwing up inside the Challenge Stradale, or possibly even over Barrichello.

I grimaced at the thought, and the profuse apologies that would follow to Ferrari, as I hosed out their Challenge Stradale, and to an apoplectic Barrichello, hopping about in a race-suit covered in my dinner from the night before.

'Enjoying yourself?' Rubens shouted above the din of the motor.

'Yeah, great, fantastic,' I lied back.

Finally, and mercifully, Rubens slowed down and veered the car back into the garage. After a couple of minutes my nausea evaporated and I was able to make out the whole experience had been not only a blast, but one that someone like me could take with my eyes closed which, in hindsight, might have been a good idea.

Barrichello, his role as 'first loser' seemingly forgotten now, was eager to talk more. The more he thought about his predicament, the more he realised there wasn't much he could do about it. 'I didn't deserve to win the world title this year,' he admitted, with a philosophical shrug of his shoulders. 'I've tried really hard, and maybe I should have won a race or two, but if I had become world champion after winning two or three races, and Michael came second by failing to finish the last five races, having won virtually all the others, that would not be part of my dream. I'm not happy with second place. It's better than third, I guess, but I'm already thinking about next season and what I have to do to beat Michael. I won't be entirely happy unless I achieve this.'

The irony behind the reasons for Schumacher's incredible season is not lost on the Brazilian, either. 'In 2003 Michael won the title, but I reckon I overshadowed him quite a bit because I often out-qualified him and won the last race at Suzuka when he could only finish eighth. That meant he was on a bit of a downer at the end, and I was on a high. It gave me a real motivational kick, but nothing like the one it gave Michael. He'd scraped home by just one point as world champion and he knew he needed to improve. As a result, Michael started this season flying because of his near miss. He has found a couple of extra gears and left the rest of us, me included, behind. It is a lesson to any young sportsman that you must always find ways to better yourself.'

Even though Schumacher's post-race antics in Spa suggests his hunger is far from dissipated, Barrichello recognises the positives of being partner to the best driver in the world. 'It's obvious Michael is far from finished. His hunger is as massive as ever. Half an hour after the end of the Belgian Grand Prix, Michael's won the world title again, and I could be forgiven for thinking that he would not be attending the race post-mortem with me. Instead he arrives and starts talking about the car, the race, and the next race. So, you see, he remains motivated.'

Maybe Rubens's best chance is when the German retires. After all, at thirty-two years of age, he is three years younger than Schumacher. Yet that is to misunderstand the mind of a competitor. 'Look, if it happens where he steps down and I become world champion then fine. I'll take it. But I don't want or need him to retire for me to win the world title. I want him to carry on and I want to beat him fair and square and become world champion.

Then there would be no buts. It's not a question of ability. I've won in so many categories against so many good people over the years. I know I have both the experience and mental toughness to be world champion. The day I believe I can't beat Michael is the day I return to Brazil and drive karts.'

Which is where, of course, it all began at the age of six in São Paulo when he started racing karts and won the Brazilian championship within five years. 'My father told me to do what I want to do in life, to be myself, to enjoy life, and to remember those people who have helped you. My grandmother lived between turns one and two beside the Grand Prix circuit, and I remember watching Emerson Fittipaldi [former Brazilian world champion] by climbing up and looking over the wall. In 1993 I got the chance to race there myself, alongside my hero, Ayrton Senna. Towards the end of Senna's life we talked a lot and had good times together. I was always the kid to him. He was thirty-three and I was only twenty.' He looked wistful just for a second, then laughed. 'He was the man,' he added, before reiterating the point. '*The* man.'

The day was virtually over. Barrichello was about to leave for Monza, where he would be testing the following day, but only after he had first completed a round of golf. 'My new love,' he admitted.

Someone mentioned to Rubens that I had enjoyed some experiences with golfers in my previous book. His eyes seemed to light up at the mention of Nicklaus, Els and Faldo, but when I mentioned I had met and talked with Tiger Woods, he wanted to know more about the supreme golfer.

I talked of his talent, his application, his fitness and his mental strength. 'Sounds like someone I know,' Rubens suggested, with a knowing smile.

'Ah, but since I wrote that book Tiger's gone downhill,' I replied.

The door of Barrichello's snazzy, yellow Ferrari opened and the engaging Brazilian hopped in and sat behind the wheel of one of the biggest head-turning cars in the world. 'Then there is hope for us all,' he said, as jerked his head back and laughed. 'Please hurry up with your book.'

His shoulders appeared to be shaking as the car drove through the main entrance of the Fiorano test site and sped off into the Italian countryside.

chapter nine

DC

The Columbus Hotel is the place where anyone who is cool stays in Monaco. Situated in the fashionable Fontveille district of the Principality it is a two-minute walk from the helipad and the various choppers that whisk and whirl visitors to and from Nice Airport, and just around the corner from the Stade Louis II, one of the most architecturally pleasing football stadiums in the world.

Inside the hotel, with its bright, Mediterranean decor and stylish interior, the invariably pretty receptionists and female concierges wear brown T-shirts with the slogan 'Live Life Love Life' emblazoned on their chests. Fashion TV blasts out from the dark, candlelit bar and people who use the place as a meeting point nod nonchalantly at each other as they air kiss all and sundry.

My arrival at reception caused a little consternation. I had returned to Monte Carlo, the scene of my bonding weekend with Brad and George, to spend some time with David Coulthard, the Scottish F1 driver universally known throughout his sport as 'DC'.

He part-owns the Columbus – hence this choice of hotel – and asked his office to make the booking.

'But we expected two of you,' announced a surprised-looking receptionist. 'There is a definite booking for a room for two.' This made me remember my American golfing buddy, Chip Thomson, who still referred to me as Ians after a schizophrenic joke that had stemmed from the world ice-golf championships in Greenland two years previously. 'Perhaps Mr Coulthard will be sleeping with you tonight?' This last comment was met with all-round laughter from the girls behind the desk.

Mr Coulthard, my potential sleeping partner, was engrossed in a business meeting with his manager and associates in a small corner of the reception area. He would be a good half an hour, I was informed. I decided to take a stroll, taking in first the gym, then the swimming pool. The usual sight at a high-class, Côte d'Azur hotel greeted me at the outdoor pool. Middle-aged women, overtanned and in an obvious battle with the onset of time, strutted around in dental floss G-strings covering barely any of their gnarled, walnutty buttocks, designer bikini tops, their nails manicured immaculately, and with not a dyed strand of hair out of place.

Who was this cool, debonair Englishman? they must have wondered, as I sauntered through the turnstile like Cary Grant, I imagined, down the step and straight into twelve inches of water that immediately engulfed my boots and jeans up to and beyond my ankles. I've never done that before, and it would be interesting to observe how I attempted to remain unperturbed in appearance as I jumped out of the crystal-clear water and shook my legs. On hearing this confession later Coulthard, as he eyed my still damp jeans, explained how everything that goes on at the pool is caught on CCTV cameras, and that he would be personally looking out for this unwitting moment of Norman Wisdom-style comedy as hapless Brit meets cool Riviera. Once again suburban man was attempting, and failing, to become Monaco Man.

We met in the hotel bar. I had been sitting there accompanied by a fruit cocktail drink with so many umbrellas, sticks and pieces of fruit that it made Del Boy's orders down at the Nag's Head seem positively conservative in comparison. It was a little more than a day after Coulthard had finished sixth in the Italian Grand Prix at Monza won by an ecstatic Rubens Barrichello who, ironically after his conversation with me at Maranello a fortnight earlier, beat off Michael Schumacher into second place. I'd like to take some of the credit for Rubens's first victory of the season. After all, was it really just a coincidence that as soon as he had driven a guy offering him penis enlargement pills around Fiorano, he then speeds off to win at Monza?

Martin Brundle and David Cawthorne were with him. Brundle, apart from being a Formula One commentator for ITV Sport, was also Coulthard's contractual manager. It was he, you may recall, who had to watch me drive his Jaguar F1 car at Santa Pod prior to the Regent Street extravaganza. Cawthorne is a lifelong friend from the Kircudbrightshire village of Twynholm who now lives in Monaco and works with Coulthard. Sounding just like his friend, and with the same initials, this has often caused confusion which has worked sometimes for and occasionally against the pair.

Coulthard suggested we should dine on his boat, *Highlander*, which was moored just a stone's throw away in the nearby Fontveille harbour. It was a nice gesture, and if he ever comes to visit me in Kent I will endeavour to find the rubber dinghy we possess somewhere in the loft, blow it up using the foot pump in the garage, and serve sandwiches as we sit in it in the garden.

It would prove to be a surreal evening, and a merry one, too. The three beers in the hotel bar started the rot, the non-stop flow of rosé wine on board the *Highlander* merely confirmed the mood for the night. Brundle, Cawthorne and a couple of DC's friends joined us. At around two o'clock the following morning we were served scrambled eggs as an early breakfast. Later that day

Coulthard could not recollect the eggs moment at all, but he did recall the haka, performed by Corrie, his Kiwi chef with Maori blood that made his performance very genuine, and copied by the rest of us. Gone midnight on a boat in Monaco, and six grown adults are sticking their tongues out, wide-eyed and snarling, as they reproduced the famous Maori war dance made universally popular by the New Zealand All Blacks rugby union team.

Coulthard was supposed to phone me at nine in the morning. He had muttered something about a bike ride the night before. I arranged a wake up call for 8.30, something I immediately regretted when the phone in my room stirred me from a deep slumber and my head started immediately to thump. I had no pills in my room, the receptionist lent me the last paracetamol in her handbag, and the pharmacy did not open until nine. A stagger later to the shop, two more pills, and a further two hours in bed repaired some of the damage. Nevertheless, whether it's down to champagne on a yacht in Monaco, or bitters in a pub in Kent, a hangover is still a hangover, and worse for a forty-year-old writer than it is for a thrity-three-year-old racing driver.

DC called just after midday. We would be assembling for lunch at Saliere, a popular, Italian restaurant just around the corner from the Columbus, his boat and, indeed, his apartment. He never mentioned the bike ride. When we met I complained that I was ready to go on the ride and had been let down by someone who had not revealed the same commitment and professionalism as me.

Simone, his Brazilian girlfriend, joined us. She discovered that I had once trained with the Rio de Janeiro-based football team, Flamengo, alongside such luminaries as Romario. Soon we were discussing the merits of Rio and São Paulo, the latter city being her original home, and the enormity of the Fluminese versus Flamengo Rio derby match known locally as Flu-Fla.

Afterwards Coulthard had some more business to attend to at his 'David Coulthard Associates' office, on the same floor of his apartment. As we agreed to have a lengthy chat that afternoon, he suggested I made myself comfortable in his pad.

Now this, I thought, as I sat on the balcony gazing at the view, was something I could get used to. Okay, so I may be a man who wades inadvertently straight into a swimming pool with his trousers on, who drops olives on to the passing stilettos of supermodels, and who nearly vomits over Rubens Barrichello. True, the chances of me owning a similar apartment in Monaco due to my prowess as a racing driver were remote bordering on negligible. But at least for an hour or two I could enjoy the luxury.

Below me was the harbour, with *Highlander* bobbing slightly up and down to the right. To the left, above me, was the magnificent Grimaldi Palace, home to the late Prince Rainier and once Grace Kelly. A rain shower broke out that turned into a thunder storm. Soon forks of lightning were flashing across the harbour. I moved inside to avoid a typically dramatic Mediterranean storm, and started to look around.

Against a wall DC rested a large, framed poster of a Paul Newman motor-racing film. *Virages* also starred his wife, Joanne Woodward, and Robert Wagner, but it was Newman, all ice-blue eyes and racing leathers, who dominated the poster. There were various pictures of Simone, Simone and DC, and Coulthard by himself, often donning a kilt. In pride of place stood one of his helmets, complete with the Scottish Saltire that he has worn faithfully ever since entering F1.

Coulthard returned and made us both a cup of tea. The storm had ended and we decided to venture out again on to his balcony. Over the next hour I discovered that beneath the jokey, fun-seeking exterior lay a deeply serious and intense character, and one hurting at that moment because of the predicament he found himself in.

By rights he should have been testing with McLaren in readiness for the Chinese Grand Prix in less than a fortnight's time.

Any other year in the past ten in which he had been one of the world's leading F1 drivers, he would have been. But not now. Despite his thirteen Grands Prix wins, despite his prominence in the drivers' championship for much of that period, and despite his renowned polished approach off the track Coulthard, at the grand old age of thirty-three, had no guaranteed drive for the next year. In fact, with only three races left before the end of the season, his F1 career could be coming to an abrupt halt.

'I don't want it to be over,' he said, gazing out beyond the harbour below him and into an uncertain future. 'It's not that I don't want to let go. It's just that I still enjoy it very much. I'm good at it, so why stop now?'

I sat there wondering whether he was talking to me, or perhaps more to himself. All of a sudden his whole demeanour had changed from happy-go-lucky to sombre. He waved a hand towards the multi-million dollar boats bobbing in the harbour, and then around in the direction of his apartment. 'It's not about all this,' he insisted. 'It never has been. It's all about the racing. All about winning. It's the most important thing in my life. If it were to end I'd be very, very disappointed.' He paused for a few moments and looked out again at sea. 'I guess I'll just have to handle it and move on.'

It seemed almost incredible that the Scot, after 172 Grands Prix, sixty podium finishes, twelve poles and 475 points, which put him sixth on the all-time list in the sport, may be close to an end. Coulthard was hoping that a seat might still become available either at BAR, if Jenson Button's attempts to vacate it in order to join BMW–Williams were successful, or indeed at Williams if Button failed. There was a decent chance that one or the other may come. But these were all ifs and buts. And it was now the second half of September. 'It has never been anywhere near as late as this in a season where I have had no guaranteed drive for the following one,' he added.

His predicament came about because McLaren, for whom he has driven since 1996 – making him the longest-serving driver for one team on the F1 grid – announced in 2003 that they would be dispensing with Coulthard's services when his contract was up at the end of this season. 'I suffered under the one-lap qualifying system last year, got the motor-racing equivalent of the golfing yips, and became too mechanical and fearful of making mistakes. McLaren saw a chance with Juan Pablo Montoya, considered his potential, recognised him to be younger than me by quite a bit, and took him from Williams. After that it's been difficult to show one's worth this season because we've not had the most competitive car.'

It must have been a numbing moment to hear the news that his contract had not been renewed. 'Well, when I was summoned to meet Martin Whitmarsh, the Managing Director at McLaren, I knew what was coming. I knew I'd been doing a bad job so I wasn't too surprised. He told me he fully expected me to want to go and kick McLaren's ass in the future, but I didn't see it that way. I was determined, though, to make the most of it since. The problem, though, is that I've been around a long time and there's been a lack of availability in other teams.'

Hence Coulthard's blank diary for 2005. He did not appear bitter. That would not have been in keeping with the Scot's pragmatic approach to his sport. But with more time on his hands that he was used to, he had come round to analysing his career a great deal.

There had been plenty of highlights over the years. 'Winning twice at Silverstone in the British Grand Prix, twice also at Monaco, and beating Michael Schumacher in straight fights such as at Magny-Cours in 2000 come to mind,' he recalled. But there were plenty of lowlights, too, such as when he was twice winning but ordered by McLaren to move over and allow Mika Hakkinen to pass.

These are events that have clearly eaten away with him ever since. 'My desire to do the right thing has cost me, to the detriment of my success and career. I think about it a lot. I was the first driver to move over for a team-mate. I was leading in the European Grand Prix in Jerez in the last race of 1997 when I was told over the radio to let Mika through. For the next fifteen laps I was arguing over the radio with my team, while trying to keep my lead in a Grand Prix. In the end I felt that if I didn't comply I would be seriously compromising my future employment and position within the team. After the race it's fair to say I had a heated discussion with Ron Dennis, the team boss. It happened again in the first race of 1998 in Australia. Mika went on to become world champion that year. That's two races I could and should have won. I think those decisions shaped people's opinions of me. I've had to live with them ever since and it's bugged me to this day.'

Unsurprisingly his relationship with McLaren had been far from perfect. 'It's fair to say that the chemistry at McLaren has never clicked because the damage was done early on with those two Mika incidents. We've tried to do the best we can ever since. In hindsight I've been at McLaren for far too long. We've not had a competitive car for a long time, even in 2003 when Kimi [Raikkonen] pushed Michael [Schumacher] close in the championship. That was down to Kimi having a reliable car and Michael not having one. I look back to 1996 and realise I made a big mistake by signing for McLaren.

'I went from leading the last race of the 1995 season when I was driving a Williams, to finding myself in thirteenth place on the grid for the start of the 1996 season in a McLaren. I sat on that grid and realised I'd sold out. I guess money meant a bit more to me back then than it does now, but you should never take payment over performance. It was a big mistake. That year Damon Hill won the world title in the Williams. The following year

Jacques Villeneuve did exactly the same thing. I can't help but assume that if I'd stayed at Williams, as I could have done, I too would have become world champion. I have a great deal of respect for Ron Dennis although he's not the kind of guy you ever feel entirely comfortable with. I look back now and realise that it was a wrong call to go to McLaren in the first place, and wrong calls to allow Mika past.'

I asked him, despite all this, if he was happy with his achievements in F1. After all, he had established himself as one of the best-known figures in the sport, had won a good number of races and made his fortune as a result. Coulthard answered immediately without a moment's thought. 'I've been in this sport to become the world champion,' he said. 'That hasn't happened. I've been close, I've been unlucky at times as well, and I've won some major races. But I haven't achieved what I set out to do, and as far as I'm concerned there's still unfinished business. I believe there is time, still, to achieve my goal, but that time is fast running out. So, in answer to your question, no, I'm not happy with it, and if I'd been offered it at the start of my F1 career, I would have turned it down.'

This obvious hunger has been doubted only once and that, understandably, followed a plane crash near Lyon in May 2000. Coulthard, his then fiancée and his trainer emerged with their lives from the mangled wreck of the chartered Lear jet, but both pilots died.

'It was a life-saving and a life-changing experience for me,' he explained, as he delved back into the dark memories of his past. 'I decided to sharpen my focus on life, to become a little more ruthless. Before I'd always been available for everything, and for everyone. I was too easy-going, too soft, too accommodating. I had to toughen up.'

He was driven back to Monaco with his shaken trainer, arriving home at gone eleven. Up until this point Coulthard had handled a truly horrific experience incredibly well. 'Maybe it was my experience as a racing driver but amid all the noise, twisted metal, fire and fuel, I seemed to gather everyone up and lead them away. I was very cool at the time.'

The more so because it was very evident both pilots had not survived. 'There was nothing left of the plane where they had been sitting. The cockpit had been ripped away. One pilot was under the wreckage, the other somewhere else in the field. I went to take a look, obviously, to see if they had survived. At the time it didn't shake me up. I guess having been in big crashes in racing has prepared me for this type of happening. But it hit me later.

'That night, as I lay in bed back at this apartment, I spent ten minutes asking myself a series of questions. This is when I started to physically tremble. Would I fly again? Did I ever want to race cars again? Did I want to put myself in a situation where I might not come home one night? I answered yes to everything, raced four days later at the Spanish Grand Prix and made the podium with two broken ribs. I learned a lot about myself that week.'

Which is why he was desperate to grab another chance. If he were to get the nod from BAR Coulthard was convinced his career, far from being in its twilight, would enjoy a fresh and successful lease of life. 'Jenson Button's a friend of mine whom I respect as a racing driver, but I believe if I'd been driving his car this season I would have won a Grand Prix or two. It's just down to experience. Jenson will win many races in due course, but right now I know how to win and hope I get the chance to prove it again next season. If I do then there's no reason why I can't challenge for the title.'

But what if none of this materialises? What if he has just three races left in his F1 career? 'Then I become David Coulthard, former F1 driver, I suppose. It will be interesting to see how I fare.' He grimaced, collected his belongings in readiness for a fitness session and shook his head. 'But I don't want to find out. Not yet. In fact, not for a long time.'

We were both to report for a fitness session. Waiting for us in the gymnasium at the Columbus Hotel was Gerry, DC's personal trainer and another Scot. The fact that he was a former semi-professional footballer hardly fazed me. The fact that he was also a former marine did, however. After a few stretches he asked us to take turns performing pull-ups and chin-ups. Now I am more than capable of many things in the gym, but never have been much good at hauling the weight of my whole body over a bar using merely my arms.

Coulthard, still lean, muscular and devoid of much if any muscle fat, went first, easing his body up and down over the bar in a smooth, languid movement. We were to do ten each over five sets. I managed six on my first attempt, and only after much writhing and dangling. Coulthard produced another flawless ten, I scraped through five, although the last one was extremely suspect. And so this process went on, with Coulthard only beginning to struggle towards the end when he would manage eight, while I succeeded at two and a half. Those eighty-seven glasses of rosé the night before were clearly now not such a good idea. More annoying still, Coulthard seemed to have recovered completely from his alcoholic excesses, while I had clearly not. 'It's an age thing, I guess,' he reasoned, helpfully. This, of course, was the last thing I wanted to hear. And he knew it.

Next came a series of press-ups, with DC producing thirty each time, and me twenty, each of us cajoling the other to do more. After five sets of these I was asked to move on to the rowing machine while DC was told to cool down on the treadmill beside me. 'I've never been able to run,' he informed me. 'It's partly due to the conflicting exercises I do, and also because of the various crashes over the years that have damaged my knees and legs.'

I told him I had completed the London Marathon the previous April. That made me feel a little better after resembling a fool attempting pull-ups. Gerry asked me to warm up on the rowing machine for five minutes pulling at a rate of 2 minutes 20 seconds per 500 metres. Then it became a lot tougher. I would need to pull flat-out for a minute at 1.50, taking in sixty seconds' rest in between at 2.00 minutes. This exercise would be repeated five times.

Towards the end of this I was, to coin a phrase used by virtually every football and rugby trainer I've ever met, blowing out of my arse. At least Coulthard was understanding. He did try and strike up a conversation, as I slid backwards and forwards on the rowing machine, until I explained that it was growing increasingly difficult to talk. Afterwards he was complimentary about my efforts. I told him how he had been a great deal kinder than the former racing driver, Eddie Irvine, who challenged me to beat his time of 9 minutes 30 seconds over 2,500 metres a couple of years back.

Unbeknown to Fast Eddie I had just completed training and playing rugby league for the Wigan Warriors in their traditional Boxing Day derby match against St Helens. I was, by my standards, big, bulky and muscular. Not much good for racing cars, I grant you, but very good for rowing machines. When Irvine realised midway through that I was going to beat his time he started using questionable tactics. At first, as I slid up and down on the machine inside his Jaguar motor home, it was clean and harmless. 'Umm,' he'd emphasise, as he swigged from a bottle of water. 'I'm enjoying this water. Shame you can't have any of it.'

I carried on, past 1,500 metres, then 2,000. That's when the abuse started to fly. 'You're really quite fat, aren't you?' he stated, as the sweat began to drip from my forehead. 'In fact, I think you look like a faggot.' Still I ignored him, now in some pain but confident I was going to smash Irvine's mark. Then came Eddie's pièce de résistance. With a final, almighty effort, I accelerated my stroke rate for the remaining 300 metres and started to grunt and groan in the process. 'You know what?' Eddie said, as I started to shout and scream. 'That's exactly the noise your missus was making when I was shagging her last night.'

Coulthard, who knows Irvine well, was amazed at this. 'No, he didn't really say that, did he? Come to think of it, I can well imagine it. I hope you beat him.' I did, by twenty-two seconds, even if it half-killed me. Of course, then I was the right side of forty. Now, as I towelled away the sweat and drank copious amounts of water, I was on the wrong side. And I was starting to feel it.

Dinner was taken at the Columbus. David Cawthorne joined us, as did a very amusing and interesting American friend of the two DC's called Vittorio who, it transpired, happened to be a plastic surgeon. Over hors d'oeuvres and, indeed, the main course, Vittorio regaled us with lovely stories of the various penis extension operations he had conducted. Now this might strike you as both puerile and tasteless, as indeed the food might have been as well under the circumstances, but it's amazing how a writer, a motor-racing driver and a manager can become engrossed in such a subject, even if some of Vittorio's story made you want to cross your legs and cover your eyes. As I listened to what Vittorio had to say, then looked across at a fascinated Coulthard, I wondered how such a subject matter should feature both in Maranello with Barrichello, and now here in Monaco.

At eleven that night Coulthard excused himself. 'Bike ride in the morning at nine,' he announced, looking at me. 'And you're coming with me.' We had moved on to the bar by then and, having ordered a Cointreau as a nightcap I was presented with a glass the size of a vase full of the clear alcohol.

I mentioned to DC his transformation from the haka-performing, rosé-swigging Scot on *Highlander*, the night before, to this. 'Yeah, I know, and I feel bad about that,' he admitted. 'It forced me to miss morning training today, which was very unprofessional of me. I had a commitment and I didn't follow it through.' He gave me a knowing look. 'That's why we'll be making up for it at nine in the morning.'

At 8.45 the following morning, my telephone rang in my room and the dulcet tones of one David Coulthard could be heard telling me to make my way over to his apartment immediately. He was waiting for me with a spare bike, helmet, top and shorts, and within minutes we were zig-zagging our way through the morning Monte Carlo traffic. 'It's quite a tough, uphill ride,' he explained, as we cycled through the streets. 'And it may take a little time. But the view at the top is special, and it's nice coming down.'

First we had to get to the top. The more we climbed, the less I was inclined to talk to DC. Once we had left Monte Carlo behind we cycled first up and through the village of Eze, then on to and through La Turbie, where so many movies in recent times, such as *Leon*, have been shot. The higher we rose, the more the sun started to beat down on us. While I puffed and panted, often raising myself from a saddle that was making my backside increasingly sore to a standing position in order to pump harder on the pedals, Coulthard would amble along effortlessly. Perhaps the most irritating aspect of all of this was when he would make and receive calls from his mobile telephone while climbing up an increasingly steep hill, with now just one hand on his handle bars, and the other clasping his mobile to his ear.

This was yet another reminder of how much I had slipped. There was never a time when I would have matched Couthard in the gym performing pull-ups, and now on the bike as we headed further and further up the mountain, but I would have given him a good run for his euros. My outward attitude to this was self-deprecating. Inwardly, I was fuming. It wasn't Coulthard's fault. It wasn't really mine, either. It was just nature's way of reminding me that my time for doing this kind of thing at this kind of level was almost up.

Towards the end, at the steepest part of the whole climb, Coulthard suggested that he should forge ahead and wait for me at the top. I agreed reluctantly with this idea, knowing that I was holding him back, and also that he was forcing me to go beyond my limits. It took no time for his figure to become smaller and smaller as he shot away from me. When I finally reached the summit and came across DC sitting beside his bike on the phone once more, I had taken twenty minutes longer than him, although that was partly due to a call of nature at a four-star Best Western Hotel halfway up the mountain. My riding partner seemed quite impressed with that aspect of my journey. 'You mean to say you just waltzed into the hotel in your cycle gear, went to the toilet, and walked straight out again?' he asked.

'Well, I did say '*bonjour*' and '*où sont les toilettes*?' I replied.

At last, after one-and-three-quarter hours of uphill riding, we could take a breather before the long descent back down to the city. After guzzling virtually the whole contents of my drinks bottle, I took in the view of Monte Carlo below us. From up there you could see everything, from the Stade Louis II and helipad next to Fontveille harbour, to the Grimaldi's Palace, and on to Casino Square. 'Don't you ever pinch yourself?' I asked my cycling partner. 'After all, it's a long way from Twynholm.'

Coulthard's answer was not one I expected. 'Never. It was all mapped out for me, you see. My Dad, Duncan, made it happen. He was a Scottish karting champion in his time, and he believed I had the ability to go all the way. From when I was eleven years old onwards every weekend was spent karting, all over Britain and then, later, all over Europe. I'd do my school homework in the car going to or coming from the races. Every weekday evening was geared towards racing, too. I'd strip the car down on Monday nights and clean it. On Tuesdays I'd clean the motor home. On Wednesdays it would be my racing leathers. And so on. My dad instilled a work ethic in me, but the money he spent in getting me into motor racing was phenomenal. Then, when I was fourteen, he told me that as soon as I'd broken into Formula One I'd have to move to Monaco. It would be the most tax-efficient way to lead my life. So, here I am.'

Here he is, indeed, but surely it could not have been quite as easy as that. 'Oh God, no, there were plenty of upsets and arguments when I was a kid. If it had not gone well my Dad would say to me, 'We're wasting our time. We may as well put the kart back in the van and go home.' That used to motivate me to do better. When I won anything my Dad and I used to have a little ceremony where we used to put the trophy on the shelf in the cabinet together. It was always a nice moment for both of us. Dad's kept everything, from my first helmet, gloves and racing suits, to my first kart. They're all in a small museum back in Twynholm now.'

But what about his childhood? Or lack of it? Didn't he miss the excesses of youth, even if he appeared to be making up for it now? 'Well, it was a small village where I lived. There were only about five boys my age there, and one of them was Cawthorne. I was pretty quiet in any case, and obsessed with my racing. But I was enjoying myself. I really was. Okay, so I didn't laugh my way through my childhood. I didn't go clubbing or pubbing. In fact I've drunk a lot more since I've been involved in F1, funnily enough. Yet I was as happy then as I am now.'

The only time David and Duncan Coulthard had any doubts over DC's career came about in 1994 after he had been undertaking some testing for Williams and driving in the Formula 3000 championships. 'My Dad told me he couldn't find any more money to sponsor me. That's when I wondered whether I was destined to test drive and race touring cars for the rest of my career. But I managed to get a car lent to me and raced on the Bank Holiday Monday the day after Ayrton Senna was killed. I finished second, which was the best result I and the team had had, and was then asked by Williams to come down to Jerez to test and see if I could take Senna's place with the team.'

This sounds incredibly cut-throat, considering that the greatest driver of the time had just died. 'Oh, everyone in the sport was shocked about it. If it could happen to Senna, it could happen to anyone. I had received a fax from Williams on the morning of his death wishing me luck for my race the following day. Ayrton had signed it, adding 'Good luck to you' on the bottom of the fax. So it was obviously upsetting to hear the news from Monza but, at the same time, I had a job to do, first in my race, and then when I was asked basically to audition for the spare Williams seat.'

He thought he had blown his chance when he crashed the car just as Frank Williams arrived at the circuit. 'I really felt there was no way Frank would offer me the seat after that but instead he told me the crash would not affect his decision, that I would be driving in the next Grand Prix at Barcelona for Williams.'

What about his mother, Joyce, though? Was she happy about her son's chosen career? 'Oh no, she would much rather I'd done something else. I tried to cheer her up after I crashed at Silverstone in 1995 and was knocked out. It was a great moment for me because I realised that if I was going to die in the car my last few moments would not be filled with fear but instead a recognition of the situation and an absolute belief that I would recover. Then I'd wake up, I suppose. Or not. I wanted my mother to know that if I got killed I didn't want her to be haunted by the thought of me screaming towards a wall. That's how I'm sure Senna would have felt. All he was thinking about was how he was going to beat Schumacher. Then the lights went out.'

Well, I'm sure Joyce Coulthard was happy to hear all this. 'Er, actually she didn't want to know and kept asking me to stop talking like that.'

We climbed back on to our bikes and began the descent down. This was far more pleasurable. We stopped along the way to pay homage at the scene of the fatal crash of Princess Grace of Monaco (aka Grace Kelly), an inconspicuous, even tawdry corner, marked by an empty plastic drinks bottle filled with a single flower.

Then it was down, down into Monte Carlo. To underline how steep the climb up was, the first time I pedalled one revolution of the wheel on the return journey was a couple of minutes away from Coulthard's apartment. When we reached our destination I managed to scrape the bike across my ankle and gouge a lump of skin away. 'What has he been doing to you?' Simone asked, as I stood in their apartment, munching away on an energy bar, downing a pint glass of juice, and dabbing away the blood that had congealed into a large lump on my right leg. 'You've only been on a bike ride, haven't you?'

Well, yes. Albeit a two-and-half-hour bike ride up a bloody mountain. Coulthard winked. 'My Dad told me to always keep away from women when I'm racing.'

I wish my Dad had told me to always keep away from racing drivers. After a hideous hangover, a cruel session in the gym, a monstrous, mountainous bike ride and gouged leg, I thanked DC for his time and companionship, caught the helicopter back to Nice and flew home to England.

By the following evening I could barely move my arms, I was having difficulty breathing and I couldn't sleep due to the pain in my shoulders, neck and back. I looked like Popeye, too. My biceps had suddenly blown up so large that I made Arnold Schwarzennegger look like Woody Allen in comparison. I'd like to say this was due to the muscle I had piled on. The truth was both arms were inflamed.

A trip to my physio the next morning confirmed the worst. 'You have severe tendonitis in both biceps and shoulders, and damage to your lats and pecs,' Paul, the physio, explained. 'And your shoulders have been misplaced. What the hell have you been doing?'

I told him the story of the pull-ups, my hurt pride, the rowing machine and the bike ride. Paul shook his head and, without warning, snapped my shoulders back into place. My cry of pain provoked the receptionist to run into the treatment room to check that Paul had not just shot me.

I bet Coulthard wasn't suffering from any after-effects. Later that day, in the search of some sympathy, I contacted David Cawthorne to tell him the news. 'I guess that dispels the myth that F1 drivers don't need to be fit,' he said.

Once again I returned home in a sorry state. The last time was due to too much alcohol, not enough sleep and hanging out with Brad and George. I expected no sympathy and received none. This, however, was down to excessive exercising.

My wife had lived through this particular scenario. She told me not to go to America and fight Roy Jones Jr. I returned home with a broken nose and concussion and took to my bed for the best part of a week. She thought it unwise for me to play in an actual rugby match for the Leicester Tigers. I contracted a broken rib and could not sleep properly for a fortnight. She considered my idea to become a professional wrestler downright crazy, and maintained this view as she drove me to the hospital after it was all over to examine my whiplash injuries. Now this.

'That'll teach you,' she surmised, making me feel like a naughty little boy with a grazed knee and a tear in my first proper pair of long trousers. 'When are you going to learn that these people you insist on competing with are the best in the world and you're not. And when are you going to realise that you're no longer a young man.'

I was happy to concede the first point. But the second really hurt, the more so because it was probably true and she was probably right.

chapter ten

SPACE AGE CITY

The message pinned to the back of the taxi driver's seat was the most bizarre I had ever read. 'No schizos, drunkards or psychotics are allowed in this taxi' it demanded.

'Well,' I said to my driver, as I sat alone on the back seat making my way from the airport to the city centre. 'Me and myself had better get out then.'

It was a joke, albeit a pretty poor one, that was totally lost on my Mandarin-speaking driver, who blinked at me and then laughed anyway, once I had given him a gentle prod accompanied by a big smile to denote I had just cracked a funny one.

I had recently arrived in Shanghai, the 'Paris of the East' or, alternatively, the 'Whore of the Orient', as it was once famously dubbed. I'd been in the back of a few taxis in my time, in a fair few cities around the world. Quite a number of them had asked for good behaviour, politeness or clean clothing, but never before had I been warned not to be a 'schizo' or 'psychotic'.

It would be the first of countless surprises I would come across over the course of the next few days during my first ever visit to China, a trip that would climax with the inaugural Chinese Grand Prix.

My adventures with Barrichello and Coulthard had whetted my appetite for more Grand Prix action. Time had healed my various physical ailments following my exercise regime with the latter in Monaco, and I had embarked on a fitness campaign to ensure that the next time I found myself thrown into a challenge against a younger, fitter man, I would at least make a good account of myself.

As a result I was already feeling considerably better all round as I boarded the plane to take me to one of the few major countries in the world I had never visited before. Despite flying the world for the best part of twenty years, travel continued to excite me, the more so when a new culture presented itself. China had only recently opened its barriers to the West and I felt as intrigued to witness this fascinating country as I did when visiting a Russian under the rule of Brezhnev on a school trip twenty-five years previously.

Shanghai is, to put it mildly, flourishing again. I say again because in the 1920s and 1930s it enjoyed a decadent image, a city sporting more than its fair share of gangsters and prostitutes, spy rings, drugs and brothels. Lured by such hedonism the likes of Noel Coward, George Bernard Shaw and Charlie Chaplin would all spend time on the eastern Chinese coast.

It was, and is, a city of vast contradictions, the result of a truly multicultural population arriving initially by sea at the great port of Shanghai and, latterly, by air, now that China has opened its arms to the west. Apart from the Chinese the city has been clearly influenced by the many thousands of British ex-pats living there over the years, not to mention Americans, Russians and Germans. Always one of China's pre-eminent conurbations, Shanghai has never quite seen itself as part of the rest of the country, but more as an individual enclave and a gateway to the world.

After the Roaring Twenties and Thirties came initial occupation from the Japanese during the Second World War, followed by many years of relative wilderness when China was under Communist rule after Chairman Mao marched into Shanghai in 1949 to declare the People's Republic of China.

From the moment Mao died in 1976 Shanghai, emerging from the darker depths of the Cultural Revolution, has never looked back, especially since 1990 when the Chinese Government decided that Shanghai, and no longer Hong Kong, would become the financial capital of the country.

In just the past fifteen years an entirely new city has been developed on marshland east of the Huangpu River the size of Singapore. This area, known as Pudong, boasts as many as 150 skyscrapers, including the inspirational Oriental Pearl Tower, modern Shanghai's signature building. Pudong is Manhattan, eastern-style, and this contemporary miracle of planning and development, coupled with the Bund across the river – a curved sweep of numerous buildings constructed between 1920 and 1940 with imposing entrances and marble halls which housed the old banks and institutions that mark the influence of colonialism – as well as the old town area, make Shanghai one of the most exciting and interesting cities in the world. The rice and paddy fields I had stupidly envisaged exist all over China. But not here. Not in the city of the future.

Even as I drew up to my hotel, the JC Mandarin, I had an example of the heady cocktail that is Shanghai, and a minor portrait of a past now hanging on desperately to the city's new-found pace. There, before me, stood my modern, skyscraper-style hotel. Across the street a couple of prostitutes were attempting to persuade a middle-aged, Western businessman to part with his money. And right in front of the hotel, beside the pavement, two classes were taking place. One, ballroom dancing, was played out by a dozen elderly couples, clasping each others' hands close to their hearts and oblivious to watching passers-by as they glided slowly across the concrete to accompanying Chinese music.

The other was a tai chi gathering, smaller in numbers, and dominated by an old man who took his tai chi extremely seriously. Each of the three mornings I was in Shanghai I would watch this same old man performing his tai chi. Through a nearby bus operator who could speak good English I asked the man, a Mr Tianshu, how long he had been doing this.

'Over thirty years,' he replied. 'At the same spot. Every single morning.' He paused for a few seconds deep in thought, before adding: 'Except a couple of days when I've been ill.' A couple of days in thirty years! Whatever the man was taking I wanted to sample some of it. It might have been the opium that had riddled the city in the nineteenth and early twentieth century. Or it could have been plain clean living.

Whatever the case, he had performed his tai chi through many years of Communism, including the final days of Mao's life, and through the sudden explosion of space-age technology and development that had spread over the city like an outbreak of smallpox. 'The city has changed,' Mr Tianshu added. He looked up at the JC Mandarin. 'That wasn't there when I started.' Then he looked across at a woman who was either a prostitute or had seriously underestimated the coolness of the late summer breeze when she got dressed that morning. 'But people like her were. She should try tai chi, like me. I think it is better for you.'

Mr Tianshu laughed out loud at that final comment, his opened mouth revealing a higgledy-piggledy collection of multicoloured teeth, before he raised his arms aloft again, spun his body around, and continued with his slow, oriental movements.

I had to dash to a Ferrari conference at the Hyatt Hotel, which meant taking another 'no schizos' ride across a city where such inconveniences as traffic lights and traffic cops failed to prevent determined drivers from pursuing their own course. As Rubens Barrichello pointed out during the conference, if Formula One gets a hold on China then, judging by the speed of the Shanghai taxis, there should be a number of potential motor-racing stars emerging from this part of the world.

The Ferrari conference was a major PR coup. Excitement was quite evidently building in the city as the teams and their drivers began to arrive, but none more so when the sign of the Prancing Horse was hung up for business. I must have been one of half a dozen Westerners present in an auditorium otherwise filled to capacity by hundreds and hundreds of Chinese journalists, reporters and cameramen and women.

Barrichello walked on to the stage first, to be met with enthusiastic applause. Then Michael Schumacher, basking in the success of his seventh world title now secured, appeared. The room erupted. The Schumacher legend had clearly reached this corner of the globe. 'What do you think of China?' one questioner asked him. 'Are you going to win on Sunday?' asked another. 'What is your favourite colour?' enquired a third.

I should have been growing used to seeing Schumacher by now. After all, I had observed him from close quarters at Monaco and at Silverstone. But the stories I had been told about him, and the character portrait painted by the likes of Dernie, Brawn and Barrichello, made me as fascinated by him as my oriental media chums.

Schumacher, in a rather polished manner, had paused following that last question. Eventually, after a perfectly judged pause, he pointed at a poster of the Ferrari F1 car. 'Red, of course,' he replied, an answer that was met with spontaneous, loud and prolonged laughter. So besotted were the Chinese media with the best driver in the world that Schumacher could have said anything and still received side-splitting chortles. He may have been desperately shy in the past. He may still not especially enjoy this aspect of his job. But boy, he was good.

Dinner was taken in the city centre with Nav Sidhu and his friend, Alex Wooff, from Formula One Management. It was Alex who kindly had arranged for me to spend time with his boss, Bernie Ecclestone, the following week back in FOM's offices, a rare audience, indeed, with the main man in motor sport. And it was Alex, together with myself, who was wondering why, on our first ever night in China, Nav had chosen an Austrian restaurant and plumped for Wiener schnitzel.

'Well, I'm hungry,' was his only explanation, as he ordered himself an Austrian stein of beer from a Chinese waiter wearing lederhosen. Alex looked down at his schnitzel, while I played with my goulash, wondering just how nice a plate of special fried rice with chicken and crispy duck might taste in Shanghai. For goodness' sake! Next we'd be hearing from a Mr Woo who would serenade us with 'Edelweiss'.

The next morning I made my way over to the Shanghai motor-racing circuit, courtesy of another taxi driver with similar, anti-schizo demands. If there is such a thing as a 'World Schizophrenics Society', then I only hope it is not based in Shanghai.

It took the best part of an hour to reach the circuit, situated in the Jiading District, a reconnaissance journey not only necessary before the following day's Grand Prix, but well worth making once I had been deposited in front of something resembling a space centre in the year 2150. There, before me, stood the best track, the best circuit and the best facilities in Formula One, and all this from a race with no history, making its F1 debut. Five years previously stood only scrubland and rice fields. Now the Chinese had created a masterpiece.

I thought about the Pudong area of Shanghai, of this new circuit, and the fact that the 2008 Olympics would be staged in Beijing. This, it seemed, truly was the time of the Chinese. Third World? Hardly. At the rate of knots this country was moving, China, and a good many other parts of South East Asia, would soon be supplanting Western Europe and North America.

During the course of the day anyone who was anyone had their say on the matter. 'It's the best race track I've seen,' insisted Schumacher, in another press conference staged this time at the circuit. 'The commitment that has been put into building the new facilities, and also the circuit layout, are exceptional,' added Jenson Button. 'It's gorgeous, very beautiful,' said Jacques Villeneuve.

It also served as a nasty wake-up call to the European tracks, many of which, such as Silverstone and Magny Cours, had been around for fifty years. If people did not believe these circuits were beginning to look understandably dated, then all they had to do was to take in the Shanghai circuit.

'This is another example of what Asia can do,' gushed the Benetton-Renault team boss, Flavio Briatore, whom I had last seen in Monaco's Amber Lounge with Naomi Campbell. 'We've seen Malaysia, we've seen Bahrain. Now this. It is so much better than Europe.'

It was impossible to disagree. Ecclestone was there, of course, his diminutive figure bedecked in his trademark white shirt, taking in everything. For him this was a particular triumph. Rumoured to have made £25 million out of the deal to bring Formula One to China, he was a few days away from initiating a process that almost saw the end of the British Grand Prix and Silverstone until last-ditch negotiations would save the day. Standing in the centre of the Shanghai circuit, it was little wonder that Ecclestone's thoughts turned to Britain's premier circuit, and his mood darkened.

I sat down next to Button for five minutes to take in the view. He, in between a multitude of publicity commitments, was doing very much the same thing. 'I've never seen so many bloody skyscrapers as I've seen here,' he said, clearly excited by this new venture in the Far East. 'It's an unbelievable place. Look at this circuit,' he added, waving his arm frantically towards the main grandstand. 'It's like being in a futuristic airport. I'll tell you something. China isn't pumping so much money into sport if it didn't believe sport has a long-term future in this country. I think F1's gonna be massive here.'

Been busy, then, Jenson, I asked, as I looked at his slightly frazzled expression. He let out a big blow of air. 'Just a bit. I've never had so much publicity, not even in Britain. And I'm British! Everyone's gone crazy!'

The circuit was designed by the German, Hermann Tilke, who had already designed the new tracks in Malaysia and Bahrain, as well as in Turkey, the latter to be used in 2005 for the first time. Costing £250 million to build it is shaped like the Chinese letter 'Shang', which means 'rise' or 'above'. Just under four miles in length, it boasted a capacity crowd of 200,000, 29,000 of which would be seated in the main grandstand overlooking the starting grid and finish.

The paddock was pretty special, too. Ordinarily each of the teams at other circuits could be found beside their large trucks and motor homes, with temporary hospitality and dining units constructed. In Shanghai each enjoyed their own bungalows, built on stilts and surrounded by beautiful fauna and a lagoon.

In one, the FOM bungalow, Alex Wooff introduced me to Niki Lauda. The Austrian legend appreciated our story of eating Wiener schnitzel the night before. 'A wise choice,' he declared, failing to appreciate my 'when in Rome' (or Shanghai) argument. He did, however, agree to spend a day with me in Vienna in a few weeks' time. 'Just remember, Niki, Ian is a family man,' Alex said, as the legendary driver, complete with red baseball cap, chuckled to himself like a boy planning a raid on a school tuck shop.

In another bungalow could be found Ferrari. Luca Colajanni, whom I'd met the day before at the Ferrari conference, had invited me over for a coffee. Luca was head of media operations and was trying to think of a way in which I could challenge Michael Schumacher in some kind of a head-to-head.

'Do you know how hard this request is for me to arrange?' he reasoned with me, as he sipped an espresso and I some Chinese tea. 'It's impossible. He is in more demand than even the Pope. There is just one thing, possibly, I may be able to do. In January Ferrari will have a day in the Italian Alps. You can be a guest of Ferrari and you can race Michael there.'

I felt my heartbeat make a couple of jumps. With one simple meeting my quest, hitherto impossible, looked likely to happen. This, on the face of it, sounded like fantastic news, until a tiny doubt crept into my mind. 'Er, did you say Italian Alps, Luca? I didn't know there was a circuit there.'

'There isn't,' Luca replied. 'I meant that you and Michael can have a downhill ski race. Just the two of you. Head to head. What do you say?'

I shook Luca's hand, thanked him repeatedly and, of course, said 'yes'. With that I took my leave from the Ferrari pod, walked over a bridge across a pond until I was well out of sight of Luca Colajanni. 'Shit!' I said, loud enough for Eddie Jordan, the Jordan team owner who was passing by on one of those paddock scooters the drivers so like to use, to turn round and wobble. 'I can't ski.'

Why, in God's name, had I agreed to something I could not possibly do and, more to the point, how I was going to dig myself out of a snowy mess? My dilemma was that I could not see any other way to have a 'showdown' with the maestro, at least not in a car. But what, thinking about it, was the point of taking on Schumacher in a downhill ski race? I may as well challenge Tiger

Woods to a game of ping-pong. Why not turn this into a whole new genre? Challenging famous achievers to take me on in an activity they are not known to have excelled in. The three tenors versus me, at who can build a garden shed quicker. The proverbial bed had been made now, and I had just better start planning to lie in it.

The Schumacher conference in downtown Shanghai the day before had merely underlined the point that asking to race against the man, in a car, at least, was akin to attempting to cancel your *Reader's Digest* membership through customer service. It just wasn't possible. Unless a sudden opportunity could fall my way I resigned myself to learning the rudiments of skiing, turning up in northern Italy, and no doubt breaking both my legs in pursuit of the German. It would be another fine mess of Stan Laurel proportions I had made for myself, and I could already envisage my wife's expression as I returned home with both legs in plaster.

I was still deep in thought when Peter Phillips, who arranged my working weekend with BMW–Williams at the British Grand Prix, tapped me on the shoulder and led me to a young Chinese man surrounded by a mass of local photographers. 'This,' Peter announced, sounding like a master of ceremonies, 'is Ho Pin Tung.'

Ho Pin Tung, so it transpired, is China's most famous motor-racing star. That may not be saying much right now, but the young man is on the verge of becoming one of the most famous sportsmen in the world, due to the simple fact that, with a population of 1.3 billion, the Chinese are looking out for their first F1 driver.

Ho Pin, who grew up in Holland where his parents own a Chinese restaurant, is likely to be that man. By virtue of winning the 2003 Formula BMW Asia series he earned himself a test drive in the BMW–Williams F1 car at Jerez. Having received one-to-one tuition from Juan Pablo Montoya the night before, Ho Pin did enough to get noticed by the higher powers at BMW. 'He has serious potential as a racing driver' was the verdict of BMW's Mario Theissen, for example.

The test drive soon hit the Chinese news stands and TV channels. And, with the Chinese Grand Prix almost upon us, Ho Pin was making the most of his paddock walkabout. 'Even though I was born and raised in Holland everyone in China sees me as Chinese,' he explained, with a smile, as he signed countless autographs. 'There is a tremendous will here for me to succeed. But it's important to me that if I do become the first Chinese Formula One driver I do it on merit and merit alone. Otherwise I may also be the last Chinese F1 driver.'

You instantly recognise his point. The Chinese Grand Prix had created a feeding frenzy for the West, not only in banking and electronics but now, it appeared, in the car industry. China, not surprisingly, has the fastest growing car market in the world. By 2010 it is estimated the country's demand for cars will have reached ten million. There was big business to be secured here, and everyone connected to any of the F1 teams was here. Ho Pin's own backers, BMW, had just started production in China, so everyone knew the importance of the young, Chinese driver.

Wang Ying, the circuit's vice-general manager, summed it up succinctly. 'Right now it is very important to have a Chinese F1 driver,' he explained. 'We have the track but to raise interest we must have a driver, too. It will send China car crazy, and that will help car sales, But we don't just see him as China's first F1 driver. We want him to be the next Michael Schumacher.'

No pressure there, then, for Ho Pin, although as he bowed, shook hands, signed more autographs and smiled at everything and everyone, the full brunt of expectation from the largest population in the world may not have quite hit him yet.

It was not just the car industry that was looking to benefit from this Chinese extravaganza. Norbert Haug, the Mercedes sporting director, referred to this Grand Prix as the most important in the history of the sport. With European legislation clamping down hard on the tobacco industry sport, which has shamelessly sought to be happy bedfellows with the various cigarette companies over the years, is looking for new markets, none more so than Formula One. Of course, the teams would argue differently. Business, after all, is business, and faced with possible extinction or a new-found prosperity, would a bank, an airline or an electronics firm operate any differently?

Besides, everyone was making money out of this. From Bernie's £25 million to the prostitutes in the streets of Shanghai, to the merchandise stalls charging £35 for a trademark Michael Schumacher cap or £1200 for Jaguar racing overalls that would soon become obsolete.

For, amid all the big business and novelty of this first Chinese Grand Prix, plenty was happening within the sport, as well. Jaguar had announced that they needed a buyer after Cosworth decided to end their partnership with the famous green livery. Otherwise their total workforce would be out of a job. The only happy note from this, purely from a selfish viewpoint, was that now that Mark Webber had announced his departure to Williams, which had been one of the worst-kept secrets all season, it looked as if I might avoid the physical workout Jaguar's Nick Harris was planning. 'Keep yourself in shape, though,' Nick warned me outside the Jaguar bungalow. 'I might just spring the test on you in any case.'

Jordan and Minardi faced difficult times, too, as a result of Cosworth's decision to withdraw their engines. Meanwhile Ralf Schumacher was making his long-awaited return for BMW–Williams after his horrific crash at Indianapolis, and Jacques Villeneuve had been drafted in to replace the departed Jarno Trulli at Benetton–Renault.

I made my way back into town in a minibus with Nav Sidhu,

Jaguar's concerned head two, Tony Purnell and Dave Pitchforth, Alex Wooff, and Sonia Irvine, Eddie Irvine's sister, who is based now in Monaco and looks after, among other things, the Amber Lounge.

Dinner was taken close to the top of the Oriental Pearl Tower. Finally, as I went round and round the city of Shanghai in the tower's revolving restaurant, I had laid my hands on some Chinese food. It had taken the best part of two days!

The Pearl Tower is, quite simply, awesome. Standing 1,500 feet (468 metres) high, it is the tallest building in Asia and the third highest in the world after the TV towers in Toronto and Moscow. With its unique architectural design, a collection of eleven differently sized spheres piled on top of each other, it is as much the soul of new Shanghai as the Yu Gardens, Shanghai's number one tourist spot, is of the old city.

A few too many beers later, courtesy of the Shanghai Grand Prix who had laid on the hospitality for the world's media, I went to bed and grappled with the confused combination of the eight-hour time difference, a hotel room revolving and the noise of a city that barely sleeps.

The paddock was alive and thriving, even first thing the following morning, like the Soho district of London, with the aroma of coffee wafting its way from the various team bungalows and blasting through your senses to erase the results of a bad night's sleep.

I had been forced to make an early start and a dash to the circuit to beat the majority of the 200,000 spectators expected to witness the inaugural Chinese Grand Prix that afternoon.

David Coulthard was already surrounded by autograph hunters and more Chinese photographers when he emerged from the McLaren–Mercedes bungalow. I told him about the damage his workouts had done to my body, news that he seemed to find amusing. 'You didn't have to do it,' he responded, knowing full well that anyone with even a minor streak of competitiveness inside him would not have turned down the challenge. 'Like I said at the time, it's probably an age thing,' he added, now being mischievous. He may as well have been my wife.

Despite my raw nerves being touched by this comment I was in a good mood. The sun was shining, the atmosphere around the Shanghai circuit had the kind of buzz exclusive to the morning of a Grand Prix and, best of all, my mobile phone, having been left on the back seat of a taxi the night before, was in my hand. The hotel concierge had informed me that my taxi driver, clearly deciding that I was not a schizo, had discovered my phone and driven back to the hotel to hand it in. Somehow, I could not see that happening in London. I had endured twenty minutes of blind panic before the concierge stepped in. Oh my God! I'd lost my mobile phone. Life, as I knew it, was now not worth living. I may as well end it all. And yet, twenty years ago, when I was making early inroads into my professional life, mobile phones barely existed. Strange, isn't it, how we all got on with our business completely unaffected by this?

Outside the main entrances a small city of stallholders had suddenly mushroomed, and a battalion of touts offering everything from tickets at exorbitant prices to binoculars and, of course, 'genuine' Rolex watches that would set you back only £50 and would break within a fortnight.

Inside the circuit the pre-race entertainment hotted up. Behind the main grandstand could be found a model of an oil refinery run by Sinopec, the state-owned sponsor of the race. A Chinese girl dressed in a PVC bikini stood having photographs taken of herself next to a Grand Prix car made entirely of Coca-Cola cans while, on the track, a carnival of singers, drummers, dancing girls with pink streamers and sparkly skirts and men dressed in white sailor suits carrying a huge, red flag, marched by, followed by a mass kendo exhibition, the air punctuated by the sound of hundreds of 'arghs' and 'huhs'. In the stands, meanwhile, most of the Chinese racegoers sported T-shirts and flags with one black emblem surrounded by red: the prancing horse.

The race itself, played out in front of 157,000, a few less than expected but still by far the biggest Grand Prix attendance of the year, was one of the better spectacles of the season, too, mainly because Schumacher, the world title claimed safely once again, failed to finish due to a puncture. It would have been tough going, in any case, after he started the race in last place and from the pit lane having spun in qualifying the day before. 'Nothing to win, nothing to lose, nothing to prove', was his summing up of his worst result (twelfth) in nearly six years. The seasoned cynics muttered dark deeds of public relations commitments and giving others a chance to make the first Chinese Grand Prix a memorable race, as opposed to a procession. Whatever the case, it resulted in Barrichello winning his second Grand Prix of the season, with Button second and Kimi Raikkonen third, but only after numerous overtaking manoeuvres rarely seen, a trading of fastest laps, spins and collisions.

Never mind the race on the track, though. The race to the airport, via my hotel to collect all my belongings, was a far hairier affair. It was in this mayhem that Peter Phillips narrowly escaped injury, and it was during this ride back to the JC Mandarin that I realised that schizos, drunkards and psychotics may be a problem in the back of a cab, but by far the biggest danger was the taxi driver himself.

I could have taken the taxi all the way to the airport but chose, instead, to take the 'Maglev'. Standing for 'magnetic levitation', Shanghai's Maglev is the world's fastest train, driven by magnets that replace conventional wheels and rails hovering just above a flat track. It makes Japan's famous 'bullet' train seem like a two-carriage, district locomotive in Scotland in comparison.

Inside each carriage digital monitors inform you of the increasing speeds you are travelling at for the twenty-mile journey. Midway through the journey it reaches its top speed and announces it with pride – 430 kph, or 266 mph – before almost immediately having to begin its sharp decline in speed to prevent it from crashing straight through the rail terminal and on to the airport runway.

It seemed an unlikely but somehow fitting way to end my short trip to Shanghai. I had come with ridiculously preconceived conceptions of ancient traditions, environments and lifestyles.

And now I was leaving on a train straight out of a *Star Wars* movie, having left a city that resembled a set from *Blade Runner* and a Grand Prix staged at a venue befitting the kind of world we are all supposed to be living in a couple of centuries' time on the moon when mankind has finally succeeded in achieving total self-destruction.

Perhaps only then will Mr Tianshu's daily tai chi class cease to exist.

chapter eleven

BERNIE

You can see a lot in a person by their office. The one I was standing in just three days after the Chinese Grand Prix was as good an example as any. Although often referred to as Britain's richest man, Bernard Charles Ecclestone's personal style, like his waiting room, is mainly understated, save for a few, tell-tale snippets of evidence hinting at a personal fortune estimated in the region of £2.6 billion.

Thus, on one sideboard, stood a metal sculpture of four mini-tower blocks of dollar bills. Nearby a golden handshake, albeit in bronze, was placed on a chest, underneath a framed cartoon caricature of an untrustworthy ducker and diver entitled 'Mr Bob Big Time – Bachelor of Bull'.

The plush offices of Formula One Management can be found just a stone's throw away from Hyde Park in London. After six months of following the Yellow Brick Road I had come, finally, to the resting place of the Wizard himself. Up until now I had gorged myself in his empire, played a small part in its running and met many of its star turns. Now I had been granted an audience with the man at the top of this multi-faceted, money-making pyramid. Mr Ecclestone, I was informed, would be with me 'shortly', although, bearing in mind his diminutive physical stature, I wasn't sure this was the best phrase to use.

Funny thing, that. Why, I mused, as I played with his sculpted dollar bills, does his incredible success seem less likely simply because he is short. What has that got to do with anything, unless he wanted to become a professional basketball player, or a second-row rugby forward? The same may as well be said of my red hair.

Ecclestone – or 'Bernie' as he is universally known within motor racing and indeed sport – earned more than four tower blocks of dollar bills out of Shanghai. 'I was told I was being an idiot approaching China for a Grand Prix,' he explained, once he had appeared and gestured me to sit down opposite him at a boardroom-style table. 'Three or four years ago people didn't want to know. Literally. Three or four years ago.'

He looks straight at you, a particular habit of his, blinks and examines your facial reaction first to the unlikely alliance between a totalitarian power and sport's greatest entrepreneur, and then the resulting scepticism in the project that would prove so unfounded.

'Look at the facts and figures,' he added. 'There are 1.3 billion people in China. Right now we have a total television viewership in Shanghai and Beijing alone which exceeds the total viewership in the whole of Europe. I've been working for ten years to make this work. Four years ago there were just ricefields and dirt there. Certainly there was no sign of a road anywhere near the circuit. It just goes to prove that when the Chinese want to do something they are truly committed.

'The West is going to be in for a big, rude shock. You've seen what's happening in China. Well, the same will be said of India and Russia very soon. Within ten years Europe will become a Third World continent, with its minimum this, maximum that and thirty-five-hour weeks.

'And do you want to know something else? The agreement was made with the Governor of Shanghai over a handshake. He's now become a very important person as a result of the Grand Prix. Today people need a lawyer to accompany them to the toilet. It doesn't have to be that way.'

There is no particular triumphalism in this little speech. Bernie does not do triumphalism. In fact, he does not show much emotion about anything, keeping his carefully chosen words down to a quiet and clipped whisper. Indeed, he would often quite happily use one or two words to provide what he believed to be a full and concise answer.

Was he happy, for example, about the way it went in China? 'Oh yes, very,' came back the reply accompanied by maximum eye contact. But the Shanghai experience is as good an example as anything the man has achieved and, with both India and Russia honing in on staging their own Grands Prix in the near future, there is more to come.

China was not the first time his methods were questioned. 'I can look back to the first ever Hungarian Grand Prix, which I put on behind what was then the Iron Curtain. Everyone back then said I was mad as well. The whole place was run by the KGB in those days but I persuaded them to build a race circuit. I'm proud of that, and China. When I'm on my deathbed I can at least look back on achievements such as these and believe I'd managed to do a thing or two.'

A long weekend in Shanghai proved to be rather lucrative for him, nonetheless. 'Yes, I made some money out of it,' he admits, when asked about the £25 million earned from fees and trackside advertising. 'But it's always the same. People have a problem with me earning a living, even if it means my living earns them money too. There are certain people in Formula One, especially the teams, who would rather earn 10 per cent if it meant I earned 10 per cent, than taking home 30 per cent if it meant I was earning 60.'

He has a point that seems to be forever forgotten in the cut-throat and often back-stabbing environment that is the big business end of the sport. Back in the mid-Seventies, with the approval of F1's ruling body, the FIA, and the team owners, Ecclestone agreed a deal whereby he received a third of any profits from television rights which, at the time, were non-existent. He appeared to be the only man who recognised that TV rights would remain at zero for a very short time. Today his power is omnipotent. His company receives all commercial and TV revenues from Grands Prix with the circuits pocketing only ticket money.

In the process he has created an unbeatable winning formula. The sport not only attracts the billion-dollar sponsorships that have made team owners such as Sir Frank Williams, Ron Dennis of McLaren and Eddie Jordan millionaires in their own right, but also new countries and markets. Bahrain and Malaysia, for example, joined China as new venues, prepared to invest up to £350 million to become annual hosts of an event which gives them a global standing and attracts new and big business, as well as tourism.

Not surprisingly, the five-foot-four-inch Ecclestone has become a big player on the international economic, sporting and even political stage. His luxury silver motor home, which sits royally on every paddock at every Grand Prix, has become a regular visiting site for heads of state and royalty, leading global business figures and film stars.

'It's just been a case of a lot of hard work and a lot of luck,' is his reason for how he landed so very much on his feet. Is that it? 'It's about recognising opportunities and taking them.'

Ah, now we were talking. I told Bernie about the time when I bought copies of my first ever book – an innocuous tome that may still be found on a few remainder lists – and sold them on for a profit. I must have made £500.

The first smile of the day spreads across his face. Up until this point he had remained stony-faced, revealing little. Underneath that shock of Andy Warhol floppy white hair is a face designed for playing poker which, of course, he has effectively been doing in business for the past fifty years.

'Now we're talking the same language,' he replied. 'What you did with your books is what I've been doing all my life in business. You saw an opportunity, took what others may perceive to be a risk, worked hard, and made a profit at the end of it. We are similar people.'

I suppose we are. Similar people in that Bernie's recognition of opportunities has thrown him £2.6 billion, and mine, £500. We could almost be business partners!

Bernie's wheeling and dealing started early. Born seventy-four years ago in the Suffolk village of Wangford, he was the son of a trawler skipper and first worked at a gasworks, but he puts his sharpness of mind down to his wartime experiences 'I had a country background but lived in Woolwich (in south-east London) during the war. It forced me to think quickly on my feet, something I've been doing ever since.' His first love, despite seeing his father leave for North Sea duties, was bikes. 'At fifteen I used to race them,' he explained. 'Then I moved on to 500 cc Formula Three cars. I had no real ambition to be Stirling Moss. I did it for fun. It was a hobby. It was all rather amateurish in those days.'

At the same time his business interests were piling up. There were motor cycle showrooms, car retailing (he remains proud of his second-hand car professional background) and property deals. His time for racing became limited and, after a crash, virtually negligible. 'I had an accident,' he said. 'Nothing too terrible.

And I was lying there thinking that maybe I might not have been able to have got up from it. I was beginning to run successful businesses and I realised it wasn't important to me to race cars.'

He had muttered something else, as well, which was said so quietly and dismissively that I had to double-check that he had said it at all. 'I was born blind in one eye,' he reiterated. 'I managed to win a few races and get a record or two with the use of only one eye so I guess I couldn't have been too bad at driving. But it most probably would have prevented me from reaching the top.'

Has this adversity motivated him to go on to achieve his feats? Ecclestone almost chokes at the notion as he takes a long sip from his glass of water. 'No,' he spluttered. 'Why should it?' Very Ecclestone. The man has the use of just one eye and laughs at the suggestion that it is an adversity. So nonsensical is the notion that it is not worth discussing any more.

Even during his early forays into business the principles he has maintained to this day were being utilised. 'One way or another I've been wheeling and dealing ever since I was a kid,' he tells you. 'You buy cheap, keep the costs down, and sell anything. I've kept to those principles all my working life.'

He stayed close to the sport, though, planning to run his own F1 team in 1959 with his close friend and driver, Stuart Lewis-Evans. This came to nothing when, during the 1958 Moroccan Grand Prix, his future partner's transmission in his Vanwall seized up and he crashed. Lewis-Evans, badly burned, died in a Casablanca hospital a few days later, yet another damning statistic in the sport at a time when it was safer scaling Everest than driving in Formula One.

Undeterred Ecclestone first bought the Connaught team, then managed his good friend, Jochen Rindt, the brilliant Austrian driver. The former Cooper and Brabham star was driving for Lotus when he won the 1970 Monaco Grand Prix after what was regarded as one of the most spectacular drives of all time, but later set a record that no one would want. During a routine testing session at Monza Rindt, unwilling to buckle the crotch strap of his safety harness, he was killed in an innocuous accident. He became the first and, thankfully, only posthumous world champion.

After Rindt's death Ecclestone bought the Brabham team from Sir Jack Brabham and thus began an era of considerable success. With drivers of the calibre of Nelson Piquet, Niki Lauda (who remains a great friend and spent much of the Chinese Grand Prix in the Formula One Management bungalow) and Carlos Reutemann, the Brabham team would win twenty-two Grands Prix under Bernie, and two world titles for Piquet.

Despite all this success as a team owner Ecclestone was broadening his horizons and becoming an increasingly influential figure within the running of the whole sport. It would be this course that he would choose to take so successfully.

'To this day I miss being a team owner,' he admits. 'The best thing about it was that you knew what you had done by the Sunday evening. I had to stop because I was beginning to neglect the team. I realised I couldn't run a team and be so heavily involved in the sport in general. Something had to give.

'But I look back on those days with a great deal of fondness. There are different people in the sport now. The likes of Enzo Ferrari and Colin Chapman are all gone. They were the interesting ones. If one of the teams were ever in trouble, like we needed an engine or something, we'd help each other out.' He paused for a few seconds and gazed out over my shoulder. 'I miss them.'

Forming the Formula One Constructor's Association (FOCA) proved to be another inspirational move. 'People forget that I took all the risks early on,' he explained. 'Up until then the sport was so very amateur. It was a gentleman's sport played out by gentlemen. I guess I've turned it into a business. I formed the company and wanted to split it up between all the teams, but the teams didn't want to know. All they wanted to do was race. The money, which was non-existent to start with, suddenly started to come in. Then the teams were interested. And that's what I'm saying. Suddenly everyone's concerned about what I'm earning, and not recognising what I've brought to the table for them.'

They would have to admit, however, that Ecclestone, practically single-handedly, transformed Formula One from a loose-knit, self-interested gaggle of constructors into a multi-billion dollar global business that has maximised the commercial potential of the sport. During 1980 and 1981 he fought a long and often bitter battle with the FIA head, Jean-Marie Balestre, ultimately winning and, more or less, gaining complete control of the sport when his friend, Max Mosely (son of Sir Oswald, the fascist politician, and Lady Mitford), became the new President. Since then neither Ecclestone nor Formula One has looked back.

Again, the name Ferrari cropped up at this juncture. Like I had done a couple of months earlier, Ecclestone visited Maranello regularly to inform the man they called the 'Commendatore' of all things Formula One. 'Up until the time he died Ferrari knew what was going in Formula One and with his team. I used to brief him three or four times a year and he was always very supportive of me.'

He's had plenty of detractors, though. Amid much suspicion concerning the manner in which he has amassed his fortune, the most interesting accusation levelled against him was that he was the mastermind behind the Great Train Robbery. 'Evidence' for this comes from the somewhat flimsy fact that he was introduced many years later to the driver of the getaway car by Graham Hill, the former twice world champion and late father of Damon.

Then there was the episode of the £1 million donation to Tony Blair's Labour Government, a move dubbed as 'Cash for Ash' by the media when it emerged that the Prime Minister had supported the exemption of F1 from a ban on tobacco advertising.

The money was paid back and tobacco promotion is on the way out in the sport, at least in Britain. 'I don't vote,' he admits. 'Governments can do what they want to do, and I'll get on with what I want to do.'

Do his detractors – and there are enough to fill the new Shanghai circuit – hurt him ever? 'No, not at all,' he replies, again with a dismissive whisper and a quick shake of his head.

Why does he think he has so many? 'I'll tell you why,' he answers almost before I have completed my question. 'It's because, save for Ferrari, Formula One is still more or less an English cottage industry. It was started in England, it grew up in England, and most of the teams are still based in England. So this Bernie-bashing is an English trait. You go to America or Australia and you'll find people delighted in your success. In England it's the other way round. I accept that I'm a target, but I not only don't care, I don't even see the bullets. But I do feel sorry for all those bitter and twisted people.' He takes another sip from his glass and utters a withering conclusion. 'You know, jealousy is a terrible thing.'

Even his critics will be forced to accept that Ecclestone, together with other figures such as Jackie Stewart, played his part in ensuring a safer sport. This, after the deaths of Lewis-Evans and Rindt and, more recently, Senna, who was also close to the man, was inevitable judging by the scar he still feels.

You can tell this not by what he says, but by what he does not say. Mention Lewis-Evans and Rindt and Ecclestone appears either lost for words or, more likely, unwilling to talk about such close friends. He has an interesting take on Senna, though, or rather on the Austrian driver, Roland Ratzenberger, who was killed the day before Senna during testing at Imola.

'Everyone was so shocked by Senna's death that nobody really cared about Ratzenberger,' he said. 'But they all cared about Senna. That was very wrong. When I started out deaths in

Formula One were the norm so it became accepted. Of course it was totally unacceptable, but that's how it was back then. I decided something had to be done about this. You can't stop accidents but you can improve the safety, and that's what we've done. It's good to see guys not being killed any more.'

Today he is happy with his lot. China, after all, was 'a job well done'; he and his sport are exploring brave new worlds, the money keeps rolling in and Formula One is faring extremely well. But after seeing the domination of Schumacher's Ferrari in the still-ongoing 2004 season, he has his concerns.

'We're in the entertainment business, and that means it is our business to entertain,' he explained. 'Whatever else may go on during the weekend, the whole event should, is and must be judged by the race. It's a bit like sex. It's not what you think is going to happen, it's what actually happens that counts.'

He paused for a few seconds to examine my response to this analogy. I hadn't really looked at it that way before and, besides, it does depend on what exactly you are expecting pre-sex. It was an area that could have been explored further, but probably not in the offices of a seventy-four-year old multi billionaire.

Having received no real response, save for a slightly bewildered look from his questioner, Ecclestone continued with his theme. 'The problem about this season is that it has been more about the anticipation than the real thing. Can Michael be beaten? Can any other team get their noses ahead of Ferrari? The answer has been mainly been no.'

Not good for the sport, then? 'Well, it's been good and bad. Frankly, as soon as it became clear Michael would win another world title, which was pretty much after the first race in Australia, I would rather he had won every single race of the year. Up until Monaco it was on, of course. At least the prospect of a man winning the whole lot for the first and probably last time in the history of the sport would have kept things interesting.

'Without Michael the racing's been good. Look at Monaco. Look at China last week. That was a great race. This is no sleight on Michael. It's not his fault, nor his problem, that he is so good. And China proved that it is far more Michael than it is Ferrari, even if Barrichello won. I don't ever care who wins the world title. I really don't. All I'd like is for it not to be decided until the final corner of the final race in the Grand Prix season.'

It almost sounds as if Michael Schumacher is becoming an embarrassing thorn in the side of Ecclestone and Formula One. 'Actually we are lucky to have him,' is the reply. 'In my mind he is the greatest racing driver of all time. I think if you look at his record, and what he has achieved, it is difficult to argue against this. The only remaining question mark is that, in general, he hasn't really had anyone chasing him hard. I would have loved to have seen Senna take him on. Senna, after all, had to fight some pretty formidable opponents. Michael's not really had to do that. Still, we'll never know.'

It is almost time to go. I had been sitting in the presence of Mr Formula One for close to two hours now, a spell of time in which he could quite easily have made many millions. 'I'm not in it for the money,' he insists, as we walk out towards Hyde Park. 'Never have been. If I wanted to make money I probably would have done something else.'

I gently mocked him after this comment, very gently, I should add. Yes, after all, there are so many other ways to make a great deal more than £2.6 billion. 'Well, it's true,' he replied, not taking my comment personally. 'Money is just a means to keeping the score. To me it's about doing things right. That's what gives me my inward satisfaction. I sleep well at night, I'm not ashamed about anything I've ever done, and I certainly don't analyse myself. That's a pointless and dangerous thing to do. I certainly don't look back. I live for today.'

And tomorrow? I shake his hand and point out, with the best

will in the world, and accepting the fact that for a man of seventy-four, he was in sprightly shape, that he is still, nonetheless, seventy-four.

'No I'm not, I'm forty,' he says, producing the biggest smile of the day. Again, he paused long enough almost to enforce a debate concerning this issue. 'I mean that I feel the same as I did at forty, and I'm as motivated the same now as I was at forty. Why should I stop? There's so much still to be done. I'm excited by the globalisation of the sport. And I very much want to be a part of it.'

There was just enough time to tell him that I was planning to race Schumacher myself over some kind of course in some kind of car. Okay, so I had no idea how this would materialise, except for on the ski slopes, but there was no time to elaborate. Did such a prospect whet his appetite?

Bernard Charles Ecclestone looked me up and down (well, mainly up, it has to be said) and ended the meeting with another, no-nonsense conclusion. 'If you were a stunningly attractive twenty-five-year-old girl and told me what you were planning I'd still not be interested.'

The fact that I was a pasty-faced, red-headed forty-year-old bloke didn't seem to do it for him either. I hailed a taxi, climbed into the back and pondered as we drove back towards Knightsbridge. It was good to know that I was such a significant figure in the world of Formula One.

© SANDY MYHRE

Lapping the original Michael Schumacher in Auckland.

© IAN STAFFORD

Passed at Last! Stamp of approval from Susie Stoddart at Silverstone.

© SANDY MYHRE

Chris Amon aboard the Eff 1 in Taupo.

© SANDY MYHRE

Sir Stirling Moss at his gadget-ridden home.

© IAN STAFFORD

With Sir Jack Brabham in Adelaide.

© IAN STAFFORD

"This is your captain, Niki Lauda, speaking." – Vienna Airport.

© IAN STAFFORD

© IAN STAFFORD

And this is Niki's plane.

Peter, Beverley and Tilly Brock in Nutfield, Victoria.

"That's how you kart."
– Ian Stafford.
"Can I go home now?"
– Michael Schumacher, Auckland.

Cracker, his teeth and his teddy.

An uncomfortable Jody Scheckter as he becomes acquainted with his buffaloes.

Nigel and Greg Mansell at Woodbury Park.

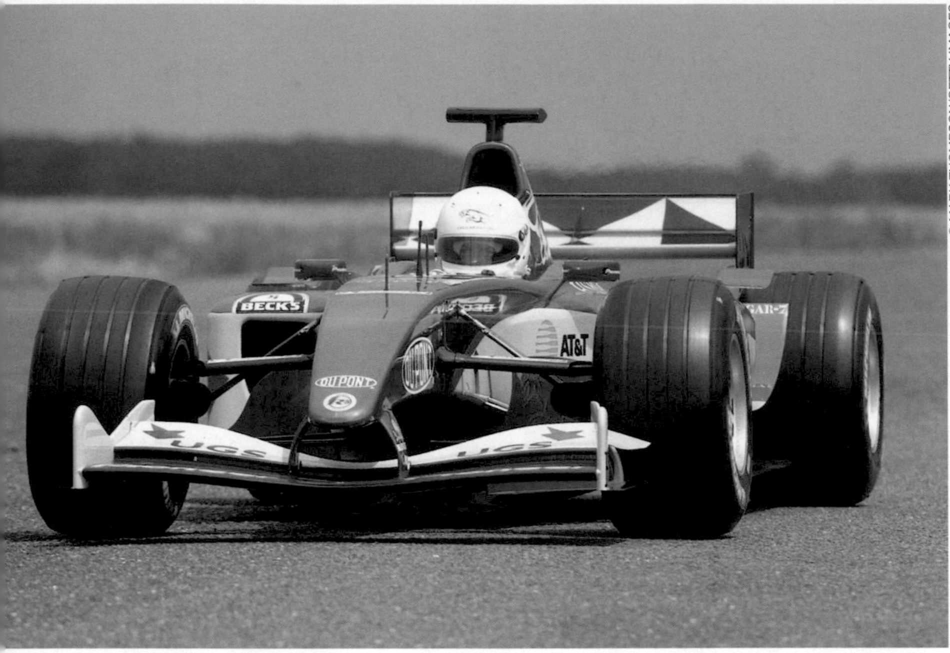

© MARK THOMPSON/GETTY IMAGES

In charge of the Jaguar F1 car at Santa Pod.

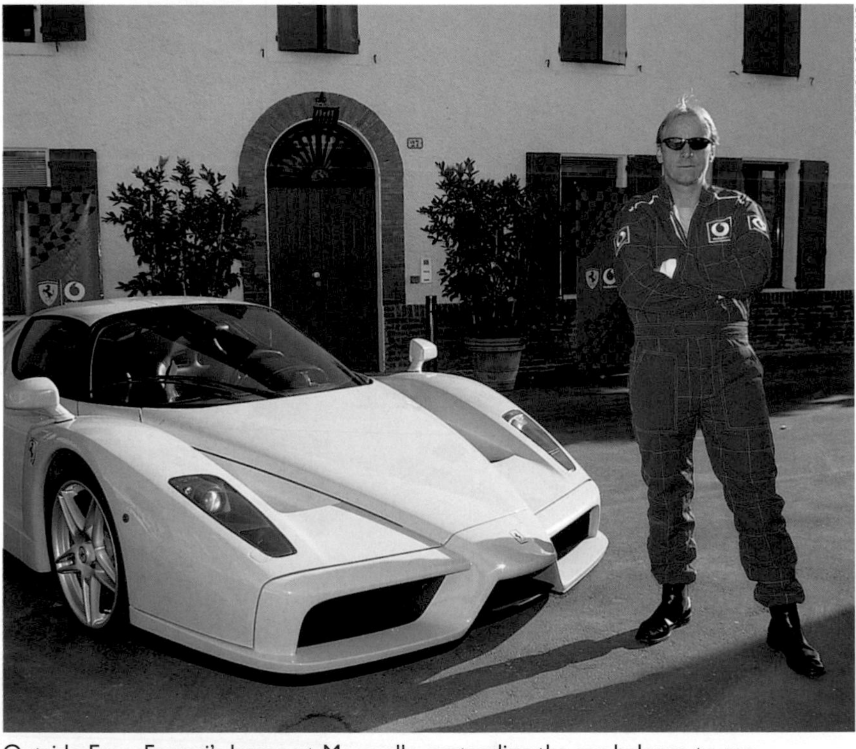

© PATRICK GOSLING

Outside Enzo Ferrari's house at Maranello pretending the car belongs to me.

The Space Age Shanghai Grand Prix.

BMW–Williams reveal their new pit board operator to Juan Pablo Montoya as he speeds past in the British Grand Prix.

Rubens Barrichello enjoys his efforts to make me vomit.

Patrick Head feigns interest as I tell him how it all works.

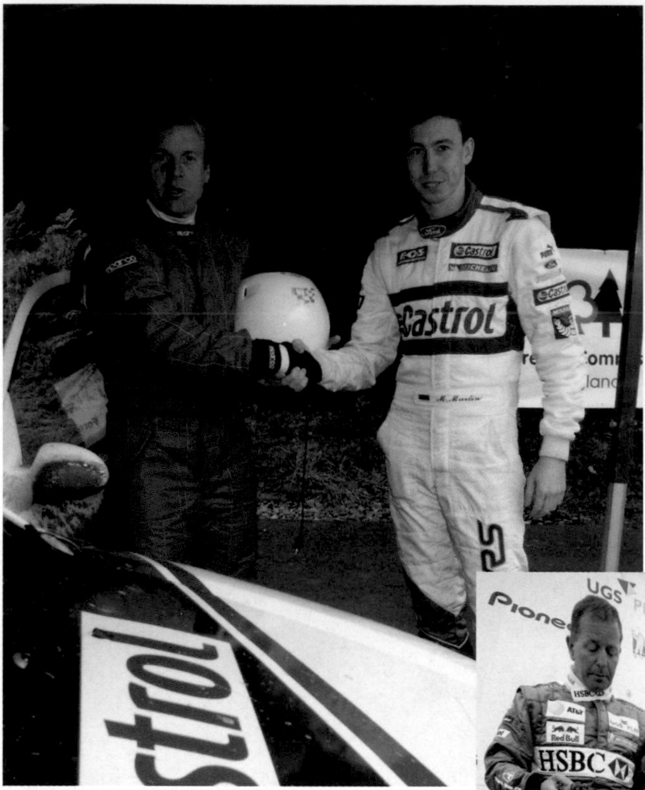

© IAN STAFFORD

Post rally in Cumbria with Markko Martin: One man happy to win, the other happy to live.

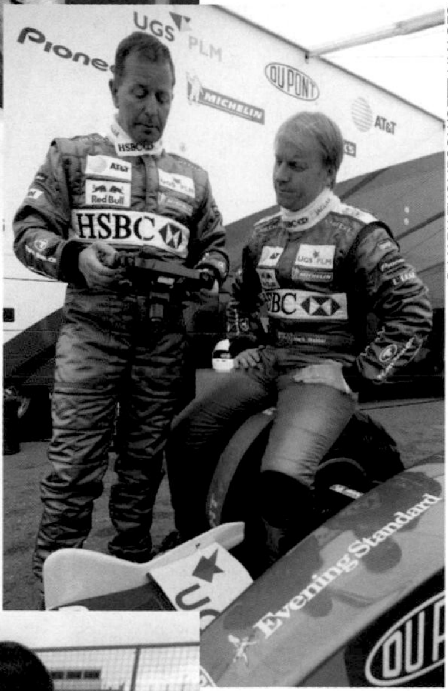

© MARK THOMPSON/GETTY IMAGES

Memo from Martin Brundle – this is a steering wheel.

© LAT

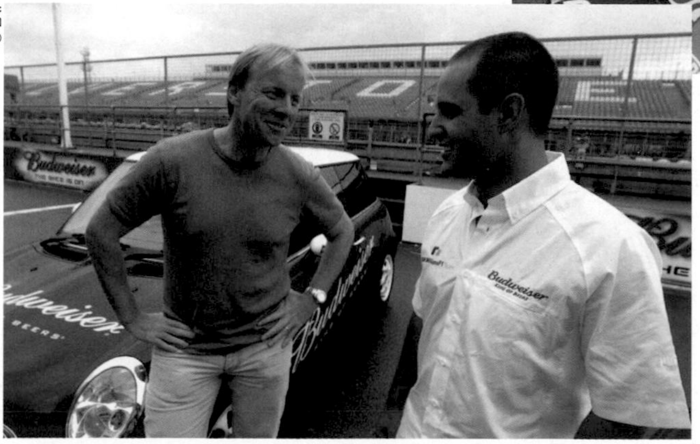

Montoya calls me a crazy f****er.

© MARK THOMPSON/GETTY IMAGES

At the Monaco Grand Prix with Nav Sidhu and a couple of irritating hangers-on called, I think, Brad and George.

© IAN STAFFORD

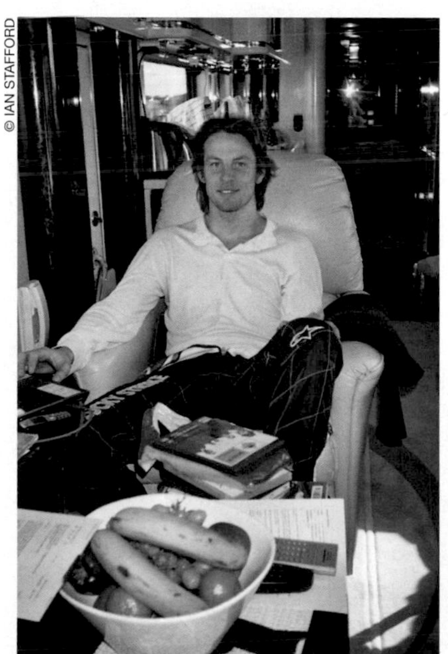

A bowl of fruit, a motorhome, and an F1 driver called Jenson Button.

© IAN STAFFORD

Life's a bitch for David Coulthard at his Fontveille home.

© IAN STAFFORD

Kenny Brack and his Chief Motivational Officer plan their assault on the Race of Champions in Paris.

© SUZI PERRY

The man synonymous with Formula One, and Michael Schumacher.

chapter twelve

IT'S A MINI ADVENTURE WITH JUAN PABLO

Examination day was almost upon me again. It had all been very well hanging out with the drivers and the main man of Formula One, but this constituted the vegetables on the side of my plate. The meat was actually driving myself and this meant obtaining my racing driver's licence.

A lot had happened since my dismal experience at the Silverstone Drive School back at the start of summer, when I was deemed a danger to myself and to others, and was sent packing with my tail between my legs, not least the fact that I had beaten Michael Schumacher in a head-to-head in Auckland and had successfully driven a Formula One car.

Part of me did not want to retake the driving part of the ARDS. The previous experience had been so humiliating that I wished it would just go away. Yet I also knew that there were things I still wanted to do which would require me to possess the necessary driving qualifications. There was also a matter of pride. Stupid, male pride. I had mucked up quite a few things in my time, especially as a wannabe sportsman. I had been injured on countless occasions by bigger, better and stronger sportsmen than me, making the most of being confronted by my questionable challenge. But I had never actually walked away from anything.

Besides, this time it would be different. Steve Warburton, the Silverstone Drive instructor who had threatened to lodge a cone up my backside if I continued to drive so badly, had made it his personal mission to see me pass. It was on his suggestion that I switch the day of my ARDS test from the initial Thursday to the following Sunday so that I could avoid taking the test once more on the complete Silverstone Grand Prix circuit and, instead, be examined on the smaller 'National' circuit, which was less than half of the British Grand Prix lap. In doing so it meant I would have to perfect four corners and not thirteen.

The day before I watched a special Silverstone CD-ROM on my computer which provides instructions on how to tackle each of the circuits. I even made notes, learnt that I would be taking on famous corners in motor sport such as Copse, Maggotts and Becketts, and envisaged in my head the circuit until it remained lodged indelibly in my mind.

The following morning I made a decision based partly on superstition. Last time I made an embarrassing situation toe-curlingly worse by turning up in my flash, red racing overalls, red booties and fancy, personalised helmet. I was the only one looking the part out of the group of examinees, and I was the only one to fail. This time I made my way north towards Silverstone dressed in a grey T-shirt, blue jeans and trainers. If I failed this time, then at least I was going to look the part.

Within half an hour of leaving home a text message flashed up on my mobile telephone. It was Steve Warburton informing me that he had food poisoning. 'I can't be more than a couple of feet away from a loo,' he explained, more graphically than was possibly necessary. The good news was that, unlike last time when I drove a Lotus Elise, this time I was down for an Audi A3 which, according to my sickly friend, would be 'far more forgiving and easier to drive'.

This was excellent news, but the fact that Steve would not be there was bad news. Very bad news indeed. I had left home confident. My family, having now fully accepted that a man had to do what a man had to do, wished me luck. My mate Steve was going to see me through the test. He'd promised me. After nearly two hours of instructions with him I was certain I'd be able to pass.

Now the confidence was seeping away. Who would I get as my instructor? What would the examiner be like? If I failed this time I would feel so useless, so inadequate and so pathetic, that I would quite possibly return home, throw thc car keys to my wife and ask her to drive from now on. Every criticism she had made of me over the years in which she had been a passenger would be justified. I really would be as bad as she had made out.

On arrival at the school I, along with four other hopefuls, first sat through a briefing delivered by Steve Deaks, a former F3 and GT racing driver, who presents the official ARDS video. I had seen all this before – racing lines, the correct places to turn, how oversteer or understeer can happen if your speed or braking is wrong, and the importance of planning ahead all the time – and was itching to get out on to the track. The problem with theory, as important as it is, is that it is still only theory. I knew what I needed more than anything else was practice, and that meant time out on the circuit driving.

At midday a woman looking young enough to be a teenager approached me. 'Hi, I'm Susie Stoddart,' she said, in a soft, lilting

Scottish accent that came, so I discovered later, from the Firth of Lorn town of Oban. 'I'm your instructor today.'

I had a woman instructor last time and look where that got me! Now I was going to be taught by a girl. I'd been driving for over twenty years. What could Susie teach me? This was clearly a trick being played on me by some greater power. Not only had my assertions of superiority on the road been shattered by my experiences up to this juncture, but a succession of women were hammering home the point. The irony was delicious, if rather painful, and not lost on my wife when I told her later.

Susie, when I examined her credentials, explained that she was on the short-list for the British young driver of the year award for the second successive year. Not only that, but she would be racing in the Formula Three championships in 2005, the only female to be doing so. At twenty-one years of age her aim was to become a Formula One driver.

Now even I was impressed, impressed enough, indeed, to concede that she might be able to teach me a trick or two. But Formula One! I'd heard it all before from virtually every young racing driver I'd ever met. This time in two years I'm gonna be an F1 driver. Yeah, right!

Nor for the first time Susie put me straight. 'I mean it and I will do it,' she insisted, in no uncertain terms. 'Just watch me.' Her conviction demanded immediate belief.

We stepped into the Audi A3 and Susie drove us on to the National Circuit, blitzed around the track for a few laps, then returned to the pits and told me it was my turn. Strangely enough, we parked exactly at the spot where I had been working for much of the British Grand Prix weekend with the BMW–Williams team, Cracker and his teddy bear and fake teeth!

I pushed down on the accelerator and headed for the track. I thought I knew what I was supposed to do. Take the right-hand Copse Corner staying in fourth gear reasonably fast, veering out to the left-hand side of the resulting straight afterwards to make full use of the track, before then moving across to the right in readiness for the approaching Maggotts Corner. Actually, Maggotts is barely a corner, but you are venturing in the opposite direction to Becketts which, with its U-bend, requires a hard brake, turn and switch down to third gear while still completing Maggotts. You should be ending up on the left-hand side of the track again as the corner straightens out. Then it is hard down on the gas and into fourth, veering over to the right once more in readiness for Brooklands corner, a large, sweeping turn which you make in third gear. An acceleration, then a quick dab on the brakes, then round Luffield Corner before heading for the minor turn at Woodcote and on to the start again.

So much for theory. In practice I just could not seem to get it. Just not get it at all. On one lap I would complete Copse near perfectly, only to muck up Becketts by turning too early and emerging at far too steep an angle which meant frantic steering and a loss of speed. I'd meet Brooklands with the correct swing to the left, only to repeat my Becketts mistake at Luffield. I'd be too far from the posts marking out the slight turn at Woodcote, swinging over to the right too early, or then too late in readiness for Maggotts, or braking too hard at Copse.

Susie would swing from complimentary to a growing impatience. 'You did it perfectly last time, why cock it up now?' she'd reason above the noise of the Audi revs. 'You should be getting it right by now.' She'd ask me to pull into the pits so that she could draw diagrams of the angles I was taking coming into corners, and the correct angles I should have been taking. We would then return to the track where I would repeat the very same mistake. 'I just don't understand,' Susie would add. Neither did I.

I had a forty-five-minute break between the first session and the second, the session which would include my ARDS test. My confidence had plummeted. I knew, without Susie saying a word, that on the evidence of the past hour, I would fail the test.

As I sat in the reception area of the Silverstone Drive School I observed a lad seemingly no older than eighteen clutching a certificate stating that he had just passed his ARDS test and once again I was eighteen and suffering the ignominy of retaking that maths 'O' Level exam four times.

Susie interrupted my thoughts. 'Come on then, let's go and pass this ARDS test.' She was smiling and upbeat, which helped, although within a couple of laps with me at the wheel, and more near misses on kerbs and corners, we were back in the pits drawing more diagrams. This was looking really bad now, and I was feeling miniscule in the company of a twenty-one-year-old junior female driver.

Then something strange and rather timely happened. I began to get the corners right. I started to relax, trust Susie's advice and discover how, even by going against my nature, the driving would seem a great deal easier. Take the Maggotts and Becketts corners, for example. Before I was entering Maggotts too slowly, then turning for far too long around Becketts and not accelerating enough. This meant I would lose time and end up nowhere near the edge of the track. Suddenly I was pulling out of my turn earlier, stepping on the gas and discovering that the momentum of the speed pulled the car out to the place it was supposed to be. It helped that I started to look further ahead, too. By looking at where I was supposed to end up, as opposed to the corner I was turning through, a combination of my eyes and hands did the rest.

Luffield, my bête noire up until now, was a similar case. Time and time again I'd end up at too acute an angle as I exited Luffield, forcing me to make a radical extra turn of the wheel to prevent us from flying off the track. Now I was making just the one turn, having learnt where the spot was to brake and then accelerate.

We pulled over into the pits and Susie suggested we take a 'mock' exam. For ten minutes I drove round and round the National Circuit in silence. Corner after corner, save for one visit to a curb, was dealt with correctly. We returned to the pits once more. 'If you drive exactly like that you will pass your ARDS test,' Susie said. 'Are you ready?'

For the first time ever since driving at Silverstone I was. Ready and confident. Within a few completed laps of silence I realised I was going to pass. Initially that made me relax and even start enjoying the experience. Towards the end I started telling myself not to make a mistake at this late stage. After all, a trip to the grass or gravel outside the kerb would result in automatic failure. I was going fast, too, certainly fast enough to hear the screeching of the wheels as we made our way around Copse. I felt I had driven better than even in my 'mock' ARDS.

Susie would be a pretty good poker player, if she was not already a pretty good motor racing driver. We returned to the pits and she remained silent long enough for me to wonder if I had, in fact, got it all wrong and still managed to fail. Her face at first revealed nothing. It was almost as if she was purposefully keeping me in suspense. If she had been a game show host on commercial TV she would have said at this point: 'We'll take a short break first.' Finally she spoke. 'Well, Ian,' she began, with a tone and expression that filled me with more doom. 'I'm pleased to say you have passed your ARDS test. Congratulations.'

I thought about re-enacting the archetypal scene played out by the learner driver flinging her arms around the driving instructor but thought better of it. Instead I just muttered a hundred thank yous. Here was a funny thing. The seeds of my quest had been sexist. How could my wife ever criticise my driving? She was a woman and I was a man. Enough said. Now, thanks entirely to a woman, indeed a woman young enough to be my daughter, I had passed the test and could now be described as a racing driver. In the previous two hours she had criticised and encouraged me in equal measures. She had me cowering with fear, and high with confidence. I was holding on to every word she uttered, and eating out of the palm of her hand. And now, at the end of it all, she and only she had the power to release me into the world of racing cars.

The fact that I had passed the exam meant a great deal more to me than the notion that much of my initial argument had been totally undermined and disproved. Susie passed me the form to read.

Under Section 1 she ticked 'pass' boxes alongside the following requirements: demonstrates adequate forward and peripheral vision; shows awareness of and consideration for other vehicles on track; is able to drive at a reasonable pace so as not to be a danger to faster cars; is able to retain full control of vehicle and stay on the track surface for the whole session; is able to drive two laps consistently, predictably and showing an understanding of track positioning and line without instruction; and finally, a question: is there any other reason in the instructor's opinion not yet ready to hold a national 'B' licence?

Under Section 2, Driver Skill Level, I received a series of marks. 'A' equalled good, 'B' average and 'C' poor. I received seven Bs for braking, down-change technique, cornering vision, transition braking to cornering, mechanical sympathy/smoothness, relaxed/confident driving style and dealing with traffic, and seven As for not riding clutch, correct choice of gears, upshift technique/revs, steering technique, consistency, line and throttle technique. In the box entitled Instructor's Recommendations/ Comments Susie added: 'Overall very consistent good strong driving with no real faults'.

I felt elated, but tired and relieved at the same time. It would have been unbearable to have failed again. Maybe passing on the second attempt is similar to passing your ordinary driving test on the second attempt, which is what I did after causing a car to screech to a halt at a junction during my first test. They say the best drivers are those who pass second time round. Or have I just made that up?

The tiredness was down to the release of tension, but also the obvious fact that after an early start that Sunday morning, plus a two-hour journey to Silverstone, I had just completed two hours of high-speed driving on the circuit.

Susie handed me over her report, plus an official certificate stating that I had 'successfully completed' a national circuit PTU. What I liked best about this certificate, apart from the 'successfully completed' bit, was the fact that down the left-hand side of the sheet is a list of all winners of the British Grand Prix. I won't name them all, but there is something rather nice about being mentioned as a motor-racing driver next to the likes of Juan-Manuel Fangio, Jim Clark, Jackie Stewart, Alain Prost, Nigel Mansell, Ayrton Senna and, of course, Michael Schumacher.

A text message on my mobile phone interrupted my thoughts as I sat in the Silverstone Drive car park gazing at my certificate and all these wonderful names. It was Steve Warburton. 'Fucking brilliant,' it began. 'No more cones up your arse!' I hadn't thought of that point. Steve ended his message with: 'Still feel terrible! Glad to call you a true racer now.' It sounded like Steve could have done with a cone up his backside that particular day.

A true racer! I read that bit over and over again. It sounded beautiful. When I reached home that evening and walked into the kitchen to tell the family the news I felt a foot taller. 'You're looking at a true racer,' I announced, news which precipitated raised eyebrows and looks to the heavens from my wife and daughter. 'Now I can not only drive fast, but I know what I'm doing. It's official.'

If there had been secret hopes harboured within my house that another failed driving test would end the quest, then these were dashed by Susie Stoddart. I was on a real high. All the humiliation of my previous visit to the Silverstone Drive School had been left behind me now. I still faced the alarming prospect of racing against the real Michael Schumacher on the slopes of the Alps, and still had no idea how I could possibly engineer some other kind of challenge on tarmac, but I was happy and hungry to add more to my quest.

Within days such an opportunity came. Budweiser, one of the main BMW–Williams sponsors, were promoting a competition which resulted in giving away Mini Coopers as prizes and asked me if I fancied racing the cars around the full Grand Prix circuit back at Silverstone with Juan Pablo Montoya.

Montoya really interested me. The dark, often brooding, sometimes menacing Colombian represented the most likely challenger to Schumacher's dominance, certainly in his own mind. While others accepted the German's superiority, Montoya refused to take his bows. Give him the right car, he was convinced, and he would be world champion.

The only other time I had met him was the previous summer at the Goodwood Festival of Speed. I remembered the occasion well because I made a fool of myself in his company. Seated next to him at an impromptu press conference consisting of primarily German media figures, I began the first question of the whole conference by saying, 'Hello Chris, thanks for your time, I was wondering . . .'

That's as far as I got. 'It's Juan Pablo,' he said to me, with just a flicker of irritation.

'Sorry?'

'It's Juan Pablo.'

I thought this was very odd. 'Er, yeah, I know what your name is.'

'But you called me Chris.'

'No I didn't.'

A German broadcaster leant forward at this point. 'Actually, you did.' Meanwhile the BMW press officer was shifting around on his feet looking uncomfortable and miserable. He was called Chris. I knew this because he wore his Christian name on a large badge, the same badge that I had been staring at when I began my first question.

So, the press conference, scheduled for ten minutes only, and set up primarily for the benefit of the German media because of BMW's major role within the team, had already been going three minutes without a question completed. Instead, now wishing I was anywhere but sitting a foot away from the Colombian, I inflamed the already sorry situation by trying to argue with the rest of the German media. 'Nope, I definitely said Juan Pablo. It doesn't sound anything like Chris. How can you possibly think I said Chris?'

By now we have all turned our backs on Montoya, who is sitting there bemused and bewildered by this strange turn of events. Eventually he tapped me on my back. 'You definitely said Chris,' he said.

'Must be my accent,' I offered back, slightly timidly. Yes, that was it. Maybe Juan Pablo, and the Germans, had mistaken my Juan Pablo for Chris. Easily done. Very similar words, you see.

In the end there were only three questions asked before the press conference came to an abrupt end and I made my excuses and left before I was lynched by two dozen German media folk.

Happily Chris – sorry, Juan Pablo – did not seem to recall the moment nor recognise me when I shook his hand and stepped inside a Mini Cooper with him. The plan was that he was going to drive around the full Silverstone circuit first for a number of laps, then get out and watch me tackle the Grand Prix circuit from the safety of the control tower overlooking the winner's podium.

Just to complicate matters it had been raining heavily that morning and, although the rain had stopped, the circuit was damp and drying out, which made the conditions treacherous. The fact that Montoya was used to driving F1 cars at speeds up to

200 mph meant that driving a Mini Cooper was akin to Lance Armstrong riding a penny farthing, but a Mini at 80 mph in these conditions on this circuit was fast and scary enough.

Montoya was under specific instructions not to drive faster than 80 mph. 'Can you believe that?' he asked me, as we sped away from the pit lane and on to the circuit. It was instantly obvious that he had no intention of keeping to that. The speedometer soon shot past the 80 mark, and on to 90, then 100 and finally 115 mph, by which stage the car sounded as if it was about to self-combust.

No point giving Montoya advice at this moment, I reasoned. God knows what a volatile Latin might do, especially with me strapped in beside him. Instead I took the approach I had already adopted with Barrichello at Maranello, namely suck in some air, hold my stomach tight and act as if everything was just dandy.

Just to show how completely relaxed and cool I was with the whole event, I began to chat away to Montoya. How well-known, for example, was he back home in Bogota? 'Oh, massive,' he shouted, above the scream of the engines. 'Stupidly massive, actually. I go home to Colombia four times a year and every time I need amazing levels of security. It's like being David Beckham over here. The only peace I can find back home is when I escape to a golf course.'

Does the imagery of Colombia to the rest of the world annoy him? 'Yeah, well, everyone makes a joke about Colombia, don't they? I get it in F1 and I get it everywhere else, too. "Bloody Colombian drugs," that's all I ever hear. That's why I'm proud of what I do, and what I have done. I hope I am helping to give Colombia a better name.'

He paused as the wheels made a screeching noise around a corner and the Mini felt as if it was on the verge of tilting over. 'And coffee.'

'What?' I shouted above the din.

'And coffee. Me and coffee. We're both good for Colombia.'

Right. I had thought for a moment he was offering me a coffee, which would have been interesting seeing that we were driving at over 100 mph on a wet and slippery Silverstone.

We came to a halt after five laps and chatted more. Like for Barrichello, Senna was Montoya's hero. 'When I was ten and twelve, he was the man,' he explained, his eyes glinting almost with pride. 'Not because he was South American, particularly, but because he blew everyone else away. I was eighteen when he died. I couldn't believe it. It was like telling a kid that Superman had just been killed. I was go-karting in Colombia that day and I remember racing around the circuit in a complete state of shock. Actually, it was just about the most shocking day of my life.'

Would he have fancied racing against his hero? 'No way,' he replied. 'No way,' he emphasised. 'I would have felt awkward. What if I was in a position where I was about to overtake him. That would have been hard. I'm not sure I would have carried it out through respect for the man.'

And that kart race in Colombia? 'Uh?' he asked. The day Senna died? 'Oh, I won,' he answered, with a slight smile. 'Of course.'

This was Montoya down to a tee, encapsulated in that small exchange of words. To be fair to him, too, he was popular in the grandstands because he represented something of a bygone age, when caution was thrown to the wind and drivers raced. 'That's why people like me,' he confirmed. 'They can see I'm trying. All the time. I don't see myself as wild. That accusation has been levelled at me a few times. But I always try my hardest, pushing myself to the edge. I like to do it my way.'

Nobody would disagree with that last statement, certainly not BMW–Williams who he informed midway through the previous season that he would be joining arch-rivals McLaren for the 2005 season. This might have made the remainder of 2003 and the whole of 2004 uncomfortable at the best of times, but bearing in mind it was Frank Williams who nurtured Montoya, sent him off to America to serve an apprenticeship highlighted by becoming the Indycar champion, and then introduced him into F1, it could have been downright embarrassing.

'Well, it's fair to say Frank was a little shocked when I told him,' Montoya admitted, which by all accounts is some understatement. 'It was a bit awkward at first, I'll confess. But you can't put a friendship over your career, can you? Frank's done more for my career than anyone, but I hope I've repaid him. I'm sure we'll remain friends.'

It hadn't been the best of years, though, had it? I tried to say this, incidentally, as gently as possible, seeing that I was still trapped inside a small car with him. 'No, but the car's not been up to it. I'm driving to my optimum and finishing fifth. That's got to tell you something.'

If you really want to get him going, though, you just have to mention Schumacher. In fact any Schumacher will do. Take younger brother, Ralf, for example, his erstwhile team-mate at Williams who was also leaving, for Toyota, at the end of the season. 'I've never really seen Ralf as a rival, not like his brother,' is Montoya's friendly offering. 'I think the world of F1 knows the score there.'

That's Ralf dismissed, then. And his big brother? 'He's had the best car. That's why he's world champion. As soon as the title was clinched Ferrari concentrated on Rubens and Michael stopped winning. Don't get me wrong. Michael's good, especially when he's in front, but look what happens when he doesn't have the best car.'

I've noticed Montoya is physically unable to sit still, something that's been levelled at me a few times. 'I can't relax,' he explained. 'No chance. I went to a Malaysian island with Connie [his wife] on holiday and all she wanted to do was lie on the beach and read.

After half an hour I couldn't stand it any more and went and played golf.'

His other love, believe it or not, is radio-controlled planes. Heaven help the small kid with his rubber-band-propelled wooden plane at the park when Juan Pablo comes along with his life-sized jumbo jet and starts flying it high above the swings and duck pond. 'Now that I could happily do all day,' he admitted.

Will he become world champion one day?

'I have to,' came back a rather surprising reply.

Have to? What does that mean?

'It means this,' Montoya said, moving around in his seat until he is looking at me squarely between the eyes. 'When I started to do well in racing all I wanted to do was to get to F1. Then, when I reached F1 I wanted to race. Then I wanted to win races. And now, having achieved all that, I want to be world champion. If you want something enough you have to work your ass off for it. That's what I do, and I believe I will be rewarded for it sooner or later.'

There was a tap on the window. A Silverstone official let it be known that if I wanted to drive the Mini I had to go immediately. Montoya and I clambered out of our seats but, while I made my way over to the driver's side of the car, he started walking towards the control tower.

'You don't fancy sampling my driving then?' I asked.

'No fucking way,' came back the disappointingly emphatic reply as he all but ran up the stairs.

With that glowing endorsement I set off, intent on showing the Colombian that I, with my ARDS test safely under my belt, would show him a thing or two about exciting racing. I was permitted three laps and, in that time, I'm not sure I taught him anything in the racing department, but I certainly ticked the box labelled 'excitement'.

By now the circuit was like an ice rink, at its treacherous worst because it was half-dry, half-wet. I managed to climb to just over 100 mph in the main, Hangar Straight but, in doing so, approached Stowe Corner too fast. The result was a magnificently dramatic spin.

A couple of weeks earlier the experience would have frightened the life out of me. Now I enjoyed it. The Mini completed two and half revolutions, which took some doing, before I was able finally to point the car back in the right direction and complete the lap.

When it was all over I strode over to Montoya who was shaking his head and looking at me. 'That was a spectacular spin, my friend,' he announced.

'Thank you very much,' I replied.

Montoya looked a little taken aback by my reply. 'No, no, I mean you ended up pointing the wrong way, you lost valuable time on the lap as a result, and you could have had an accident. You really could have.'

Oh! But didn't the most volatile, exciting and spectacular racing driver on the circuit appreciate my few moments of motor mayhem, my few seconds of spectacle, my brief visit to spin city?

What he had to say next was on a level with George Best accusing me of having drunk too much alcohol, or Warren Beatty suggesting I was over-sexed.

He raised his hand, pointed his finger straight at me, and smiled. 'You are a crazy fucker,' he announced. 'A crazy fucker.' And with that he stepped into a waiting helicopter, hovered momentarily above the circuit and then disappeared into the clouds, leaving me to smile rather self-consciously at the watching gaggle of Budweiser representatives.

Perhaps that was a Colombian compliment? The deathly white faces of those from Budweiser and BMW–Williams watching all this suggested not. Still, I was happy. I quite liked being referred to as a crazy fucker by the craziest fucker of a pretty crazy bunch of fuckers on the Formula One circuit.

chapter thirteen

I'M NIKI, FLY ME

'This is your captain speaking, Niki Lauda.' The voice boomed over the plane's intercom in a heavily accented English. 'There is a slight delay in Rome due to fog, but we hope to make up the lost time. In the meantime, settle back, enjoy the flight, and thank you for choosing Niki.' He turns the microphone off, leans over to me and raises his eyebrows to the sky. 'Fucking Italians!'

Welcome to the world of Niki Lauda, where a spade is most definitely a spade, and where the talking is straighter than a Roman road.

We – that is former three-times F1 world champion Lauda, myself and a co-pilot – are sitting in the cockpit of an 'Air Niki' Airbus A320 on the tarmac at Vienna Airport minutes away from departing for a day-trip to Rome and back again. The co-pilot, Hans, is dressed as all co-pilots should be. Crisply clean white shirt, black tie, three stripes across each of his shoulders. Lauda, in contrast, is in a casual stripy shirt, a light green jumper, blue jeans and his trademark red baseball cap, this one sporting the logo 'Laudamotion'.

Should he really be dressed like this? Two points here. First, it's his airline, so he can do what the hell he likes. And second, he does not give a damn what anyone else might think in any case.

The story of Niki Lauda is one that, quite simply, could not be made up. One that would have Hollywood film producers laughing in your face and ordering you to clear out of their office if you ever had the temerity to offer it as a script. It is almost ridiculous beyond words.

The gist of it is as follows: an Austrian F1 driver becomes world champion in 1975 driving a Ferrari. In 1976 he is involved in a horrendous crash during the German Grand Prix and is horrifically burned, the accident that prompted Chris Amon to quit the sport. He lies close to death in a hospital bed for several days, and is even read the last rites. Just six weeks later, and with burns to his head, face, upper body, lungs and hands a long way off being healed, he returns to Formula One and finishes fourth at Monza. It was seen to be one of the bravest drives in the history of the sport.

At the final Grand Prix of the season, the Japanese at Fuji, Lauda needed only to finish fifth to clinch a second, successive world title. In treacherous and wet conditions he withdrew after just two laps of the race, an action that resulted in his great friend, Britain's James Hunt, becoming world champion by one point.

Criticised for this, Lauda, his head and face so badly scarred that to his day he chooses to wear a baseball cap to hide his deformity, bounces back in 1977 to win his second world title with something to spare. Angered by Ferrari's reaction to his crash (more of which later) he then walked out of Maranello and joined Bernie Ecclestone's Brabham team.

Still with me here? There are more unlikely twists yet to come. Two seasons later Lauda sensationally walked out of Formula

One, citing that he had better things to do than drive around in circles. Aviation was fast becoming his new love but, after founding Lauda Air, he realised he would lose the battle against his country's state-owned Austrian Airlines, who were far from pleased with this sudden competition, especially from such a national hero.

Disillusioned with this, and realising he still had the F1 drug in his bloodstream, Lauda returned to the sport with McLaren after an absence of three years. The unwritten law in F1 is that once a driver has retired there is no way back, certainly not to the top. In his third race Lauda won at Long Beach, USA. Within two years he had claimed the world title for a third time and become the first to do so having previously retired.

Then, with the job done and the challenge met, he quit again, returned to aviation and, this time, succeeded in getting Lauda Air up and running. One of his aircraft, a Boeing 767, then crashed in Thailand in 1991 killing 223 passengers and crew. 'This, and the days and weeks following, were the darkest days of my life,' he would tell me, once we had taken off. Eventually investigations proved it was a design fault with the aircraft, not the airline, but it is a memory that has scarred him as much as his crash at the Nurburgring.

In 2000 Lauda, despite being the airline's chairman, was ousted in a boardroom clash with Austrian Airlines, which had amassed a major shareholding in his company after buying Lufthansa's shares. Now, at the age of fifty-five, he is back, this time with his own, new airline, 'Air Niki'. His goals are simple: to make a greater success of running his own airline and to be, in his own words, 'a pain in the arse'.

I was told to strap myself in and sit in between Lauda and Hans, the co-pilot. Goodness knows what the 150-odd passengers behind us thought of this. Niki is a low-cost airline. In fact, it's a cleverly conceived low-cost airline with free, high quality food and the space in between the rows of seats you find on normal priced airlines, as opposed to the sardines-in-a-can effect of most low-cost outfits. Yet there might still have been one or two passengers wondering whether low-cost meant that anyone from England could just turn up and chat away to the pilot in the cockpit at 35,000 feet for the whole journey.

As we taxied along the runway towards the point where we would fire up the engines and accelerate I noticed that in between us and another Niki plane was a 'Lauda Air' flight. That, I presumed, must rankle.

Lauda laughed, his booming guffaw filling the cockpit, and then slapped the same leg that sacrificed much of its skin in a graft to replace that burnt away on his head. 'It's the best advertising campaign I've ever had,' he explained. 'And it's all, totally free. Everyone knows the Lauda planes, everyone knows what they did to me, and everyone in Austria knows I now have a new airline. So now I'm taking passengers away from an airline bearing my own name.'

I decided instantly that I liked the man. He had a mischievous grin on his face, the sort of expression that tells you that he likes lobbing a proverbial stink bomb in a lift, whether it may be full of Austrian Airlines executives, or the powers that be in Formula One who left him for dead and wrote him off after first his accident, and then his retirement.

His stewardesses were dressed in silver outfits that made them look like crew members of the Starship Enterprise. A few of the passengers took photos when the cabin door swung open. It is not every day, after all, that they are flown by one of Austria's enduring heroes.

We gained speed and shot down the runway. Lauda eased up the throttle and we were up and away. I remained quiet for a while, deciding that I should wait until Niki was able and willing to talk. He winked at me as we soared through and then above the clouds, leaving the tarmac of Vienna Airport behind us now, sweeping south towards Graz and then on to the Adriatic.

His first world title he dismissed with a nonchalant wave of his hand. 'I'd won a few races the year before in the Ferrari so it wasn't the biggest surprise,' he explained. 'Then, in 1975, I had the best car. It was easy to win the world title as a result.' This begged for no debate.

Then came 1976, the single most stand-out year of his life. 'The accident?' he said. 'Well, I could have done without it.'

He'd already won four and finished runner-up in the other two out of the first six races of the season when, during the second lap of the German Grand Prix, his Ferrari lurched into the barrier, bounced back on to the circuit and straight into the path of Brett Lunger's Surtees. The Ferrari, now awash with flames, was shunted down the track before coming to a halt, with Lauda now unconscious. With no marshals, medical teams or safety cars nearby, it took Arturo Merzario, assisted by others, to wade into the fire and haul Lauda out of the cockpit. 'I don't remember any of it,' Lauda admitted, as he took a coffee from a smiling stewardess.

But he remembered the days afterwards, and the struggle between life and death he witnessed at first hand. 'My eyes were bandaged so I couldn't see, and a tube stuck down my throat meant I couldn't talk, but I could hear everything,' he recalled. 'When my wife first saw me at the hospital in Mannheim she freaked out and started crying. I thought to myself, "Shit, I must be in a bad state." She told me later the only way she could recognise me was by my feet because I was so fucked up.'

He was moved from a first hospital to a second and lay there listening to every doctor dismissing any suggestions on the grounds that they would all kill Lauda. At one point he was convinced the dying process had begun. 'I felt myself falling down backwards into a black hole. I thought: "Shit, I'm in trouble." My body was giving up on me because of the pain. I was frightened because I felt as if I was dying. I told myself to stay awake, to fight it.'

His optimism received a further dent when he heard a priest read him the last rites. 'That really pissed me off,' he said, grinning at the absurdity of a man, bandaged up like an Egyptian mummy, aware of everything, but unable to do anything about it. 'That stupid priest didn't say a word to me because he thought I was unconscious and all but dead. Instead he read me the last rites. I wanted to scream at him: "I'm not dead. I'm not fucking dead yet." But I couldn't.'

Reactions to his malformed head, and half-burnt-off right ear, were far from encouraging. 'When I first looked at myself in the mirror I swear my head was as wide as my shoulders. When I finally got home to Salzburg I asked my wife to fetch my neighbour round. He was a farmer, a country man, and one used to unseemly sights in his time. As soon as he laid eyes on me he had to look away. That, more than even my or my wife's reaction, confirmed how bad I looked.

'And at a press conference I had to do after I came out of hospital one of the questions a journalist asked me was, "Is your wife now going to divorce you?" I asked him why. He replied, "Because of the way you look." For a time no one, and I mean no one, would look me straight in the eye. I was never saved from gasps from people as they enacted double-takes at my condition. I reckon it took six years for this to stop.'

The defending world champion came to Monza six weeks later a dreadful bag of nerves. 'My no fear attitude had gone,' he confessed which, given the circumstances, was hardly surprising. 'I sat in the car for the Friday qualifying and I nearly shit myself. I couldn't drive it at all.' The next day he resolved to start all over again. 'I took it easy, as if I was learning to drive the car for the first time. I finished fourth qualifying, then fourth in the actual race. Old man (Enzo) Ferrari didn't want me to race. He told me not to. Better to use the excuse of losing the championship because of the accident. But I wanted to get back in the car, otherwise my problems would become worse. You know, I admired the old man. He was the most charismatic person I've ever met, but also the most egocentric.'

Lauda's confused state of mind at Monza also resulted in a faux pas that he clearly regrets, but has happily resolved. It involved Arturo Merzario, the driver who hauled him out of the flames. 'He was the only one who actually pulled me out. It was him, more than anyone else, who saved my life. Of that there is no doubt. But at Monza he was upset because I never came and thanked him. He was right to be angry, but I was under so much pressure that it slipped my mind. I was so nervous. Will I drive? Can I drive? I was in a terrible state. I gave him a gold watch the next week in Salzburg but he was still pissed off. Then, years later, I flew a Lauda Air plane down to Havana, Cuba. By chance Merzario was in a race there. I said to the Cubans: "This is the man who saved my life." Then he was happy.'

The monsoon had hit Japan by the time of the final race of the 1976 season. Lauda took one look at the water cascading on to the track and did not like what he saw. 'It was ridiculous. Who would have cared if we'd raced the next day instead? Quite a few of us pulled out of the race. I lost the world championship by one point. Everyone in Italy blamed me. They didn't stop and think that if my crankshaft hadn't broken during the French GP earlier in the season when I held a big lead I would have won the world title even with the accident. Anyway, I lost the title to James, so I didn't give a fuck. If I'd lost it to someone else I would have been really disappointed.'

At this point he laughed, thumped me reasonably hard on the shoulder and added: 'Let me tell you a couple of James Hunt stories.' He took a final swig of his coffee, downing the final dregs in his cup, afforded a quick glance out of his window as we crossed the eastern Italian shore, and began.

'You know the first thing James said to me when I came out of hospital following the accident? He said, "It's done you a big favour, Niki." I asked, "Why's that?" And James replied, "Because it's made you a lot better looking than you ever were before."' Lauda laughed, and so, too, did Hans, his co-pilot, who was supposed to be studying a map but had half an ear cocked in our general direction.

'I held my birthday party in Vienna one year and I invited James along,' he continued. 'At midnight I went home, telling James that we both had testing at Paul Ricard the next morning and that I would fly us both there. "We have to leave at seven," I told him. "If you're not there I'm going because if I'm late Ferrari will sack me."

'At seven James turns up with a girl he'd met the night before, and his stupid radio on his shoulder. He's completely drunk and giggling like a child. We arrive at Paul Ricard and we go our separate ways, me to Ferrari and James to McLaren. Half an hour into testing my engine blows up so I'm back in the pits doing nothing when suddenly there's a cry and big panic: "Accident, accident." I heard it might be James so I jump into a rented car and drive on to the circuit until I find James slumped in his McLaren at the side of the track. Shaking him he wakes. "I'm so tired I must have fallen asleep," he announced. He'd decided to pull over on to the side of the circuit for a quick nap.'

Now we were all laughing, Niki, me and Hans. Lauda shook his head and murmured to no one in particular: 'Ah, James. We had some good times.' Like many other stories in Formula One, it was all to end in tragedy, although this time not inside a car. In 1993, aged just forty-five, James Hunt died of a heart attack. 'You know, James complained of chest pains for some time before but nobody did anything about it. His life might have been saved. The most ridiculous thing of all, though, was that for the last three years of his life he led almost the perfect life. He didn't drink, didn't smoke, didn't do drugs. Then he dies. F1 misses characters like James. And I miss him as my best friend in the sport.'

The laughter of a few seconds ago had been replaced by a thoughtful lull. Niki ordered me to fasten my buckle again as he switched on the intercom. 'Hello, this is your captain speaking, Niki Lauda. We have started our descent and we will be landing at Rome in ten minutes' time. Please ensure that your seat belt is on and your tray tables stored away. Cabin crew, prepare for landing.' He gesticulated to me, a sign that said he had to concentrate on his flying as he steered the Airbus down though the clouds again, out across the Mediterranean and back along the western Italian coast and into Fiumicino airport.

We were late, due to the morning delay and then circling above a busy Rome. The turnaround of passengers should be fast. Those departing took further snaps of Lauda sitting in the cockpit as they head for the stairs. The local ground staff became excited when they realised who was sitting at the gate. A twice Ferrari world champion had just flown in. Signed photos of the former F1 star were distributed. One man, clipboard in one hand, signed photo in the other, showed it to his fellow workers, kissed Lauda's picture and exclaimed: 'Niki Lauda. *Bellissimo*.'

There was a natural break in proceedings on the ground. It was frustrating to be so close to the eternal city, but yet so far. I'd like to have described a pleasant couple of hours in Rome, perhaps with a plate of pasta, a glass of chianti, a stroll around the Vatican or an excursion to the magnificent Coliseum in the still warmth of the autumn sunshine. There was no chance of this. The 'Niki' flight was itching to be on its way again. As far as its owner was concerned, he couldn't get out of Rome quickly enough.

I stayed with Lauda on and then beside his plane as he made notes, chatted to his crew and looked repeatedly and impatiently at his watch. 'Where the fuck are my passengers?' he asked on a number of occasions. Finally they arrived in two bus loads, took more photos as they saw who was flying their plane, and settled themselves in their seats. Niki insisted I sample a 'Niki' salmon sandwich and a *mousse au chocolat*. 'It's good, yes?' he asked, even as we jerked back in our seats and began the ascent again into the clouds. We reached 35,000 feet, and then continued with our conversation.

In 1977 Lauda, burns and all, took his second world title with Ferrari. 'It was a challenge,' he explained. 'A challenge to me to see if I still had it, and a challenge to everyone else in the sport who wondered whether I should be driving at all. Do you know, old man Ferrari offered Emerson Fittipaldi a two-year contract one hour after the crash? I know this because Fittipaldi told me himself. So I won the championship and then left Ferrari because I'd had enough.'

Lauda joined up with the Brabham team led by Bernie Ecclestone. 'I stayed there for two years but grew more interested in aviation as I lost interest in racing. One morning I woke up in Montreal just before the Grand Prix there. I had a brand new car, a new, £2 million contract, a new and fast team partner in Nelson Piquet, but it was a miserable foggy day and I looked out of the window and thought to myself, "What the fuck am I doing here?" I told Bernie I was going to retire. I remember Bernie's reaction very clearly. He first asked me if my mind was made up. Then he told me to make sure I left my helmet and overalls behind.'

His absence from Formula One proved to be relatively short-lived. Tired of a losing battle with Austrian Airlines, he began to wonder if he could win a third world title and be the first man in history to become world champion having previously retired. Accepting a lucrative offer from Ron Dennis at McLaren, he returned to the fray in 1982, won at Long Beach after just three races and took the world title again in 1984. One year later, after seeing his McLaren team-mate, Alain Prost, take the world title, Lauda quit, this time for good. 'There really wasn't anything left for me to do. I'd driven a Ferrari, which is every racing driver's dream, survived the crash, won three titles in total and had come back to do so. I had no more challenges.'

At least in motor racing. In aviation it was a different story. Within a year Lauda Air was off and running. In 1991, though, came the worst moment in his life. The air crash and the resulting 223 deaths in Thailand became a living nightmare for the man. 'When I raced around the Nurburgring in 1976 and crashed it was my decision. I knew all the risks. But I sent over 200 people off in my plane and they never came back.

'The worst thing was that I didn't know the reason. In fact, I didn't know for six months. I went straight to Thailand as soon as I'd heard the news. I'll never forget the sight that met me at the scene of the crash. The worst thing was the smell, and the fact that dead people were scattered all over the ground. Some of the locals were stealing rings from the corpses, or robbing their luggage. This was worse than anything I'd ever seen in motor racing, and I've seen a few things in my sport. If it had turned out to be my fault I would have quit the aviation industry and never returned to it. In the end they discovered it to be a fault with the plane, and not with Lauda Air. It was a huge relief, of course, but it did not bring back all those people.'

There was another lull in the conversation as Lauda stared out of the window, alone with his thoughts. I stared out of the other window, not entirely comfortable about having just discussed the horrors of a plane crash from 35,000 feet in the air. Hans just stared into his map.

After being ousted from Lauda Air in 2000 Niki, with time on his hands, took up a new position as CEO of Ford's Premier Performance Division, overseeing both the Jaguar F1 team and its engine supplier, Cosworth. This would prove to be short-lived.

Lauda's contract finished the following year due to poor results, even though the budget at Jaguar's disposal was far less than the top teams.

That's when Lauda decided to become a 'pain in the arse' again. Teaming up with Air Berlin he launched 'Niki' and now flies one of his planes two or three times a week – he gained his flying licence just weeks after his crash in 1976 – and is already eating away at Austrian Airlines' and Lauda Air's customers. 'We had 970,000 passengers in our first year,' he informs me. 'I don't think Austrian Airlines like me very much. But I'm motivated to do even more against them.'

We were close to landing again in Vienna. Time had flown by. Lauda touched down, started talking to the control tower and, in the same sentence, invited me to dinner that night at a well-known restaurant called Do & Co. I had just enough time to go for a half-hour run along the banks of the River Danube, that great European thoroughfare that winds its way through some of the continent's major centres and serves as the main artery on the city map of Vienna, reach my hotel, shower and change before I found myself being ushered to a table in a corner of a seventh-floor restaurant in the city centre close to the imposing Viennese Cathedral. Although a dozen people are already seated, there is a vacant place next to Lauda who, on seeing me, waved and pointed to the seat.

'You must have the Wiener schnitzel,' he insisted, as I pored over a menu in German. *Mein Deutsch ist nicht so gut*, so he saved me the embarrassment of failing to understand much of what was written inside the menu. 'I'm having it too,' Lauda announced. I'd watched Nav Sidhu eating Wiener schnitzel a few weeks earlier in Shanghai, but this time, in Vienna, it felt absolutely the right dish to sample.

I'd never been to Vienna before. The fact that it boasted a magnificent assortment of churches and cathedrals, domes and palaces, theatres and mansions did not surprise me. After all, as the capital of the Austro-Hungarian Empire, it was the very centre and seat of power for much of Europe for a considerable length of time. What did take me aback, however, was how Eastern European the city felt. You might think the capital of Austria would have a similar atmosphere to the major German cities, or even other Austrian cities such as Salzburg and Innsbruck. Yet Vienna is very much of an Eastern persuasion. A glance at the road signs tells you why. Whereas other Austrian cities are a long drive away, the Slovakian capital, Bratislava, is just fifty kilometres to the east, Prague not a great deal further to the north, and Budapest well within radar to the south-east.

'So, where were we?' Lauda asked, as he squeezed a half a lemon over his schnitzel and started to eat. I thought I should ask what he felt about Michael Schumacher, seeing that the German and I would be 'getting it on', albeit on the slopes.

'The greatest driver ever,' came back Lauda's reply. 'No question.'

I wasn't prepared for that answer. Even though Sir Jack Brabham had reached the same conclusion a few months back in Adelaide, I expected something different from a man who raced against some of the greats. 'Really. Better than Senna? Than Prost? Than you?'

'Oh yes,' Lauda responded. 'I can't speak for people like Fangio, but I reckon so, yes.' He took a gulp from a glass of wine. 'I'll tell you why. First, because he has won the title now seven times. Seven times! That shows he has a greater hunger than anyone else in the history of Formula One. Anyone can win the world title once. To win it twice means that it was not a one-off. To win it three times shows a hunger and the fight for a challenge. But to win it seven times is remarkable.'

But hasn't he often had the best car? 'Well, not always. Not necessarily with Benetton, and not necessarily with Ferrari early on.

Besides, the fact that he has the best car has much to do with him. It is no coincidence. Schumacher, more than any other driver I know, has an enormous input into the Ferrari car. He has played a major part in its development, so we mustn't penalise his achievements now that he drives the quickest machine.'

It's a fair point, and well argued, too. He hadn't quite finished, though. 'It's not Michael's fault, but he is not the most colourful of characters, is he? Neither are any of them, really. Not any more. I suppose Eddie Irvine was. But he's gone. And Jacques Villeneuve is back, but he seems to have mellowed. But none are like they used to be. None are like James Hunt, or Clay Reggazoni, or Carlos Reuteman or Gilles Villeneuve. The sport misses those kinds of characters.'

I have a few more enquiries. Lauda ordered himself another wine, and me one of those hideously large litre-glasses of beer that you can only really find in Germanic or Scandinavian Europe. I put to him the following: racing F1 cars or flying his planes? 'They are the opposite. In F1 there are no rules. You can screw anyone, anyhow. You can be an egocentric arsehole, if you like. In flying there are only rules. The best pilot sticks best to the rules. So, when I was racing, I'd fly myself to all the races. As a pilot I respected the rules. I'd drive my stupid races, then be disciplined on the way home again. It was a nice mix for me to have.'

I'd heard that he'd given away all of his trophies.

'Ja, that's true. I've given them all to my local garage.'

Why, for God's sake? Lauda looked at me and blinked, as if it was obvious. 'They'd wash my car for free every time I gave them a trophy. I don't need fucking trophies to look at. I can remember every race I won. You can get rid of or lose a trophy, but you can't lose a memory.'

I knew, after this, how he would answer my final question. Lauda had clearly never had his head turned by all the trappings of success, glamour and fame of F1. He'd remained unseduced by it all, hence the large trophy cabinet now adorning an Austrian garage. The notion of cosmetic surgery on his damaged face, head and ear had obviously never really been an issue.

'What's the point?' he asked. 'Everyone knows who I am, everyone knows what happened to me, and everyone would know that I'd had it done. Anyway, there's only so much you can do with a head like this.'

The evening is now late. One of Niki's long-standing friends sitting opposite ordered a bottle of disgustingly strong, Eastern European vodka and six glasses. What was supposed to be a quiet night after a long day that had seen us fly to Rome and back was degenerating rapidly into a late session.

Niki suddenly remembered the point he was going to make before the vodka arrived. 'Anyway, do you forget what James Hunt said?' he asked, prodding my shoulder in the process before pouring me a first of what would prove to be too many vodkas. 'Why should I have plastic surgery? I'm much better looking now.'

chapter fourteen

NASTY CORNERS, NASTY DROP

The head-to-head with Schumacher was no nearer fruition. I was clueless about making it happen, and growing more concerned by the day about the impending ski-slope disaster. For some reason, however, I imagined everything would end on a happy note and that, in the meantime, I would broaden my driving experiences and turn my attention to rallying.

The weekend after my flying adventures with Herr Lauda the next stage in the World Rally Championships was held in Corsica. The Frenchman, Sebastian Loeb, finished second but was crowned 2004 world champion as a result of yet another impressive performance, this time on home soil.

What caught my eye more, however, was the man who won the race. Markko Martin's victory meant that the Ford driver had forged ahead of his nearest challengers into third place in the drivers' championship, and was honing in on the second-placed Swede, Petter Solberg.

This meant that he would be in fine spirits three days later in the Lake District where, apart from undergoing some testing, he would be fronting up to another stiff challenge – namely me.

Ford, to my surprise, had agreed to set up a stage in the Cumbrian forests to see which of us – the current number three rally driver in the world, or a forty-year-old bloke from Kent – would be the fastest. It seemed like a tricky one to call at the time, but by the end of the day there would be a winner, and a crystal clear loser.

The night before had been spent at the Lakeland Sheep and Wool Visitors Centre just outside Cockermouth. Ford had made the overnight arrangements and as I drove the long journey northbound I was wondering just how I was expected to sleep in a pen surrounded by sheep. Happily the biblical scene I had envisaged never materialised. Instead I discovered the centre boasted a small hotel.

The odds against me giving Martin a run for his considerable haul of money may not have been too favourable when the idea was hatched, but they became considerably worse as the next day unfolded. For a start, the weather was atrocious, if somewhat fitting. After all, rally driving, despite the various races staged in places such as Monte Carlo and Corsica, conjures up images of mud and rain, and cars covered in muck with their windscreen wipers frantically to-ing and fro-ing.

This was precisely the weather that met me as I made the twenty-minute journey from Cockermouth to the Whinlatter Forest where the Ford team were waiting. The rain was pouring down in sheets, the wind was sufficiently high to feel my car being buffeted, and the clouds appeared to be nestling on the tops of the numerous hills and mountains. On any other day I would have appreciated this. We were in Wordsworth country, after all, and the names of the passing towns and villages on road signs tripped off the tongue. Grasmere, Buttermere, Keswick and Loweswater.

The weather befitted the terrain. Mean, moody, raw and uncompromising, yet breathtaking at the same time. But I wasn't there to marvel at the scenery. I was there to drive a rally car and race against one of the very best in the world. In that context, none of this was helping.

I reached the Ford team by nine in the morning and by 9.10 was changed into mechanics' overalls. Everyone else looked frozen as I reported for unexpected duty in my all-in-one Ford overalls, bobble hat and walking boots. Markko was there, too, but sitting in the warmth of the motor home. We caught each other's eye and waved at each other, the type of half-friendly, half-cautious wave that competitors give before facing each other in the sporting arena. Well, at least that was my interpretation. The truth was that the twenty-nine-year-old from Tallin not only looked cosy, but anything but perturbed by the questionable challenge that lay ahead.

It was probably a nice experience for him, rather than the usual frenzy of either driving or attention that fills his life. Back home in Estonia he is just about the most famous sportsman in the country. There is a successful decathlete called Erki Nool, and a goalkeeper named Mark Poom, but Martin is the number one figure in sport. As a result of this he is unable to walk down the main street in Tallin without being recognised.

Stifling a yawn, he placed his helmet on to his sleepy head, strode out to the waiting car and sped off down a narrow, muddy lane and away through the distant trees as the Ford Focus R5 World Rally Car 03 was put through its tracks. To me this seemed pretty exciting. To him, performing a routine stage at ridiculous speeds around dangerous and slippery corners was as normal as brushing your teeth. A few minutes later he was back, announcing his return with an over-exaggerated skid and slide. Shortly afterwards a representative from Castrol, the oil giant which provides for the team, was sitting next to Martin discussing business in readiness for a quick spin.

This was when I was put to work by Neil Robinson, the Ford WRC Hospitality Manager, Gary Collister, a workshop technician and Tobias, a Swedish apprentice rally driver who was learning the ropes at Ford. The troops gave me an extremely important job title. 'Vision Technician'. This meant I was in charge of cleaning the windows! Actually, this was more important than it sounds on the basis that without my endeavours the driver could not see out of any windows, such was the level of mud thrown up by the previous drive through the mountain and forest stage.

So expertly did I wipe away the mud that I was promoted within half an hour to a full-grown mechanic. This, it struck me, was rather ironic. After all, you wouldn't ordinarily see me dead under the wheels of a car. Well, not unless I had just been knocked down and I really was dead. Not only did I not know anything about the mechanics of a car, but I had no wish to, either. Put me behind the wheel and I am happy as your next man. Put me under a car in overalls and, frankly, I'd rather be mown down by a stampede of rams and ewes at the Lakeland Sheep and Wool Centre. I went to the Goodwood Festival of Speed a few years back and could not work out how grown men became orgasmic over the sight of a gearbox, an engine, a valve or a piston. Not only were these men excited, they were taking photographs. Just how exciting, exactly, is a picture of a valve?

I decided not to divulge these thoughts to my new-found teammates, even as they seemed to be taking great delight in instructing me to do their job. Markko was the worst, now out of the car and standing with his arms crossed and a beaming smile across his face as he watched me go to work. He even started making suggestions concerning other duties I could take on. My brief was to be a corner man, not the sort you find in boxing with a sponge and a bucket, but the kind in motor sport. I was in charge of the front passenger wheel. This meant taking the wheel off, checking out the suspension, replacing the wheel and tightening all the nuts, not unlike Cracker at BMW–Williams. Then I had to rush to the nearby jack to lift the car up at the front and then at the rear, shouting out 'down at the front' and 'down at the rear' to ensure no mechanic would be squashed underneath, before descending the car down to ground level again. Finally, having pumped some more fuel into the tank, I had to check how much oil remained using a thin dipstick and trying my hardest to avoid touching severely hot metal around it. I didn't mention it at the time, but asking me to tamper with any part of a car worth £450,000 was like asking Ringo Starr to sing in the King's College Choir.

By now there was more black and brown on my overalls than the existing blue-coloured material. Thankfully my mechanic duties, after two and a half hours of honest if confused graft, were over. I had been summoned to the magnificent Dovenby Hall headquarters of M-Sport a few miles away to meet the director of the BP Ford Rally Sport team, Malcolm Wilson.

Wilson had more than twenty years' experience of rallying at world championship level, won two British national titles in the late 1970s and then the British international crown in 1994. He also spent several years as Ford's chief test driver, developing new rally cars. Under his guidance M-Sport has become one of the world's leading private teams. Now, as the director of the Ford Rally team, he had full responsibility for Ford's championship programme for an eighth successive season.

His headquarters are imposing. Set amid wild and rugged Cumbrian countryside, Dovenby used to be a lunatic asylum (as it was called during its time) and it is very evident today touring the facilities where the wards once were. Incidentally, I thought there was a neat correlation here between a home for the mentally unstable and rally drivers, but I kept that thought, too, to myself.

Wilson, a youthful-looking forty-eight-year-old, was not certain whether to laugh or cry when he met me. When he told me that if I beat Martin's time that afternoon he would be rushing up into the Whinlatter Forest to sign me up, he possessed a huge grin on his face. But when he also pleaded, nay begged me, not to write off his car, there was uncertainty bordering on fear etched across a much-changed expression. 'I don't want you, in all honesty, to even try and beat Markko,' he explained. 'Because if you do the car will almost certainly end up in a terrible mess.' He paused and stared at me for a few seconds before adding: 'So might you, too, but to be frank I'm more concerned about the car.'

Always good to understand where exactly you lay in someone else's priorities. He then launched into a long series of tips. 'You're going to find it a totally different driving experience to anything you've tried before,' he began. 'You'll be amazed, for example, at the level of braking achievable on a slippery, gravel surface. Don't underestimate it. If you get the chance to sit next to Markko first as a passenger on the stage you will find it scary because only he will be in control of the brakes. When you get your chance don't try and emulate him. If you do you might end up in Lake Bassenthwaite 600 feet below, or on the A66 dual carriageway. So treat the car with respect.'

I wondered just how good he felt his number one driver was. 'Oh, he's one of the best, for sure,' Wilson replied. 'He's a potential world champion. You'll be amazed at his skill when you sample his driving. He could have had a better season than the two rally wins he's had, but a couple of bad accidents didn't help. It is my view that the top rally drivers have more skill than the circuit drivers. Few in motor sport disagree with that. I think you'll find that when you compare yourself with him there will be a big discrepancy.'

Feigning hurt I accused the Director of the Ford Rally team that he had just made a major and unfair presumption. 'No I haven't,' Wilson replied, smirking. So he didn't feel that I stood any chance of pushing the potential world champion at all? Wilson gave this consideration for less than half a second. 'Not a chance. Let's say Markko will complete the stage in 2 minutes 20 seconds. You'll do well to finish a minute slower.'

Bearing in mind that the stage is only 4.1 kms long – albeit, so I was informed, through forests, round corners and up mountains – a minute seemed an awfully long time behind the Estonian. Malcolm shook my hand, wished me luck and felt fit to remind me again. 'Please, please don't write off my car.'

I told him how the Jaguar F1 team had made the same, pleading request to me moments before I drove their 2003 World Championship car at Santa Pod. 'I looked after them, and I will look after you,' I announced as I strode purposefully out of Dovenby Hall and was driven back to the Whinlatter Forest. Inside me, however, as my time to perform drew nearer, my guts were churning.

During the ten-minute journey back to the stage I chatted to Mark Wilford, the head of communications. He related a story concerning Martin's previous prang. 'It was in Argentina earlier in the year,' he began. 'Markko went over the brow of a hill and landed full on to a rock. The car then flipped over and over again at high speed for over one hundred metres. Amazingly, Markko was relatively unscathed but his vision was slightly impaired and still might be to this day. Psychologically he could have been affected, too. That's why his win last weekend in Corsica was such a major result for him. We're hoping Argentina will now be forgotten, both physically and mentally.'

Nothing like a story involving high-speed somersaulting and impaired vision to whet the appetite. Back at the forest Tobias had transformed himself from a mechanic to a rally driver, resplendent in his driving overalls. I, too, was told to change. Deciding not to be too flash, I decided to leave my Ferrari overalls and Rubens Barrichello-signed helmet in their bag and opted for my more modest red Sparko little number, complete with red booties. 'Bloody hell, you're early,' Neil and Chris shouted when I re-emerged.

'What do you mean?' I asked.

'You don't normally see Santa until Christmas,' came back the reply, as Neil thrust a waiver – yet another waiver – for me to sign my life away.

Tobias had been army volunteered into showing me the ropes. For the first run of the stage he would drive, with me watching and listening. We sped off in a decent hurry, or at least it seemed to me. A little later on I would discover how slow this actually was. Less than a minute into the course I noticed to my right a steep drop down, and to my left a near-vertical ascent of trees and rock. We were sliding around the edge of a mountain. 'Oh, that one's just the small drop,' Tobias explained, when he saw my expression. 'Wait until you see the big one.' Thirty seconds later we emerged from a huddle of trees into the open. To my right, again, was another drop, but this one seriously worrying. Way, way below were the serene waters of Lake Bassenthwaite. 'Make a mistake here, my friend, and you may be toast,' Tobias added, rather helpfully.

Arriving back at the start line we swapped seats, with me driving this time from the European left-hand side of the car, and Tobias the passenger on the right. It was both interesting and nerve-wracking to see Tobias noticeably more concerned now that he was the passenger about to sample my driving. We agreed that he would shout out the relevant gear changes, leaving me to concentrate on my driving. The first time around went smoothly enough, but only because I was driving at a snail's pace. Even then I found the car skidding and sliding at the muddy corners. Approaching the steep drop I slowed right down and veered off line closer to the trees. 'What are you doing?' Tobias asked, somewhat incredulously.

'Trying to live,' I replied.

We went around again, this time a touch more urgently, with Tobias shouting 'first, up to second, up to third, down to second, more speed', and so on. Afterwards he presented me with his verdict. 'You have something to learn,' he announced in his heavily accented English.

'What, in particular?' I asked.

'Braking, acceleration, corners and straights,' he replied. 'You managed to get the car rolling from a standing start, which is credit to you. Normally people take five or ten times. You went outside the driving lines quite a lot, and into the big mud. That made it harder for you because it was a lot more slippery and there wasn't much grip because we were using tyres suitable for dry conditions.'

At this point Markko walked by. 'You're not gonna find it easy to beat Ian, you know,' Tobias announced.

'We'll see, we'll see,' he replied, without breaking stride. That's all I needed. A pumped-up Estonian thrown down the gauntlet by his Swedish mate on my behalf.

The plan was this. I would sit next to Markko while he completed the 4.1 km course, a stage, incidentally, which used to be an official part of the old RAC Rally. Not only would I get the chance to experience what it is like being a passenger alongside a leading rally driver at full pelt on a slippery, mountainside stage, but I would also masquerade as the co-driver which, on added weight inside the car alone, would provide more reality to the procedure.

Then it would be my turn. Tobias would sit in with me, partly to bark out instructions, but also to level the playing field in terms of weight in the car. Mark Wilford decided to remind me once more of Malcolm Wilson's plea. 'Don't write off the car.' He added that I was the first non-Ford driver to be let loose at the wheel of the car that had been used for the whole of the 2003 World Rally Championships, and indeed for half of the 2004 season. As he walked off he had the same, pained expression that Nav Sidhu at Jaguar had etched over his face when he fixed up for me to drive the Formula One car at Santa Pod. Both were staring P45s in the face.

I sat next to Markko in the car. The straps were so tight that I needed a mechanic to delve under my backside and between my legs to haul the clamp up and shut it tight. Chris was the lucky one to get the job. 'That'll teach you to call me Santa,' I told him through my helmet. I turned round to Markko thinking I might strike up a conversation but he seemed strangely intense, his eyes fixed firmly ahead at the first few hundred metres of the stage. 'Don't worry,' I comforted him. 'I'll ease you all the way round.'

Markko failed to reply. Maybe he had taken Tobias's warning to heart. If he had, it meant two things. Not only would he post an incredible time, but I was about to experience the roller-coaster ride of a lifetime that made anything at Disney World seem ridiculously tame in comparison.

The car made a vicious revving noise, my head was suddenly jerked back, and we were off. I've been in a few similar experiences to this before, notably in the past few months with the likes of Barrichello and Montoya. Indeed, in the case of Barrichello, we were travelling a great deal faster than we were in the Ford Focus. But there was a crucial difference. These other examples were all on circuits. They possessed no slippery mud, no trees, no humps and rocks and, most of all, there were no hairpin bends and ninety degree turns on the edge of a steep mountain with a drop that would kill you if you happened to slip over the edge.

There are two states of mind to battle with as you are driven by Markko Martin in the Whinlatter Forest. One is to be logical. You are with one of the finest rally drivers in the world. He's just won the Corsican Rally. He may finish second or third at worst in the year's World Driver's Championship. He knows what he is doing. Driving at these speeds, in these conditions, in this terrain, is actually child's play. He does not want to write off the car any more than I do. Moreover, he does not want to kill me, nor die himself.

The other is to be emotional. It is now raining steadily, the clouds are hanging low over the forest and, indeed, at one point, swamping the car. The wheels below us are sliding all over the place. We are sprinting up a hill at a ridiculous rate. No sane person would be driving a Ford Focus at 80 mph along a narrow, uphill track splattered in wet mud with a sheer drop of 600 feet right beside them and a fast-approaching turn at the top which looked close to ninety degrees. There is no way we are going to make it. No way at all. We are going to be hurled over the edge and down toward a certain end. This man is indeed mad, and quite clearly we are all going to DIE!

I decided, quite wisely, to adopt the former approach, leant back in my seat, sucked in some air and waited for the stage to finish. Two minutes and seventeen seconds later it did, and with both of us still in one piece. We had survived the sharp turn at the top of the mountain after all, and although we continued to hurtle through narrow, tree-infested gaps at ridiculous speeds, around more corners with thick pools of mud, and twice went airborne as we tackled small humps in the road rendering the road ahead blind, I went through my usual routine at the end.

'Yep, not bad, Marrko. Thanks for the ride.' In all the years of doing such things, I'm not sure I've ever convinced anyone of my nonchalance and unflappable demeanour. True, there haven't been any unfortunate accidents stemming from various orifices, but the sweat on my face and the glazed eyes are usually a give-away.

Now it was my turn. I walked around the car and sat in the seat still warm from Markko. Tobias perched next to me in the passenger's seat. He wore a strange and slightly manic smile on his face. 'Okay, now we show Markko how to be a rally driver, yes?' he announced, slapping my knee hard with his gloved hand.

Markko, meanwhile, was running down to the first corner of the stage, showing far more interest in this exercise than I had previously imagined. It just goes to show how the competitive animal, irrespective of the quality of opposition, still has the need to prove him or herself.

Rather strangely, I then noticed the ambulance. It had been standing there all day but only now had it registered in my mind. The Emergency Mobile Medical Unit (EMMU) was positioned by the start line. (Incidentally, talking of EMMUs, I had received a text from Sandy Myrhe, the New Zealand journalist, the night before. Peter Brock wanted me to know that the generic noun for a collection of emus was a 'mob', too, just like with kangaroos. I was happy Brocky had finally been put out of his misery.) Anyway, the EMMU was a Land Rover, designed to cover the muddy tracks of the stage if required to aid halfway up the mountain. Chitty Chitty Bang Bang might have been more useful, though, if we ended up flying off the corner at the top of the mountain before crashing into Lake Bassenthwaite.

I had decided to give it my best shot. This did not mean reckless driving, but it did mean pushing the Focus a great deal harder than I had done before. I wouldn't mind being beaten by the better man if I tried, but if I had not the whole exercise would have been pointless.

Neil waved his arms and we were away. Within moments there was drama. Approaching the first corner I braked a little too late and too hard and we underwent a serious wobble of the car. 'Steady,' Tobias remarked over the microphone that was attached to each of our helmets. He seemed relaxed about the incident, but I could now feel my heart beating furiously. We had been possibly inches away from crashing, and this before we had barely begun.

In the previous two runs I had tried to avoid the thickest part of the mud, even if it meant avoiding the best racing lines. This, so Tobias had informed me, had been a mistake. 'The suspension is so strong in these cars that it can take anything,' he explained. This time I cut the corners and treated the stage as if it were a lap at Silverstone. I was clearly going faster than in my previous runs. A lot faster. But I was still not prepared to push too hard as we climbed the notorious hill. I tried to look straight ahead but still there, invading the corner of my eye, was the dreaded drop. Rounding the corner I felt myself relax a little more. Psychologically, it was good to have got the sight of Lake Bassenthwaite out of the way in one piece. We sped down the hill on the other side, round a couple of bends, over a hump that saw us airborne for a split-second, and across the finish line. I'd even reached the dizzy heights of fourth gear on this run, unchartered territory for me before then.

Now that felt faster. Not as fast as Markko, but fast. Even Tobias seemed pleased. 'Now we are starting to look like something,' he announced, slapping my back. 'It looked a lot better. And you made it into fourth. But I think you were scared at first when we had that wobble, yes?'

I admitted it had been a little unnerving. How about Tobias? 'Nah, not really. Well, maybe a little. If it had been me driving I would have been relaxed, but as it was you, I wasn't sure how you were going to react when the car started sliding in a different direction to the one you intended it to go.'

Markko came to join us, a beaming smile suggesting that he had enjoyed the fun and knew he remained the best driver in the Whinlatter Forest that day. Neil made the official announcement. 'Markko Martin – 2 minutes, 17 seconds. Ian Stafford, 3 minutes, 35 seconds. The winner is Markko Martin.' The winner smiled, waved his arms in mock triumph, and waved as everyone else clapped.

I was in a state of shock. I knew Markko had been faster. Let's be honest, he was always going to show me up. But I had given my all, pushed the car as hard and fast as I had the nerve to do, and I was a whole seventy-eight seconds slower. That's eighteen seconds per kilometre less, or 1.8 seconds per 100 metres.

In a moment of sympathy Markko attempted to cheer me up. 'It was a big ask,' he reasoned, his English almost perfect. 'I drove at 80, maybe 90 per cent, you know.' Actually, that made me feel worse. He could have driven the Focus even faster than the madcap speed he produced with me sitting alongside.

'You only had three runs. If you had been driving all day I think you would have knocked down the time deficit to maybe ten seconds a kilometre. You did well under the circumstances.'

That was kind of him, but it still highlighted the yawning chasm between someone like me and someone like him. It also provided inexorable proof that rally driving is unbelievably skilful.

I had experienced three and half minutes of it. Markko explained the reality. 'In rally terms half a second slower per kilometre is too much. That's considered a long time. And in a rally I drive 100 per cent, of course. Sometimes a stage can last for half an hour. That's something like sixty kilometres, which requires incredible concentration. One slip and the rally could be over.' He smiled and shook my hand. 'So now you know for yourself that it's not so easy to do, yes?'

The funny thing was, I was despondent. Everyone else seemed to be delighted. Ford were delighted that I had not confirmed team boss Malcolm Wilson's worst nightmares by writing off the car. Mark Wilford was delighted that he still had a job. Tobias was delighted that he had survived in one piece after sharing a lift with me. Markko was delighted that I had been put firmly in my place. And the team were delighted that I had discovered just how challenging and tricky rally driving really is.

Yet I saw it just one way. Once again I had been beaten behind the wheel of a car. I had been exposed, nay humiliated, by a younger man, and I did not possess the talent even to push him close. I was rather hoping, naively, it seemed, to be starting to present a challenge to racing drivers. The truth was that I wasn't even close to them.

Now we both knew this younger man happened to be one of the very best rally drivers in the world, but it still hardly enforced my belief that I, as a man, can drive better than most, nor my case in the long-standing argument back at home. This, after all my experiences, had been severely diluted. My success rate was proving consistent. Consistently non-existent. The one salvation was that I was not expecting my wife to ask me whether I thought I was Markko Martin.

If she ever did I had just discovered the answer.

chapter fifteen

OLD MACSCHECKTER HAD A FARM

'Would you mind waiting while I put you on hold and find Mr Scheckter?' shrilled the voice down the end of the telephone line.

For the next two minutes I was subjected to this. 'Old MacDonald had a farm, ee ay, ee ay, oh. And on that farm he had a pig, ee ay, ee ay, oh. With an oink oink here, an oink oink there, here an oink, there an oink, everywhere an oink oink, Old MacDonald had a farm, ee ay, ee ay, oh. And on this farm he had a duck, ee ay, ee . . .'

'Hello, Ian?'

The male voice sounding down the line lulled me out of a revisit to my childhood. When I first heard the music I thought I'd dialled the number for the local nursery school, not Jody Scheckter's house. I don't suppose there are too many former Formula One world champions who adopt 'Old MacDonald's

Farm' as their holding music on the phone.

After a while, though, and rather disturbingly, I was beginning to enjoy the old children's favourite. I was pleased to hear Jody's voice, of course, but slightly disappointed not to hear the quacks that would have sounded within seconds on the line. After that, of course, who knows what might have come next? A dog? A cow? A sheep? Maybe, but a tad boring for Scheckter. How about a boar? Or a buffalo? Now that's more up his street. Or field. Or pen.

It was one week after my adventures in Cumbria. My new best friend, Markko Martin, had gone off to the next stage of the world rally championships, but had invited me back to his home in Estonia afterwards. It meant another trip away from the family, of course, but at least this time I would not be risking life or limb.

My defeat by Martin was met at home with the same response as every other defeat achieved over the previous few months. 'What exactly do you expect?' my wife asked, almost endearingly.

I couldn't really answer that one. Did I expect to become the best racing driver in the world? Well, no. Did I expect to test some of the best drivers in the world? At first, yes, but that was clearly the expectation of a blind enthusiast. I was beginning to understand that beyond the glamour, fame and wealth was a long, hard apprenticeship, a work ethic second to none, an abundance of natural talent inside a car and an unshakeable belief despite the odds stacked up against.

I considered all this as I made the two-hour journey from my home to deepest Hampshire to meet Scheckter. The 1979 F1 champion, and indeed the last man to be crowned as the world's best driver in a Ferrari until you-know-who came along in 2000, had since his retirement from the sport in 1980 first made more millions establishing a communications business in America linked to defence, and then moved to southern England to become a farmer.

Not just any old farmer, though. That would not be Scheckter's style. Scheckter was in charge of what he termed the 'biggest smallholding in the world', a futuristic enterprise called Laverstoke Park Farm, whose aim is 'to become self-sustaining and self-sufficient, producing the best-tasting, healthiest food without compromise'.

This sounded different. I was fascinated to meet the man. Jody invited me down for the day, to talk Formula One, of his own incredible career, of Ferrari, and of his extraordinarily successful post-racing career. There was one proviso, though. I had to get my hands dirty. What he meant by this he decided to keep to himself until the day. But in the week running up to my visit I kept on receiving emails from his friendly office suggesting I should bring plenty of padded clothing, a change of clothes and definitely a pair of wellington boots.

As I drove through the large gates of Laverstoke Park, situated fifteen miles west of Basingstoke and close to the Watership Down Inn, I envisaged being gored by a particularly wild boar, of which Scheckter owned many, hence the padded clothing, or being knee-deep in manure.

In the hall of the farm house I flicked through the varied array of books on show while waiting for Ralph Hardy, the farm manager, to show me around the farm. Mixed up with books such as *Enzo Ferrari*, *Marlboro GP Guide* and *Ken Tyrrell* were the *Home Grower's Manual* and a biography of Bill Gates. You can obtain a good feel of a person by the books they have on their shelf, just as you can by the ingredients of his office, and here we had Scheckter's interests and feats encapsulated in a handful of tomes.

Jody popped his head around the corner to say hello. We would be lunching together in his grand home a little later, and then paying the water buffalo a visit as well. 'Hope you don't mind huge animals that could quite easily crush you to death,' was how the fifty-four-year-old put it.

I was still thinking about such a prospect when Ralph ordered me to jump into his Land Rover for the grand tour. There was a chill in the air, but the sky was blue and here we were meandering our way through fields and across streams in true Richard Adams country.

Over the course of the next hour we covered just about every acre of the 2,500 owned by Scheckter. Never before have I seen such an array of farm animals, nor indeed, once it was explained to me, such an exclusive bunch, either. Fourteen of the forty pure native Angus cows in the world can be found here. 'And we have semen banks from extinct families from 1950,' Ralph added, helpfully. Eighty of the world's 500 traditional pure Herefords are here, too, as well as Dairy Shorthorns and a 250-strong herd of water buffalo. 'The most underdeveloped type of bovine milking animal,' Ralph explained. 'They produce less milk than our cows, but their milk has qualities that makes it excellent for cheese-making and other dairy products such as ice cream.'

A little further on he stopped the car, switched off the engine and ordered me out. After a climb over a fence sporting a sign saying: 'Keep Out: Wild Boar', we entered the boar pens. Laverstoke sported three male pigs, a dozen sows and one hundred boarlets, all originating from Poland. One of the males was clearly the Big Daddy of them all. The size of a small rhinoceros, with tusks that would happily gore right through your torso if you happened to annoy him, he stood proudly before us in a pile of his own poo, surveying the scene. 'You don't mess with him,' Ralph pointed out, which I felt was rather stating the obvious. Besides, he'd made enough mess by himself, thank you very much. He certainly didn't need any help from us.

We returned to our car and crossed the River Test, where mink can occasionally be seen, as well as roe and muntjac deer. A hawk flew overhead, closely followed by a partridge, while a couple of pheasants scurried into a bush. For a city boy such as myself, this was a very pleasurable way to spend an hour. Or at least it was until we came across a squashed rabbit on the road. 'That's probably Bigwig,' Ralph said, referring to the hero of *Watership Down.* I rather hoped it was General Woundwort instead, if it had to be any of them. (Note to myself: We are talking about fictional rabbits here. Get a grip!)

'I have a disease.' This was Scheckter's explanation after we met up and he drove me the short distance from the farmhouse to his home, Laverstoke House. 'I'm afraid this latest venture is like everything else I do. It has to be the best. In the world. I wish I was easier on myself, and on those around me.' He sighed and shrugged his shoulders in a rather resigned way. 'Still, that's the way it is.'

Laverstoke House is magnificently grand. Designed by Joseph Bonomi in 1780, it was built for the Portal family. Henri Portal, the son of a refugee Huguenot family, established a paper-making mill at Laverstoke and, in 1727, he secured the contract for the manufacture of Bank of England pound notes since the water from the River Test was uniquely suited to making crisp notes.

The actual house, complete with resplendent clock tower and courtyard, now sits amid a Grade II listed park of approximately 275 rolling acres, including the upper River Test. The original estate comprised 12,000 acres, but after much of the acreage was sold in the last century only 500 remained until, in 2002, Scheckter added neighbouring farms to increase the land to today's 2,500 acres.

Jody gesticulated towards a grand hall where, in the middle, stood a large dining table and two settings. On a mantlepiece stood a male doll dressed in racing overalls. 'That's Tomas, my son,' Jody explained, seeing my gaze towards the figurine. Tomas raced in American Nascar and was doing rather well.

A chef, complete with tall hat and stripy trousers, marched in holding a silver platter which, once he had lifted the lid in a rather exaggerated way, revealed a large slab of meat. Buffalo meat to be precise. Home-grown, organic vegetables followed, which I spooned on to my host's plate while he carved what turned out to be surprisingly tender and tasty buffalo.

There are some of you who may be put off by the idea of eating buffalo. A few years back, while staying in a South African hotel, I ordered the meat platter in a restaurant celebrating African Week. After chewing relentlessly on a massive slice of meat I asked the waiter what the animal was.

'Elephant,' he replied.

That was not good news.

'Which part of the body?' I enquired.

'It's rump,' came back the replay.

This was even worse news.

'I thought elephants were protected?' I reasoned.

'This one would have died most probably of sickness, in which case it's okay,' explained my matter-of-fact waiter.

So I was chewing on a sick elephant's backside.

I related this story to Jody, partly to show him how eating buffalo was child's play in comparison, but also to introduce the whole subject of South Africa, and how a kid from East London could ever end up being world champion, the first and last to do so from that part of the world.

'My uncle drove on the South African Grand Prix circuit before the war, which is where I guess my interest derived from,' he began. 'I was useless at school [which was interesting, considering the success he enjoyed not only in sport but in business] but I was a good, young mechanic. I remember my dad walking into my room when I was twelve and discovering me reading a book inside my homework. It was entitled *How to Modify Two Strokes*.'

Within a couple of years he was beginning to get noticed as a junior racer in South Africa thanks to the circuit in East London. In 1971 he won the 'Driver for Europe Award' which meant he was sent north from South Africa to see if he could make it in motor racing. 'In my first race at Brands Hatch I was leading and driving aggressively,' he recalled. 'I ended up spinning, finished second, but got noticed. In 1972, one year after arriving in England, I was driving in Formula One.' He was just twenty-two.

There followed an eventful career, riddled with the kind of problems only a white South African would face. 'You might have thought the fact that Lotus had signed me up would have been big news back home, but I was viewed as a traitor for leaving a South Africa still very much in seclusion and under apartheid rule. Other drivers who stayed in South Africa received far more attention than me.' Then, in 1973, he raced five times for McLaren before losing his seat in the car. 'Marlboro, McLaren's main sponsors, didn't want a South African in the car because of apartheid. I quite clearly wasn't prejudiced, but I had no seat so I moved on.'

To Tyrrell, to be precise, where he enjoyed three years with the British team, including four GP wins, a first in Sweden in 1974, closely followed by a British GP win at Brands Hatch, then a home soil victory at the South African GP the following year, and finally the Swedish again in 1976. In 1977 he joined the Wolf Team, won three GPs and finished runner-up in the driver's championship. By then he had recorded a second and two third placings in the driver's title races, and won at home, in Britain and, that year, at Monaco. 'I knew by then I was good enough to become world champion. Having realised this, I then had to win it. It wasn't just an aim. It was an obsession.'

Which meant a move to Ferrari in 1978, and some famous grapples with old man Ferrari himself. 'I didn't speak Italian so all my views and thoughts were passed on to him by interpreters. After a while I realised that my sometimes strong views were not being correctly translated because the interpreters thought Enzo would not want to hear them. It came to a head when I told them to tell the old man that his engines were not as good as Cosworth's. They simply refused to tell him this so, from then on, all my communication with Enzo was by telex.' He threw a couple of extra organically grown roast potatoes on to my plate and added: 'In Italy then first came Enzo, then the Pope.'

By then his 'disease', as Jody put it, was rearing its head. 'Ferrari's son told me once that I was the most dedicated driver they'd ever had. I was certainly intense. Too intense for my own good. It burnt me out. I can't say winning the 1979 World Championship was an enjoyable experience. I was too intent on winning. And I was so focused that I didn't notice or care what was going on around me. I twice won the "Biggest Asshole of the Year" award from the motor racing writers at that time. I can't say I'm particularly proud of that. I was so single-minded I must have come over many times as rude. I regret that now.'

In 1979 it all came right for Scheckter and Ferrari, with their other driver, Canadian Gilles Villeneuve, finishing runner-up. 'We didn't necessarily have the best car, but we had the best tyres,' is his explanation of a triumph he was strangely keen to play down.

'To be honest, I don't have too many happy memories from the experience. Back home in South Africa, a country dominated sports-wise by rugby and cricket, there was little interest. Formula One wasn't televised. Fiat got hold of the Minister for Sport to ask if he could arrange a welcoming home reception for me, but he told them it was impossible because they needed at least three months' notice.'

Old man Ferrari appeared equally lukewarm. 'The only recognition he gave me for the feat was when he walked up to me in Monza after the penultimate race of the season which I won, said 'Hello champion', and walked straight on by. It was his policy to make the driver as unimportant as possible. To him it was all about the car. Actually I didn't mind that. I got paid a great deal of money for doing what I loved, and Ferrari helped me to achieve my goal, which was to become world champion.'

He could enjoy his success for just six days. 'The old man

wanted me to race in a non-championship race at Imola the following weekend. Although there was still the Canadian GP remaining my lead was unassailable in the title race. I refused at first because I wanted to enjoy my success and concentrate on Montreal, not a non-championship race. But it was at Imola, so it was important to Ferrari. In the end I agreed, very reluctantly, didn't really have my heart in it, and finished fifth. It was pretty clear to me then that I'd gone from a hero to a wanker in six days.'

Within a year he had quit Ferrari aged just thirty. 'I had a lousy car and I was losing,' he explained, as the chef returned to clear away the plates. 'After becoming world champion in 1979 I could only lose. Losing was even worse after having been a winner. Halfway through the 1980 season I announced I was retiring. My fascination with the sport was fast eroding, people were still getting killed, and there were many things about the sport, especially the politics, that I didn't like.'

Dessert, in the form of coffee and vanilla ice cream made from buffalo milk, was served. Creamier in texture than ordinary ice cream, it was delicious, at least until Jody suggested we paid the buffaloes a visit after lunch. Seeing that I had just helped to eat one of them, and then gorged myself on ice cream almost straight from a buffalo's udder, a little ray of guilt flashed across my mind as I realised I would soon be looking at a great deal of them in the eye.

After the end of the 1980 season a soon-to-be restless Scheckter slunk off to his Monaco home and came across a magazine article about simulators. Within days a friend told him how the US police were looking for some form of equipment, in the shape of a simulator, that could improve their gun training, especially when it came to determining the good guys from the bad ones. Up until then all they used were cardboard cutouts.

'I met a laser technician and got him to build me a prototype,' Jody explained. 'The whole business started from my kitchen table.' Within the space of just twelve years the kitchen table business had expanded into a company employing 115 people near Atlanta, which was then sold in 1996 for a cool $230 million. 'We developed first eight-foot screen projections replicating bank robberies, then a twelve-man simulator for the National Guard. It was tough-going at first, tougher than my years in motor racing. But by the end we owned 95 per cent of the world market, and operated in thrity-five different countries.'

Then his English-born wife, Clare, announced just before the 1996 Atlanta Olympics that she wished to return home to Britain. The Scheckters upped sticks and headed for Hampshire where the next adventure began.

'I didn't really have any plans, but I had a small farm in America and when a friend gave me a book on organics a hobby soon became a passion. I bought a farm here at first, and became organically self-sufficient. The problem with this was that if we killed a cow we'd be eating beef from the same animal for the next six weeks. That's when I bought the rest of all this you've seen, and became a serious farmer.'

Lunch had been finished. I complimented Jody on the quality of the food which was genuinely superior to the fare served up by most top London restaurants. He looked pleased, but added: 'Well that's good to hear, but frankly it has to be the best. I'm afraid the disease I suffered from in motor racing and in the communications business is still ravaging me. I can't do anything 95 per cent. If I do I do it badly. Most people can deliver well on 95 per cent. I can't. It has to be 110 per cent or you can forget it. I know it's my weakness. It makes me hard to be with, but it's also my strength. It means that I run this farm as firmly and as efficiently as I ran my racing career, and my business in America.'

We jumped back into his car and headed off to the buffalo pen. Along the way he waxed lyrically about his latest love. 'I've got over four hundred farming books, and nearly all of them are from the nineteenth century,' he said. 'They didn't use antibiotics and anti-oxidants then. Now look at the state of us. It's no wonder people are sick and obese, or suffering from diabetes or high sugar levels. When you look at what's put into soil these days, and into grass, it's no wonder. Did you know that a handful of soil has more living things in it than all the people on earth? If you get your soil right you get your grass right. And if you get your grass right the animals are right and thus, finally, so too are the humans. It's as simple as that.'

With that he suddenly thrust into my hand a piece of paper with two equations on it. One read: Healthy soil = healthy grass = healthy animals = healthy meat and milk = healthy people. The other stated: Unhealthy soil = unhealthy grass = unhealthy animals = unhealthy meat and milk = unhealthy people. 'That's why I've just employed a doctor in microbiology to test everything here at the farm.'

There must have been eighty of the gigantic beasts inside the buffalo pen. Jody and I clambered in, both rather gingerly, and eased our way gently into the middle of the pen. Here is a tip I pass on to anyone who wants to stand in the middle of a pen of eighty buffalo. Do not wear a suede coat at the time. Within seconds a dozen buffalo ambled their way across to me like moths to a flame. Some started to sniff at my coat, others even to bite it. Another one's backside barged into me, sending me flying into the face of a particularly large buffalo. When Jody attempted to prise some of them away from me he, too, was semi-crushed.

'I think it's time we got out,' he suggested, appearing concerned at the experience. 'I've never actually done this before, even if they are my animals, and this is my farm.' We were supposed to be mucking out the pen, then milking some of them, I was told as we clambered back over the fence. Mucking out eighty buffalo in a pen with twenty tons of poo would have been one of my jobs that afternoon. Just how much fun can a guy have? Luckily, on witnessing what one accidental collision with a buffalo could do to a human, Jody decided against the idea.

On seeing a much smaller pen with just half a dozen buffaloes inside, I suggested climbing over the fence and milking them instead. 'Actually they're bulls,' came back the reply. On second inspection, both of their horns and what was dangling beneath them, this was pretty obvious. 'Sex-starved bulls at that,' Jody added. 'Climb in that pen and try and milk them, and you'll find that first they will fuck you, then they will kill you.'

A pretty compelling reason to stay put, I considered, as we both leant against the pen and observed the bulls from the safety of the other side of the railing. Of course, I reasoned, now that Michael Schumacher has won the world title five times with Ferrari, and seven times all together, Scheckter is no longer the last man to have won the world championship for the prancing horse.

'Yes, and there are plenty of people who believed I didn't want Michael to win because of that,' Jody admitted. 'I heard all sorts of comments like that, especially in 2000 as Michael honed in on his first driver's title for Ferrari. The truth was that, after twenty-one years since I last won it for Ferrari, I'd become a cruel reminder of their failure ever since. Ferrari like to trumpet their success, but it got to the stage when it was better for them if I was not around.

'You wanna know what I think of Michael Schumacher? He is miles better than I ever was. He possesses a hunger far greater than I ever had. He built Ferrari up from a struggling team with a historic name that at times hampered them, and he's never been beaten by a team-mate.

'I respected Niki Lauda and Emerson Fittipaldi most of all as drivers, maybe Alain Prost too, while my best friend in motor racing was Gilles Villeneuve, until his fatal crash. But none of them would mind me saying that Schumacher is better than any of them. And anyone else too.'

We bade the buffalo farewell, and the boars, too, which we passed en route back to my car. Big Daddy was still standing just as proudly in his own mess, surveying his own little empire. As we drove Jody told me one more story about himself. 'Do you remember the TV programme, *Superstars*?' he asked. Who could forget the sight of Kevin Keegan falling off his bike and half-killing himself in the process. Or Brian Jacks and his controversial sliding squat thrusts?

'Well, I was invited to compete in an international *Superstars* event in 1982. I was up against the likes of Edwin Moses and Skeets Nehemiah and I, don't forget, was supposedly an unfit motor-racing driver in comparison to the others. I trained for three months for the competition back home in South Africa, then, after a series of sports such as swimming, dips, rowing, cycling, running and others, went out and beat the lot of them. Becoming the 1982 World *Superstars* champion was one of the proudest moments in my life.

'That's how I'm approaching running this farm, too. I approach it like the toughest company to be in charge of. I work until eleven o'clock every night. It's like everything else I do in life.'

I told him how interesting a day I had experienced. 'What's next for you?' Scheckter enquired. Markko Martin had emailed just the day before and was expecting me in Estonia the following week.

'Estonia,' he replied. 'Now that's somewhere I've never been to. I guess we're both on a crusade.'

He shook his head as we reached my car and I pointed my remote control towards the doors. 'It's just too tough,' he added. 'I should be on a beach, like any normal person who's made his money.'

Then he smiled, a rather wan smile, and shrugged his shoulders in a confessional manner. 'You know that beach I'm talking about? I wouldn't just lie on it, though. I'd try and make it the best beach in the world.'

And with that Jody Scheckter traipsed off in his green wellington boots back to the farmhouse, his microbiotics and his crusade to produce the healthiest food in the world.

chapter sixteen

FREEDOM TO RACE

Autumn had turned to early winter by now, at least early in the UK. In Tallinn, the capital of Estonia, the cold season had long set in. Snow was firmly settled on the ground, the locals went about their day-to-day business wrapped in so many layers of clothing that they looked as if they were about to embark on a trek across the polar cap, and your own breath became thick fog within a few inches of your mouth.

'Actually, it's still quite warm,' Markko Martin insisted. The Ford rally star, the man who had beaten me so comprehensively when I took him on in the WRC Ford Rally Car in the Lake District the month before, had just collected me from the airport in his four-by-four and was driving me through town.

To prove his point he nodded his head towards the Baltic Sea to our left as we ventured into the capital. 'See, it's not frozen.' Normally by November, and certainly by December, the Baltic is frozen solid all the way from Tallinn to the Finnish capital of

Helsinki, fifty miles away. Technically it was quite 'warm'. After all, the temperature gauge on his car read a mere minus three degrees Celsius. Very often by now it would be minus ten to fifteen, and occasionally a great deal colder than that.

'Look,' Markko then said, as we passed by a large lump of concrete jutting out of the road towards sea. 'That's the unfinished bridge to Helsinki.'

'Really?' I replied, with a genuinely surprised tone in my voice.

'No, not really, but it's a joke I like to play on anyone visiting.'

I tried to cover myself by arguing that since it took only eighteen minutes to get to Helsinki by helicopter the prospect of constructing a bridge was not such a preposterous idea after all. Actually, that's the first point about Estonia, one of the three small countries known as the Baltic States (together with Latvia and Lithuania) and a former state of the Soviet Union until independence in 1991. Estonia to me conjured up images of just that – Russia. But although there is plenty of evidence of Russian influence, unsurprising considering the Soviet's heavy influence on the place, Estonia and Estonian are far more akin to Finland and Finnish.

The language is perhaps the most obvious example of this. Estonian, despite the country's borders with Russia, is completely unrelated to Russian, Latvian, Swedish, German or any other Indo-European tongue. Along with Finnish and, strangely, Hungarian, Estonian belongs to the Finno-Ugric group of languages, thought to have originated somewhere beyond the Urals thousands of years ago.

Which is why 'One beer, please' is '*Palun, uks olu*' in Estonian, and 'Will you marry me?' (a phrase the stag weekenders who flock to Tallinn may be forced to say after an amorous, or more probably drunken accident) is '*Kas sa abielluks minuga?*'

Markko was beginning to resemble one of those tourist guides you hear blasting out their well-rehearsed mantra as an open-top bus cruises by in the streets of London. 'That's the sailing centre for the 1980 Moscow Olympics,' he pointed out as we passed a large, grey, concrete block by the sea with the unmistakable five rings of the Olympic movement fluttering above on flags. It was a long way from Moscow.

By now we had driven all the way around the large bay that dominates Tallinn and arrived at a rather strange-looking building that was shaped like a ship's hull. 'Now we have some lunch,' Markko suggested. The restaurant was called The Boat, which explained its unique structure, together with the fact that it stood just a few yards away from the Baltic, with its cold, uninviting waves crashing over the sea wall and on to the subsequently melting snow. Popular with the locals, The Boat is seen as the place to eat if you want to escape the lively Old Town that most tend to flock to in Tallinn.

Inside we sat down next to a roaring log fire as a waiter dressed in a thick, white, woollen sweater and with a splendidly shaggy beard, took our order. He looked as if he should have been out at sea guiding his vessel through the rising lumps of the almost black Baltic. The 'Kiiluaotlibi' looked nice, a chicken breast with plum sauce that Markko helpfully recommended, although when I attempted to say it I probably uttered a word meaning something very different indeed. A glass of Saku Originaal, the most popular of the national brews, washed the chicken down.

The menu was the perfect example of Estonian cuisine, a confused mixture of Scandinavian and Eastern and Central European. Thus we had marinated eel and the sauerkraut stew vying for attention with the blood sausage, all kinds of pork and omelettes, the latter a particular favourite in this part of the world. 'I miss my Estonian meat and potatoes,' Markko declared, as he looked down lovingly at his plate with his cutlery already in his hands.

At first he wanted to talk about rallying, and in particular the season just finished. It was his best ever season in the World Rally Championships, with a third place in the final drivers' table behind world champion Sebastian Loeb from France, and Sweden's Petter Solberg, as well as three rally wins to his name. But Markko, the perfectionist, was not entirely satisfied.

'I expected a bit more,' he admitted, as he tore a bread roll into two and gazed out to sea. 'There was a time, last May, when I was leading the whole world championships, but I ended the year in third place. So, I learnt how to lose the championship. Now I must try and learn how to win it.'

What probably did for him was that horrendous crash during the Argentine rally, the one Ford's Mark Wilford told me about moments before I stepped into Markko's car for the stage drive through the Whinlatter Forest. 'It was a big crash,' Markko said. 'A real nasty one. It made the rest of the year very difficult.' It didn't prevent him from winning both the Catalonian and Australian rallies, mind you.

'The biggest problem was my eyesight, particularly in one ear.'

What! In one ear? Markko's English was excellent, once again shaming a well-travelled Englishman who has not been bothered to learn any language beyond half a dozen words and phrases in French, German and Spanish. But for once he had chosen not only the wrong word, but a phrase that conjured up all kinds of images. I pointed out his mistake, which prompted a loud roar of laughter from my host, before he returned to the rather more serious stuff of potentially fatal crashes.

'My eyesight was impaired for the rest of the season because of the huge impact of the crash. I hit a rock at 110 mph, and then flipped over and over again for a good hundred yards before finally coming to a halt. There wasn't much left of the car by the time the rolling had stopped, but I was still sitting inside of what was once the front of my car.'

Did that put him off rallying? 'Oh no,' Markko replied, as he gesticulated towards our seafaring waiter. 'It just pissed me off because I thought I was going to win.'

The bill was 260 Estonian kroon (rhymes with 'tone'), or £13. And that was for our two-course meals, plus drinks. Markko insisted on paying for it, refusing to accept my pleas to cover at least some of it. We headed off back into town and to the picturesque area around where the Estonian Government can be found. Markko returned to his tourist guide guise.

'You see that big, pink palace?' he asked, which was a bit of an odd question seeing that we had just parked on Toompea Hill and stepped out of the car right next to a huge, pink palace. 'That's the parliament building.' Its legislative body, the 101-member Riigikogu, did its business there, governed by the country's current centre-right coalition comprising three parties midway through a four-year term.

You might think Markko took me here to show me Estonia's equivalent of the Houses of Parliament. You would be wrong. 'You see that building there?' he asked, pointing at a corner house in a row of smart terraced dwellings a hundred yards down the street from the pink palace. 'That's where I lived when I moved to Tallinn,' he explained.

We went to a frozen pond in a nearby park to take some photographs. A duck skidded on the ice and nearly crashed straight into an erect bandstand in the middle of what was now a shining white floor. 'That's what it's like for us when we're rallying in Finland and Sweden,' Markko commented, on seeing the hapless duck. 'Only we go a lot faster.'

Back in the car we made the twenty-minute journey from the city centre to Markko's out of town house. By now a heavy blizzard was falling. Unlike in England, when the whole world grinds to a slushy halt at the first drop of a flake, in Estonia life goes on uninterrupted. It was three o'clock in the afternoon and darkness was already beginning to fall. 'That's why I also like to live in

Monaco,' he informed me, with a rueful grin. 'There's no snow, it's warm, and it's nice and light.'

Along the way we passed by the Russian Orthodox Alexander Nevsky Cathedral, with its interior filled, so Markko informed me, with gold icons and incense. Around 170,000 Estonians are Russian Orthodox, with a further 180,000 Lutherans out of a population of 1.37 million inhabitants, but, in truth, according to a census undertaken in 2000, only 31 per cent of the country claimed any religious affiliation at all.

A little further on from the cathedral we drove past a host of ultra-cool bars, Internet cafés and anything-goes clubs. In the space of ten minutes the full and widely contrasting mix of Tallinn could be witnessed. History and tradition in this city sporting 400,000 inhabitants met an almost hedonistic embrace with the West.

We turned down a narrow track and through some woods before finally coming to the Martin residence. Markko, a famous figure in Estonia, was concerned I did not reveal too much about his home, suffice to say it is big, cool and marvellously art-deco in design. It is also unbelievably quiet there, which is the way he likes it.

After pouring us both some juice into a couple of glasses Markko led the way as we climbed two flights of stairs to reach a top, attic room, jutting out of the house like a pilot's cockpit in an old, wartime bomber. This, as Markko's expression stated without his having to say a word, was his favourite place at home. Here you could sit and watch the world go by, or more precisely the ferries as they made their way to and fro across the Baltic from Tallinn to Helsinki and back. A large telescope stood in one corner of the room from which he could study the Finns on a clear day. Maybe a large telescope stood somewhere in Helsinki where someone could study Markko, too.

It was here, in a reflective room, that Markko was able to be more reflective himself. Born twenty-nine years previously in Estonia's second city of Tartu, he was then an inhabitant of the Communist Soviet Union and continued to be so until Estonian independence sixteen years later. 'I may have lived in the Soviet Union, but I called myself an Estonian,' he explained, somewhat defiantly, before adding: 'Central Government was in Moscow. Maybe it will be similar again now that we have joined the EU (which Estonia did earlier in 2004). I guess the difference is that this time we will be free.'

Free? What did he mean by that? 'There was no real freedom for me in the first sixteen years of my life. I certainly couldn't travel freely, only in the Soviet Union. We couldn't get out. It was ironic, because we could travel 1,000 kilometres east across the Soviet Union, but not 80 kms north to Helsinki. I lived in Tartu and, although the kids didn't have radio-controlled cars or Barbie dolls, it was a happy existence in general. But in Tallinn they used to watch the Finns arrive at the port and then return again to Helsinki, but no Estonians could make the same journey in reverse.'

Being Soviet citizens meant that the Martin family were Communists. Markko dismissed such a notion, though. 'I was too young to understand all that crap and by the time it all started to matter to me the country was changing and breaking away from the Soviet Union. But I'll tell you what I think having lived under Communist rule. It's a great idea in principle. The bad thing about it, though, is that it doesn't work because human beings are human beings. It's not good to keep people down. People should have higher aims and be allowed to follow them through. They should be able to do what they want to do. It wasn't possible to do any of this when we were part of the Soviet Union.'

Now 'Communism' is almost a dirty word in Estonia. 'Not too many people look back and miss the days under Communism,' is how Martin put it, which is not the biggest surprise considering the large number of complaining Estonians who ended up in Siberia during Soviet rule. Today there is little if any evidence of fifty years of Soviet domination. Certainly not any statues or hammers and sickles. In fact the only real reminder is the population itself. While nearly 70 per cent is made up of ethnic Estonians, the Russians fill a further 26 per cent of the country's population.

It was in 1991 that the country finally regained independence and kicked out the Russians, this time for good. For two hundred years Estonians had lived under Tsarist rule, where the locals were treated as serfs to Russia. Shortly after the end of the First World War, however, the Republic of Estonia was declared, taking advantage of the confusion caused by the Bolshevik Revolution. Less than twenty years later Estonia was back in the USSR as the Second World War got underway and, although there were various outbreaks of nationalism, this would be the case until the final fall of the Iron Curtain.

This process produced a number of memorable events. 300,000 gathered in Tallinn to hear the first calls for independence in 1988. A year later two million people joined hands between Tallinn and the Lithuanian capital, Vilnius. By 1991 the Soviet army had been reinforced in Estonia, but was powerless to stop the will of the people. Lenin's statue was torn down in August of that year and, the next day, Russia recognised Estonian independence.

During all this time a teenage Martin attempted to build on his own dream of becoming a rally driver. So single-minded was he in his pursuit that much of the biggest events in his nation's history went over his head, although he can remember some of it. 'They were strange times,' he said, as we both gazed out towards sea in the gathering gloom and watched a ferry's lights twinkle in the distance. 'Very strange times indeed. I remember Soviet tanks suddenly appearing on the streets but it never got violent. The tanks and the army tried to take over the Estonian television service housed in the tall TV tower here, but they failed to do so. I didn't really know which way it was going to go.'

It still did not stop him rallying, though. 'All ships across the Baltic were stopped but I managed to drive to Finland all the way round the Russian coast via St Petersburg,' he said. 'By then anything was going on, and stopping me from entering my first rally outside the Soviet Union was the least of the Soviet's problems.' By the time he returned Estonia was free.

Markko can still speak fluent Russian. It was a prerequisite at school, although he has little to no use for it any more. 'Apart from the elderly everyone else is so pleased not to be ruled by someone else any more. But the shame of it is, in my view, the fifty lost years. Knowing my country and its people as I do, we could have been another Switzerland by now if it were not for Soviet rule.'

The man is not for complaining, though. 'Winning the small revolution was a wonderful moment not just for Estonia, but for the self-esteem of its people. There's been a huge change in the country ever since. Hotels, peoples' houses, in fact everything has been upgraded.'

If the creation of liberty in Estonia was a miracle, then the promotion of a young Estonian into the world rally series was pretty unlikely too. 'My father was a truck driver and featured sometimes in the Estonian Rally Championship,' Markko explained.

There was an Estonian Rally Championship, then? 'Oh yes. In fact there was a Soviet Rally Championship, too. That was huge, especially in the 1980s. You'd get 200 cars entered into the Soviet Championships, including many foreigners. Just think how much land they had at their disposal. But the Estonians were always the strongest. Out of the top five three would normally come from Estonia. That, and my father, got me into rallying. I entered my first event in the Estonian Championships in 1994, when I was eighteen.'

At school he had dreamt of being Soviet champion because the thought of taking the world crown was an impossibility under Russian rule. Now he was free to do as he wanted, but still the prospect of an unknown Estonian cracking the big time was remote.

'Even five years ago people said there was no chance of it happening. I guess I was in the right time at the right place. My breakthrough came in 1999 at the Swedish Rally where, in a privately run Ford Escort, I finished eighth, and in front of a number of more prestigious factory cars. They had better equipment, better tyres and more experienced drivers, but my efforts got me noticed by Toyota and the rest followed on from there.'

Now he is gunning for the world title. 'Yes, and no,' came back the cryptic response. 'Yes, I'd like to be world champion because I like to win, but no because already I have achieved the impossible, not just because I am Estonian, but because I got to drive in the World Rally Championships through merit and talent alone. I'm not saying others don't, but plenty can pay for their seats. It's more than I ever expected. Five years ago if you'd told me I'd own homes in Monaco and here, beside the Baltic in Tallinn, I would have laughed and checked to see how much Estonian vodka you had drunk. It is, after all, strong stuff. Not like your western European versions at all. So now, whatever comes on top is truly a bonus.'

It was getting late by now. Markko, the congenial host, suggested not only driving me back to my hotel in the city centre, but then, a little later, picking me up again and taking me to dinner at one of the capital's trendiest joints. I was being killed by hospitality. En route the tourist guide returned. 'See that,' he said, pointing at a house built on stilts which rose some thirty feet into the air. 'That's the craziest house in Tallinn. You have to use an elevator to get to the front door.'

A couple of hours later my hotel room phone shrilled and it

was Markko again, waiting outside in his car to take me to dinner. This time he was not alone. In the passenger seat sat his beautiful girlfriend. Mari-Liis was a student currently sitting exams at Tallinn University, but this did not prevent her from joining us for dinner. Quiet at first, she soon came out of her shell as dinner wore on.

It was noticeable how many fellow diners were staring at Markko throughout the night, something he was not entirely comfortable with. 'I'm not looking especially for money, glory or attention,' he said after a while. 'I don't want to be famous, even though I am in this country. Just the fastest.'

But he is famous. 'Too many people know me. I guess I am one of the more famous people here. Certainly the most famous sportsman. I'm the only one who is internationally known, I guess. I won the Estonian Sportsman of the Year this year and, last year, won your equivalent of the OBE after winning the Finnish Rally. I know the President well and could quite easily mix with the highest levels of Estonian society if I wanted to. But I'd much rather play basketball with my friends in Tartu and Tallinn, and see my family and friends. And it's why I live in the house you were at this afternoon. It's quiet and it's away from it all. I haven't really changed at all in the past few years. Nor would I want to, even if I became world champion.'

Maari-Liis needed to pack in some revision. It was the night before her exam but Estonians, like us Brits, seem to ignore that famous teaching cliché, too: 'If you're having to learn your stuff the night before your exam then it's too late.' I always found that learning my 'stuff' in the final forty-eight hours did the trick nicely. The fact that most of the information would leave my head within seventy-two hours made little difference to me. The important fact was that it was in my head during the exam.

Still Markko's hospitality had not ended. Refusing again to accept any payment from me that night, he told me he would collect me at nine the following morning to show me around the old town and to have some breakfast before driving me back to the airport to catch my flight back to London.

Ten hours later he was sitting behind the wheel of his four-by-four waiting patiently for me to emerge from my hotel. If he was growing sick of my company by then he was disguising it well.

Tallinn Old Town is a legacy of the prosperous past within the Hanseatic League. By all accounts the best part of all the three Baltic State capitals put together, it is compact enough to explore its cobbled streets and tall merchant houses on foot in a day. Its highlights include the medieval town hall, Raekoda, Raekoja Square, Toomkirik Cathedral and the Danish King's Garden, all of which Markko pointed out as he made his way to a particular café he liked to visit in the mornings.

Old Town also sports most of the livelier bars in town. It is a favourite haunt with British stag-weekenders, a fact not entirely welcome with the locals. 'Well, the Brits aren't too popular here because of the way they behave. They think we have cheap beer, which we have, and cheap women, which we don't. Well, not particularly. They get drunk and break the law here.'

The British tourist. It used to be the Balearic Islands, Spain and Greece. But now that all kinds of weird and wonderful countries have opened up due to a change in political climates, plus the advent of low-cost airlines, we Brits can let ourselves down all over Europe.

Markko found the café. Here, accompanied by tea, croissants and the ubiquitous Estonian omelette, he spoke of his future, a near future which may not include rally driving. 'I'm a little disillusioned,' he admitted, even though he was leaving Ford and joining Peugeot for the 2005 season, a team that also included the twice former world champion, Marcus Gronholm.

'For a start rallying is so much more time-consuming than Formula One. They only have three-day events, plus testing. Each rally takes up a week for us. Now there are only four real stars: myself and Gronholm, plus Loeb and Solberg. When I started we had Colin McRae and Richard Burns, Carlos Sainz, Tommy Makkinen, Didier Auriol, Juha Kankunnen and quite a few others too.'

But what if Markko could become world champion? Wouldn't that be a wonderful occasion for his country? 'Yes, it would, for sure. But I don't see any others to follow me. Estonian rally drivers are content in winning the Estonian championships. They don't seem to have any more ambition than that.'

There are other things Martin wants to do with his life, too. 'Live more in Monaco where the sun shines,' he said, looking up rucfully at the leaden Baltic skies. 'Race in other events, such as the Paris-Dakar, maybe Le Mans. Have a family.'

Doesn't he enjoy the respect of his fellow countrymen, though? 'Yes and no,' he answered, not for the first time. 'Yes, I am famous, I win awards, I put Estonia on the map. But Estonians, although ambitious as a people, tend to be traditional too. They don't like people doing better than them. If they find out someone is, they'll happily put them down.'

I mentioned that was a human trait, not just Estonian. 'Maybe, but after all that time under Soviet rule, you'd think we'd applaud and encourage each other to achieve. Maybe old habits die hard.'

Maybe they do. It was time to leave for the airport, but not before I finally succeeded in paying for breakfast. I asked Markko what his plans were for the rest of the day. 'Well, I really should be doing some physical training,' he said. 'After all, the Monte Carlo rally, the first rally of 2005, is not too far in the distance, and I am starting with my new team on January 1st.' Then he laughed. 'But I probably won't. Not today. I'll go and play some basketball instead.'

And then? 'And then I'll sit in that same room we talked in yesterday at home. I'll dim the lights, stare out to sea and watch the ships go by.'

Is that it? 'Oh, well, I'll obviously have a good think, and relax, too. After a year driving in the world rally championship, there's nothing better in life than to do just what I've described.'

Martin had presented me with yet more evidence that behind the robotic public persona of the racing driver was often a complex individual with an incalculable drive to achieve, and one given to considerable reflection in private.

That was the image that remained with me as I bade Markko goodbye, thanked him for his time and generous hospitality, wished him luck for 2005 and entered the arrivals hall at Tallinn International Airport.

And it was the image that stayed with me as my plane taxied down the runway, turned around and took off over the Baltic and close to where Markko may well have been sitting by then, in his cockpit, with the best view in town.

chapter seventeen

WHO DO YOU THINK YOU ARE – STIRLING MOSS?

The grey of early winter in London and the fire crackling in the front room were good to return to. When I began this quest spring, my favourite English season, was emerging from a deep sleep. I had basked in the rays of the Melbourne winter, Monaco summer and Shanghai autumn sunshine, but now the year and my journey were coming to an end.

Flying back from Estonia meant the usual descent over London, providing the tourist with a five-minute view of virtually every famous landmark. As we flew over Hyde Park I recognised the tall block that is the London Hilton Hotel, and this reminded me of my next appointment.

Way before my wife asked me if I thought I was Michael Schumacher policemen around the country used to stop drivers whom they felt were speeding to ask the following question: 'Just who do you think you are? Stirling Moss?'

The strange thing is that long, long after Moss retired from motor sport in 1962, constables, sergeants and detectives still used that well-worn, roadside phrase. Even policemen too young to remember Moss in his pomp referred to what became a cliché to equally young drivers who understood exactly what the officers were getting at.

Of course my wife, being the modern girl that she is, plumped for the greatest current racing driver in the world when she referred to my driving. 'Well, I hope you'll educate her about that,' Moss reacted when I told him of this. 'I don't mind Schumacher winning seven world titles. I don't even mind him being known generally as the best driver of all time, although I don't personally agree with that. But I do mind, very much, when policemen, and your wife, for that matter, use his name instead of mine. That 'who do you think you are' phrase was established long before I quit racing, you know.'

We were sitting in his Mayfair mews house just at the back of the London Hilton. Shepherd Market was close by, with its grocers, pubs and narrow, cobbled alleys criss-crossing the area. The Moss mews appeared small on the outside but, rather like the Tardis in *Doctor Who*, seemed larger inside. Positioned in the most salubrious part of London, it would have been worth a fortune.

I had decided early on into my project that at some point I needed to have an audience with the great man. Not only was he a throwback to a period I once thought of as glamorous but now, after conversations with the likes of Brabham and Amon, merely wasteful and traumatic, but he was as British as you ever possibly imagine.

The greatest racing driver never to win a world title – and that's another moniker he is very proud of – was waxing lyrically in the manner in which only Stirling Moss can.

'Thank God Nigel Mansell won the world title,' the seventy-five-year-old exclaimed, as he leant back in his office leather chair and peered over his desk at me.

Why, because he is British and Moss is fiercely patriotic?

'Not really,' he replied. 'More so because he didn't end up sharing my mantle when it comes to being the greatest non-world champion. I've got to the stage where I really am quite proud of having failed to win the drivers' world title. It's a very exclusive club, you know. There are a few drivers who were worthy of being a world champion who failed to make the mark, but there are plenty more world champions who really shouldn't have become so. In some cases it was farcical in the way they managed to pull it off. My exclusivity is, I guess, that I should have won the world title. Still, there are plenty of plus points. I get loads of sympathy from people about it.'

Actually Moss has only himself to blame. Or at least his principles. In 1958 he was the world champion in waiting. Driving the Vanwall he won more Grands Prix than anyone else but Mike Hawthorn's consistent points-scoring with the more reliable Ferrari beat him to the title by just one point.

The Portuguese Grand Prix that year produced arguably the greatest show of sportsmanship ever from Moss, and an action that cost him the world title. Hawthorn looked likely to be disqualified after finishing second in Portugal because, following a spin, he regained the track by push-starting his car against the traffic.

Moss, therefore, on the verge of being crowned world champion, spoke in his dear friend Hawthorn's favour, insisting that not only had he seen the incident himself but arguing that his rival was simply removing his car from a dangerous place. Hawthorn's points were reinstated and Moss lost the chance to become Britain's first ever world champion. Little did he know at the time, but this would prove to be the closest he ever got to achieving the feat. Agonisingly, he would finish runner-up in the drivers' title a further three times.

'Well, I have principles,' he explained, some forty-six years later. 'To have a man disqualified for something so petty and stupid would have been wrong. I said it then and I still say it today: I'd rather lose a race driving fast enough to win it, than win a race driving slow enough to lose it. I have absolutely no regrets about helping Hawthorn win that title.'

He won a great deal more races that he finished than he lost. This is Moss's real claim to fame and the reason why he has gained universal admiration from motor racing and the public alike. His total motor sport career up to official retirement in 1962 spanned an incredible 496 races. Of the 366 he completed, Stirling won 222. Over 50 of these were in Formula One in the days when many of the F1 races were non-championship affairs. He'd race anything, from F1, F2 and F3, to rally cars, sports cars and touring cars. Of the many famous races he won perhaps the best known, outside F1, was the 1955 classic Mille Miglia in a 3-litre Mercedes sports car, in which he averaged almost 98 mph over a thousand miles of Italian public roads.

'I'd race fifty times a year back then,' he recalled, settling back in his office leather chair. 'The F1 world title wasn't such a big deal as it is today. For example, the Daily Express Trophy was a non-championship race in Britain but it meant more to us drivers than the British Grand Prix because there was more publicity, and a great deal more money involved.'

He didn't help his world champion cause by insisting on racing for British teams, despite the advances to him of virtually every top team in the world. 'It was just my principles again,' he explained. 'I'm a great patriot and, seeing as I'm British, I thought it only right and proper that I should stick to British cars. Mind you, there's little doubt that if I'd gone to Ferrari, as I was often asked by Enzo [Ferrari] to do, I would have been world champion more than once.'

The Argentine driver, Juan Fangio, did exactly that, winning the world title five times, a record he held until Schumacher exceeded it in 2003. Despite Schumacher's better record, Moss insists it is Fangio, his old adversary, who remains the best driver in the history of Formula One. This, he says, is not just because Moss is an 'in my day' type of person.

'The reasons why I go for Fangio are simply motor-racing reasons. There's no doubt that Michael is considerably better than any other driver of the current time. His biggest contribution is not so much his driving, in my view, but the fact that he has made Ferrari a winning team again. But as a driver he makes a lot of mistakes. If he'd raced in my era making those mistakes he'd be long dead, I'm afraid. Now the sport is so much safer, and the cars are so much stronger, and other things like traction control all play their part. In my time, I'm afraid, you just didn't make mistakes. Not if you wanted to live. I admire Schumacher hugely, but he's not up there with Fangio.'

I wished I had raised this point with Lauda and Scheckter when they proclaimed Schumacher to be the greatest. I also wondered why Brabham, who drove under the circumstances depicted by Moss, chose the German first. To take risks knowing that, in this day and age of super safe F1 cars, death was unlikely was one thing. To take the same risks understanding that death was highly likely took a lot more guts and precision. Now I was beginning to understand why so many motor racing aficionados always went for Fangio.

There is one particular Moss/Fangio story that stands out. Moss took pole for the 1957 British Grand Prix at Aintree, then led the race all the way to the final corner of the final lap. Fangio was a fraction of a second behind him and, in another show of sportsmanship that would never be witnessed in today's highly competitive and highly funded game, Moss pulled over to allow the Argentine through.

'I wasn't sure he had the power nor the time left to complete the manoeuvre, but I saw it as the decent thing to do,' Moss recalled. 'Anyway, he didn't overtake me and I won the race with Fangio the runner-up. Afterwards I asked him, "Did you let me win today?" Fangio replied, "No, no, it was your day, you were too good for me." But you know something? To this day I'll never really know the truth. I'm still not sure if he just decided to let me have it on the day. He was such a gentleman, you see. Now he's dead I guess I'll never know.'

Fangio may be gone now, but at least he died an old man, which is more than can be said for many of Moss's contemporaries. 'That was always the hardest aspect of driving,' Stirling admitted, becoming sombre for the first and only time of the day's visit. 'They were always so very difficult to accept. I'll tell you the odd thing. I always had strong senses and used to love the scent of freshly cut hay which you often smelled from a circuit as you raced. When there was a death during a race – and more often than not you could tell straight away if an accident had been fatal – I used to wonder how there could be such a wonderful smell when something so terrible had just taken place. I can still smell the hay to this day, sometimes in my sleep.

'You know, Peter Collins was only driving at 65 mph when he made one mistake and died from the consequences. [Collins, a handsome and lively character who drove for Ferrari died at the Nurburgring in 1958 after being thrown from his car when it struck an earth bank and rolled into a field.] Mike Hawthorn. He was another great friend of mine. He always drove too fast off the circuit. [Hawthorn, who wore his trademark bow tie when racing, retired after winning that 1958 world title following Stirling's show of sportsmanship, but crashed his Jaguar in a road accident and was killed in early 1959.] There were many of them, and they were nearly all friends, because back then we did a great deal together off the track. We ate together, we shopped together, we genuinely enjoyed each other's company. I don't think it's like that today.'

What stands the police constable's favourite apart from nearly everyone else in motor racing, however, is his attitude to this, and to the danger which claimed so many lives. 'They all died doing what they loved, and what they were best at. And, to a man, they all knew the risks involved.'

Knowing that, though, and the potential short life-span of an F1 driver, why on earth did they risk losing their lives on practically a weekly basis? 'There's not a lot good about danger, but it was one of the main reasons why we did it,' was the interesting answer. 'Danger was an important element to motor racing in the 1950s and 1960s. It was like cooking without salt. Nobody wanted to get hurt. But it was this living on the edge way of life that gave us a buzz that could not be replicated in anything else we did. The pleasures of taking part and having some success were sufficient to gamble.'

It was a scenario that, in today's changed society, would be deemed totally unacceptable. Moss accepts this. 'Oh, Christ Almighty, no. There's no way it would be allowed to go on now.' The levels of today's safety can be put down largely to the efforts of Bernie Ecclestone and Jackie Stewart, the three-times former world champion, who led the campaign for improved safety in the 1970s and onwards. Moss can see the necessity of the campaign, but is so against the idea that he managed to persuade FIA, motor sport's global governing body, to allow him to sign a waiver to race in his old cars wearing his old gear. To this day, despite being seventy-five years of age, Stirling likes to race in old classics and exhibitions under these unsafe conditions.

'Jackie and I are good friends. He's even my son's godfather. But our attitudes to safety are poles apart. I wouldn't want to take part in modern racing. That's why I forced FIA to accept my signed waiver. It means that I can race in my old cars with no seatbelts, a weaker helmet and non-fireproof overalls.' Stirling's argument here is that a modern helmet in an old car would seem 'ridiculous'. He shrugged his shoulders and adds: 'I guess I'm an old-fashioned guy, but I've always put fun and enjoyment first when it comes to motor sport.'

Fun and enjoyment. You think today's F1 drivers live the life? Well, obviously they do in most peoples' eyes, but if ever there was an era to be a top racing driver, it was the late fifties and early sixties. Providing you survived. Hawthorn and Moss may have been tremendous rivals on the racing circuit, but, off it, they were equal predators in the bars and clubs. 'Oh, that's what Mike and I did best,' Stirling recollected, now accompanied by a quite discernible glint in his eye.

'Chasing crumpet. It was absolutely unbelievable in those days. Do you know what the very best thing about motor racing was back then?'

He looked me straight in the eye, allowed me a split-second to attempt an answer, and then gave me one anyway. 'It was a licence to get laid. I was a young man with a very high sex drive.'

Glamour and courage were strange bedfellows with tragedy and death, but this is how it was in Moss's day. The lifestyle, the availability of girls, the money, it all sounded a gas. But there was nothing glamorous about getting killed in your mid-twenties. For all Moss's stories very few of his contemporaries were still around to share them. Most were long dead.

It seemed odd listening to a seventy-five-year-old, hampered, to boot, with back trouble that would result in serious surgery a few weeks later, waxing lyrically about getting laid, let alone referring to crumpet. It seemed even odder when Suzy, his wonderfully friendly but presumably long-suffering wife, emerged smiling with some teas. As she left, seconds after her husband's 'licence' comment, I was sure I detected a swift look to the heavens.

All this prompted Stirling to rise from his chair and lead me to a hallway where he kept a horde of old, leather-bound, black and green scrapbooks. 'Newspaper cuttings,' he announced. 'The blacks are for my racing career, and the greens are for my social life.' I took a more considered glance at the books. The greens outnumbered the blacks by two to one.

'People talk about the intrusive media of today, but I can assure you it was just as intrusive fifty years ago.' He flicked through a random book and fell upon a random page. 'There!' he exclaimed. 'See what I mean.'

There, in front of us, was the a slightly gnarled, fading and browning front page of the *Daily Sketch* with a main headline reading: 'I Love Stirling Moss'. It turned out to be a story about Stirling's latest flame declaring her love for Britain's best-known motor sport star. 'I was more in the front pages of the newspapers, especially pages one and three, than I was in the sports pages. Photographers like Terry O'Neill used to follow me around everywhere.'

Sounds terrible. 'Oh, I loved it,' he replied, with evident glee. 'It was entertainment for others, and it was showbusiness for me. My quality of life in 1960 was far better than it is now, and that's not because I'm seventy-five years old. I used to earn £32,000 a year. That made me the highest-paid driver in the world. It equates to around half a million today. It was good money, but not, even proportionately, like it is today. But I had a great deal more fun.'

By far the biggest item of news, though, and the one that fills most of a scrapbook alone, is his career-ending crash at Goodwood. 'April 24th, 1962,' he says, almost to himself as his eyes for a second seem to gaze beyond the scrapbooks and to a time over forty years before. It is not surprising he remembers the day. It was the day he nearly died.

We returned to the scrapbooks. All the main newspapers of the day led their front pages with this item. 'Agony of Stirling Moss', shrieked the *Daily Mail*. '135 mph crash, then trapped inside for forty minutes', added the stand-first.

'I broke my back at Spa. That's why I've got this bloody trouble now, you see. I had eight major brake failures, and seven wheels came off in my time, so it was just the law of averages that, sooner or later, I'd have a crash that would kill me, or at least half-kill me. Luckily, I plumped for the latter.'

Half-killed is just about right. Moss was unconscious for four weeks, and paralysed for six months. 'Paralysed down the whole of my left-hand side,' he explained, in his no-nonsense manner. 'Couldn't lift my arm at all. The hospital wouldn't tell me for ages because they were worried I'd die of shock. When I talked I was terribly slurred. I sounded permanently drunk. There were daily bulletins every day on the BBC. I think everyone expected me to die.'

There then followed a brief tangent as Stirling admitted to fancying the hapless nurse who was given the job of looking after him during recovery. 'Had a brief fling,' he inevitably revealed. 'Very pretty nurse, as I recall. Her name was Christine.'

With some little difficulty I persuaded him to focus his mind on the consequences of his accident. The effects of the crash forced his hand, once he had recovered. 'I had planned to race professionally until I was fifty, not quit at thirty-three. After all, Fangio only stopped at forty-seven, and that was because he'd had enough of seeing all his friends being killed. The problem was my powers of concentration had gone as a result of the crash. I didn't want to hurt myself, and I especially didn't want to hurt someone else in a race. So I had no real alternative.

'It was a tremendous shame because, although the likes of Jimmy Clark were coming and Jackie Stewart was just around the corner I would still have backed myself against them. That was the worst bit about quitting. Normally I would have bounced back. It was the knock to the head that did for me.'

He cites that Spa crash in 1959 as the best example of 'bouncing back', using an anecdote that only Moss could use. 'Broke my back and both legs when a wheel came off. I was bandaged from head to foot. Looked like an Egyptian mummy. The chief physio at St

Thomas's wanted me to exercise my legs to get the muscles working. At first this took the form of cycling. Then I asked him if I could go dancing. I used to get a load of strange looks when people would see me on the dance floor at a club in Leicester Square or somewhere when I was supposed to be recovering from a terrible accident and was too injured to race cars for a while.'

The crash that did for him was some forty-two years ago. Ever since then Stirling has been utterly shameless, but endearing in the manner in which he has maintained his name and standing in the world of sport. 'People often ask me what I've been up to since 1962 and the best answer I've come up with is that for the past forty years I've been plugging a fading image. Basically, I'm an international prostitute and have been ever since 1962.'

A little too self-deprecating for, in truth, Stirling Moss is much-loved to this day. I asked him why he thought he was still regarded as Mr Motor Racing.

'Lots of reasons, actually,' came back the instant reply. 'For a start, the name. It stands out, doesn't it. My mother was a Scot, you see, and her wish was to call me Hamish. Can you imagine that? Hamish Moss! My father told her: 'Certainly not. Think of another name.' (He impersonates his father as he tells this anecdote, a slightly deeper, more severe version of his own voice.) So she then came up with Stirling, as in the old seat of power in Scotland. Stirling Moss. It's not a stage name, you know.'

There's more. 'My timing was right, I suppose. I was very lucky to become involved in professional motor sport when it was just starting out after the Second World War. I was young, and I was one of a very few to drive British cars.' In fact he started out at seventeen and turned pro at nineteen. 'There weren't any real established stars at first because of the war, and I suppose I helped my cause my being very accessible.'

At this point he rummages around close to his scrapbooks and finds a latest copy of the London telephone directory. 'You'll find me in there,' he said, jabbing his finger on to the book. 'Under "M". I've always been in the phone book. Frankly I consider having an ex-directory number as the height of conceit.'

I declined to inform him that I, actually, possessed an ex-directory number. Moss continued unabated. 'That's why I could never really get into all the politics of motor racing. I'm not like Jackie [Stewart, again]. He's always been very political, very polished, and very professional. Me? I'm no diplomat. I'm impetuous. I'm hard to live with, too. It comes with the territory of being the kind of driver I was. I've always been one for instant decision-making.'

Which is another factor he uses as a further reason for his popularity. 'As I'm sure many have told you, you get two kinds of racing drivers: those who drive, and those who race. I was never a racing driver. I was a racer. Jackie (Stewart) was a racing driver, so too Alain Prost. But I was prepared to take a few more risks. Ayrton Senna was the same. So, too, Gilles Villeneuve.'

It is more than a little ironic that the two racing drivers Moss uses as examples are alive, well and faring prosperously. The two racers he cites were both killed in their F1 cars. 'I know, I know,' he conceded. 'But the people loved them. The public like the racers far more than the racing drivers. This, and the fact that as I drove British cars I was almost always seen as an underdog in whatever race I competed in, all added to my image. I was proud to received a knighthood in the Millennium Honours List. But I was even more proud to be awarded it for my services to driving.'

I have another theory about Stirling's popularity, though. And it was reinforced by what happened over the following half an hour. I'd already heard rumours and tales about his fabled house. It was, by all accounts, straight out of Q's manual in *James Bond*, with the kind of ludicrous gadgets only seen in the *Bond* or *Man from Uncle* films of the Sixties.

Although we had talked in his study, and then ventured into the hallway to flick through his hundred or so scrapbooks, I had not really seen much more of his intriguing house. I did not want to appear nosy but, in this case, it was well worth the gamble.

'Would you mind showing me around the house, Stirling?' I asked, not quite knowing what to expect as an answer.

My host positively beamed with delight. 'I was wondering when you were going to ask, old chap,' he replied, and beckoned me to follow him up a narrow, spiral staircase. As we slowly made our way up the carpeted steps he explained how he'd bought what were two mews houses together in 1962 following his crash and then designed himself its unique layout. 'I only lived down the road,' he added. 'This was a bomb-site, actually. Bought it from the auctioneer.'

We entered an upstairs living room. In the corner stood a piano. I began to make my way towards it when Stirling pressed a button and the piano started to play. By itself. 'You like that?' he asked, as the piano tinkled away. 'Look, I'll show you some more.'

He took me over to a carbon-fibre lift, designed by Patrick Head, now Williams Chief Technical Engineer, and a fire lit by the press of another switch on the wall. But his true loves could be found in a small area beside the main living room he referred to as 'the nook'. Stirling told me to sit down on a sofa and 'enjoy'.

Moving around better than he had all day the world's greatest driver never to have won a world title jabbed at a few buttons. First a television set emerged from the wall. Then a rumbling noise could be heard from over my head. Looking up I saw the ceiling open up and, from the kitchen on the floor above me, a dining-room table descended until it came to a halt beside my legs. On top of this, the table was laid and sported some fruit.

'So, what would happen is that I'd sit here with some bird and watch TV, press a button and dinner would be served without either of us having to move,' my host explained. 'After dinner I'd remove the table and the TV, turn on the remote stereo for some music, and transform this area into a dance floor.'

Once his catch had been suitably impressed by all this Stirling would deliver his inimitable *coup de grâce*. 'Upstairs I have a two-seater, pear-shaped bath,' he said, sounding at first as if he was inviting me to sample it. 'Another push of a button and the bath would fill by itself as music would play, from speakers in the bathroom.'

He paused to catch his rather excited breath, examined me for a second or two, and then concluded his speech. 'Seemed to work with the crumpet, you know.'

Every time?

'Every time.'

Moss seemed to be enjoying himself even more than I was. He may have been seventy-five years of age, but he was anything but a sad old man living in the past. His natural enthusiasm, plus his ability to see the funny side of himself, made him an entertaining as well as interesting companion. And the best bit of all is that none of it seemed out of place.

Now that's what I, and no doubt others, like about Stirling Moss. There are very few men, let alone seventy-five-year-old men, who could not only carry off telling stories of his 'pulling days', but use phrases in this day and age such as 'bird' and, especially, 'crumpet', and totally get away with it.

If I went home and started referring to my wife as a bit of crumpet all hell would break loose. Stirling says this and people – and I'm sure nearly everyone feels this – love him that much more.

It is the same with George Best, by the way. Whenever he appears on television chat shows recalling his drunken days of the late 1960s onwards, retelling his Miss World and £25,000-on-a-hotel-bed stories, and giggling like a schoolkid, half the female population ooh and aah at his naughty shenanigans. Try acting like Best yourself and your partner will find your behaviour totally unacceptable.

Standing in Stirling's gadget-ridden home I felt I was in the company of a man who was a cross between Leslie 'Helloooo' Phillips and Austin Powers.

It was time to go. What was supposed to be an hour's visit had lasted half the day. But there was still time to witness one final sight before being ushered out. On Stirling's walls hung many photographs. One is of Fangio and Moss together. Another is of Ayrton Senna, with the inscription: 'To Stirling: with admiration. AS'. But what really caught my eye were two bent and battered, old steering wheels.

'Oh, those,' Stirling said, after he caught me staring at them attentively. 'From my two big crashes. Spa and Goodwood.'

He had made a point in keeping the steering wheels of the two cars involved in crashes that nearly killed him?

'Of course,' he said, in a tone that questioned why I should be in the slightest bit surprised. 'As one broke my back and both legs, and the other put me into a coma and made me temporarily paralysed, I thought if anyone should have the right to keep them it should be me.'

I shook hands with a true motor-racing legend and thoroughly enjoyable company and thanked him for his time. Turning my back and walking out on to the cobbled street I had already walked ten paces down the road when Stirling called me back.

'You know, those two steering wheels got me loads of sympathy from visiting crumpet as well,' he admitted, with just a slight self-conscious grin.

I sighed and gave him the kind of look you might present a five-year-old with when they've just slopped food down their shirt.

'Well, you may as well get something out of those two crashes,' the irrepressible Sir Stirling Moss reasoned. 'It's not that much to ask, is it?'

chapter eighteen

MANSELL

There was no chance of my place sporting the kind of *James Bond* gadgets evident in a Mayfair mews house. Never mind a descending table, or bath taps that turned themselves and, if Moss had guessed right, women on. Changing a light-bulb was seen as a minor triumph. Putting up a shelf was a once in a lifetime experience. Replacing a tyre was a job for the AA. Whatever qualities my wife married me for, it certainly was not for my practical expertise.

Besides, I was far less convincing when it came to impersonating Bond than Moss was, and he was thirty-four years older than me. I tried using some of the great man's antics the day after my visit, pulling into my drive in my Jaguar car and announcing to my wife as she stood on the doorstep: 'I'm looking for some crumpet.' I expected probable indignation, but possible excitement. I got a put-down, instead. 'Oh really, like that's going to work.'

How come it worked for Moss but not for me? I asked Nigel

Mansell this very same question. 'Well, that's Stirling for you,' the former world champion answered. 'I have to admit, having heard you say it just now, it does nothing for me, either.'

If Stirling Moss was yesteryear's hero, then Nigel Mansell was yesterday's. Like Moss and Schumacher, Mansell is the only other name to feature in a policeman's vocabulary.

There is no doubt there was a time during the late 1980s and early 1990s when traffic police asked whether overly quick drivers believed they were the man from Hall Green. I know this for a fact because someone in a panda car asked me this very question one night late on the M1 motorway.

I was returning from a television studio and assumed, when the constable in the front seat of the panda informed me of my name, that he had just seen me on TV. 'No,' the policeman replied, through gritted teeth. 'I've just looked up your car registration.'

It seemed particularly odd to be then asked if I thought I was Nigel Mansell, considering the man had just told me my name. Still, one of life's golden rules reminded me at the right time not to push my luck any further. Never act a smart arse with a traffic cop.

I mentioned this to Mansell when we met up for a day at his Woodbury Park Golf and Country Resort close to Exeter in Devon. It seemed apt to recount the story to Mansell. After all, he was not only the 1992 Formula One world champion, but had been a special constable in the police force for the past twenty years.

'I don't think Stirling will be pleased to hear this,' he warned, now minus his bushy moustache. I told him how Moss was admonishing my wife for daring to replace his name with that of Michael Schumacher's in the well-worn cliché. 'He'd prefer that to my name,' Mansell replied. 'I'm British you see. I'm stealing his mantle.

'I remember when I finally became world champion in 1992. Stirling was furious. He phoned me up and said: "You bastard.

When people called me the best driver never to win a world title I'd say: 'What about Nigel Mansell?' Now you've gone and won the title it's just me again, isn't it?"'

That's not quite the way Moss told it to me in his Mayfair mews home, but that's one of the many conundrums about sportsmen. They do tend mainly to have a cyclops's view of life.

Before meeting Mansell I had an hour to kill, so took full advantage by wandering around the Nigel Mansell World of Racing, a museum of motor sport and all things of a Mansell nature found in the bowels of the Woodbury Park Hotel.

On the walls and behind the glass of numerous cabinets could be found a vast array of varying photographs and trophies, trinkets, awards and mementoes which, when viewed from start to finish, pretty much chronicled the man's life. Thus, in the same room as world drivers' championship trophies and numerous winning F1 Grands Prix trophies, stood a cabinet with all of his karting awards as a junior, including his very first: second place at Bromsgrove Kart Club.

I rather liked that. I have a very similar trophy at home, too, on my office window sill. Winner in the 1979–80 Stamford and Rutland Table Tennis League Division Two doubles competition. It is the kind of trophy you make in woodwork at school, with a wooden oblong as a base and a thinner oblong placed on top on which a metal shield is stuck. The only difference between myself and Mansell, then, is that I don't also have a Formula One world championship trophy, an Indycar world driver's title, plus thirty-one individual GP wins next to my table-tennis triumph.

Neither do I possess two F1 cars, the Ferrari that won him the Brazilian and Hungarian Grands Prix in 1989 and the Williams–Renault of 1991 that proved to be the forerunner of his greatest triumph the following year, both sitting there shiny and resplendent.

Alongside all this were other, non-motor-sport mementoes.

Signed photos of Gary Player and Arnold Palmer underlined his love of golf. A framed certificate next to these denoted his first hole-in-one, achieved in 1992. Quite a year for Mansell, then, what with scoring his first hole-in-one and winning the world title. 'It's a close call now to say which made me happier,' he admitted.

In another cabinet stood the instantly recognisable BBC Sports Personality of the Year mounted silver camera which he won in 1986, a gold disc presented to him by motor-sport fanatic and singer-songwriter Chris 'Driving Home For Christmas' Rea, and the Manx Sword of State, a huge weapon presented to only five people in its history, four members of the royal family, and Mansell, who lived on the Isle of Man for many years.

Finally, photos of him as a special constable, swimming with 'Flipper', the 'movie star' dolphin, the jaws of a huge shark he caught in South Australia, and as a co-pilot with the 'Red Arrows' vie for the remaining few inches left on the museum walls. All in all it summed up a pretty active and fulfilled life.

Yet, for all these other postcards of his life, he is best-known as one of the most exciting, volatile, risk-taking and incident-ridden Grand Prix drivers in Formula One history. Perhaps it was the fact that he had pushed so hard to get to this point.

Breaking his neck in Formula Ford he fared well enough to get his chance in Formula Three, but only after he sold his house to pay for a drive and moved into rented accommodation, relying on his supportive wife, Roseanne, to earn much of the Mansells' wages. Colin Chapman, the then boss of Lotus, summoned him for a test drive and Mansell, despite having to swallow painkillers after damaging his spine, got the nod to join his first F1 team.

It took him seventy-two Grands Prix to register a first win, the 1985 European GP at Brands Hatch but, thereafter, he never looked back. By the time he finally ended his career in Barcelona in 1995, he had raced in 187 Grands Prix, won thirty-one of them, claimed thirty-two pole positions, 482 world championship points and, of course, won the F1 world title in 1992, as well as the Indycar Championships in 1993, making him the only man in history to hold simultaneously both titles.

But this barely scratches the surface. Whenever Mansell was about, something was guaranteed to happen. The list is endless but incidents include darting past Nelson Piquet at Stowe Corner to win the 1987 British Grand Prix at Silverstone, overtaking Ayrton Senna to win in Hungary, passing Gerhard Berger on the outside of the notorious Peraltada in Mexico, going side by side with Senna in Spain at 200 mph until the Brazilian backed off as both sets of wheels set off sparks, losing the 1986 World Championship title in Adelaide when a tyre blew with just eighteen laps remaining at 190 mph, tossing his gloves into the crowd to denote his first retirement in 1990, his acrimonious departure from Williams three years later, and so on.

The odd thing about the man was that he clearly made high-ranking enemies, even among those he worked for and served up success with. He won twenty-eight of his thirty-one Grands Prix with Williams, for example, yet Frank Williams once famously described him as 'a pain in the arse', while Patrick Head said: 'Nigel thinks everyone is trying to shaft him at all times, and that can be extremely wearing.' The media, especially in Britain, laid into him often enough as well, finding him at fault for everything from his consistent complaining to even his Brummie accent and moustache.

But the British public saw it very differently. Mansell was unquestionably the 'People's Champion', a man who could cram 150,000 into Silverstone off the back of his own appearance in the British Grand Prix. In fairness, it wasn't just in Britain, either. The *tifosi* in Italy loved him every bit as much when he raced for Ferrari for a couple of seasons, nicknaming him 'Il Leone', in the process for his undoubted bravery in races.

I was very keen to hear the man's story but Mansell, now a convert to golf, insisted that I could only if I followed him around his golf course. His seventeen-year-old son, Greg, would be joining us for a few holes, and I would be put in charge of driving the buggy.

Now, driving a golf buggy would not normally present any kind of problem to me, even if, during the process of writing my last book, I managed to prang one or two, notably at St Andrews on the Fife coast in Scotland, and at the K Club, just south of Dublin, in Ireland. But being Nigel Mansell's chauffeur seemed, for some reason, to be a nerve-wracking experience, made worse by the fact that when he asked me to collect the buggy, he watched me surge forward and into the buggy parked in front of me, when I was supposed to be reversing away from the parking area.

'I saw that,' Mansell said, with a laugh.

I'd managed by now to drive an F1 car, a world rally car, various single-seater racing cars, a Lotus and an Audi touring car at Silverstone, as well as a souped-up Mini Cooper and various karts, yet in front of one of the best racing drivers of all time I'd just crashed a golf buggy.

Unperturbed by this setback Mansell insisted that I continued and was still laughing at what he had just seen as I drove him to the first tee. His interest in motor racing, so he explained as he sized up what driver should be used from his large selection of clubs, was encouraged by his father, Eric. At seven he was driving a petrol go-kart around his garden in the West Midlands. Inspired by watching Jim Clark win the British GP at Aintree, Mansell took up kart racing, proved to be a success (as, indeed, his second place in the Bromsgrove Kart Club proves) and began his life as a professional driver in 1976 at the age of twenty-two.

Mansell and his wife, Roseanne, were so convinced that he would make it one day that they sold their house and moved into rented accommodation to fund the early stages of his career. 'Looking back that decision was bordering on insanity,' Mansell admitted twenty-eight years later on. 'But at the time we were so single-minded and we believed so strongly that I would make it in motor sport that we thought nothing of selling the house. Roseanne was right behind me. It was a belief that proved to be justified.'

Within two years he had been offered the job of test driver with Colin Chapman's Team Lotus F1 team. This was after Chapman, who founded Lotus as an engineer and had been building winning cars since the 1960s, had seen him test driving a F3 car. Typically, Mansell was recovering from that broken neck at the time, but did not want to lose the opportunity of impressing Chapman.

While he was informing me of all this he was nonchalantly playing golf, taking next to no time in sizing up his shots before depositing the ball consistently within a few feet of the hole. Greg, his son, was doing likewise, and I, already feeling singularly untalented, was hauling Mansell's clubs around.

Chapman died in 1982 and, three years later, Mansell moved to Williams, winning his first two Grands Prix and setting up what, for mainly the wrong reasons, would be a memorable year for him.

It was in 1986 that he all but won and then lost the world title, having held a six-point lead entering the last race of the season, and it was the same year when the death of a colleague transformed Mansell's approach. First, the world title that ended up in Alain Prost's hands.

'At the time it was horrible,' Mansell began, the word 'horrible' sounding especially enforced not because he had wanted to underline the emotion, but due to the fact that I had just slammed on the buggy's brakes. 'It was lap sixty-four in Adelaide when the left rear tyre suddenly exploded. It took nearly a quarter of a mile to bring the car under control. I was sitting comfortably in third place, which was all I needed to do, and after a whole season it was down to the last race, and the last forty-four miles of the race. It was the biggest disappointment of my whole career.'

What made it worse was what he discovered later. 'The president of the FIA asked me to come to the end-of-season world championship awards in Paris,' he explained. 'I really didn't want to go. I had nothing to celebrate, but he told me if I failed to show up I'd be fired. At the ceremony I sat next to a clerk of the course. He started to commiserate with me about my misfortune in Adelaide. "Do you know what would have happened if you'd crashed?" he then asked me, which struck me as odd.

'"Yes," I replied. "I would have broken both legs, or, worse, killed myself."

'He said: "If you'd crashed there would have been debris all over the track and the race would have been stopped. Because the race had gone beyond two thirds of the distance the rules state that it would not be restarted and then you would have been crowned world champion." So I lost the world title twice on that day.'

Mansell halted this story just for a second to remonstrate with me for driving the buggy down the wrong turning, the end result being that instead of depositing the former world champion next to the third tee, we seemed to have ended up in the middle of a small copse.

'Is there a moral to this story?' I asked, hoping to deflect Mansell's attention from a squirrel that had just squirted alarmingly up a silver birch.

'Yes, there is,' he said. 'When you're going at 200 mph down the home straight during the last Grand Prix of the season, and when you're just forty-four laps away from winning your first world title, take the fucking rule book and read it.'

Quite, although at 200 mph it would not be too easy to flick through the rule book. He still managed to win the BBC Sports Personality of the Year award, though, despite finishing runner-up that year in the driver's title race.

1986 also saw the death of Elio de Angelis, an incident that changed Mansell's take on motor racing and life indelibly. The popular Italian died during testing at the Paul Ricard circuit, an incident that has affected Mansell to this day. 'The most significant event of my life,' is how he put it. 'Elio's car caught fire. Keke Rosberg and myself rushed over from the pits and although we tried to extinguish it there was nothing we could do. He was upside down in his car and we couldn't get him out. For Keke it was enough. He couldn't take any more of this and quit that season.'

And for Mansell? 'For me it was the day when Formula One changed from a game to a job. I decided that if I was going to stay in this game I was not only going to make it pay, but I was going to make it successful. My whole mentality changed from that day on. F1 wasn't supposed to be real life. But watching Elio die was just about as real life as you can get. From then on it became serious shit.'

Sooner or later, when in conversation with any driver from the early 1990s and before, the subject of death came up. Over the past few months it had reared its head in Adelaide and on a yacht as it bobbed up and down in a Taupo marina in North Island, New Zealand. It had shown its horrific face again inside the cockpit of a passenger airliner, an organic farm and inside a Mayfair mews house. Now the cold stench was back again, this time on a rolling golfing fairway, on a crisp, early winter's day, with the sun shining down on the first, green slopes of Dartmoor on the horizon.

It had not quite sunk in down in New Zealand, although, judging by Amon's graphic testimony, it should have done. Maybe not even after a day with a horribly scarred Austrian. But now, finally, it had. All the glamour surrounding Formula One was a perception created by others. The drivers, certainly pre-1990, danced with death and, post-1990, still faced a danger none of us do almost every day of their lives. There were too many ghosts haunting the drivers to make it exclusively enjoyable.

'That's probably my greatest achievement,' Mansell explained, interrupting my thoughts. 'Just being here. I lost twenty-four friends in Formula One. It could, and often should have been me. We'd have a drivers' line-up at the start of each season and I'd look across at everyone and know that maybe three of us wouldn't be making the line-up the following year. We all felt we were bullet-proof. A lot of drivers changed this view after Ayrton Senna died. Mine was transformed after Elio.' He nodded at his son, Greg, who rattles in a long putt with consummate ease. 'He's never going into it, that's for sure. I couldn't put his mother through it.'

There was another, more practical reason, that underlined Mansell's own achievements. 'Look at the size of him,' he whispered, out of Greg's earshot. He had a point. Although not exactly huge Greg was on the tall side. Although one or two other of today's F1 drivers are of medium height – notably Jenson Button and Mark Webber – the majority look as if they have just emerged from a jockey's weighing room at a horse-racing course.

'I was one of the biggest and heaviest drivers in the history of the sport. It cost me a lot of time on the circuit. I gave away 40 lbs, for example, to both Senna and Alain Prost. We worked it out as 0.4 seconds per lap. Over a seventy lap Grand Prix, that's a major disadvantage.'

Like Amon and Scheckter Mansell also drove for Ferrari. 'I was the last driver to be appointed by Enzo Ferrari before his death,' he pointed out. 'The one thing I remember about the old man more than anything else was this.' He pointed a finger into the air. 'That's all he had to do. The moment he did this everyone else fell silent. That was the hold and the power the man held.'

During all this time, when not being driven down dead ends by his chauffeur, Mansell was playing golf and making it look effortlessly easy. In 1992, back with a much-improved Williams, he made F1 look effortlessly easy, too, although it was plain to see he had the best car.

The year before he had won five times for Williams, but lost out to Senna in the world championship race. Having recorded a third runner-up spot in the drivers' championship Mansell was growing increasingly desperate, but he also knew, as he entered 1992, that his would be the best car. In typical Mansell fashion, he refused to let a season-threatening injury get in his way.

'In the last race of 1991, the Australian GP, I had a big crash and smashed my left foot. The diagnosis was a major fracture, and the prognosis was that I'd be finding driving very difficult. I kept this to myself, underwent three months of rehab and had special shoes made. The media didn't know anything about this at the time, and decided that I looked absolutely wrecked after each Grand Prix because of my size and the usual effort I ploughed into my racing. The truth was that for that time I was in pain.'

Pain or no pain he rattled up wins in the first five races of the season, a feat equalled by Schumacher in 2004, and nine victories in total to wrap up the 1992 world driver's championship by August with still five races remaining. This was the year that Schumacher, driving a Benetton, won his first Grand Prix, in Belgium, to provide a taste of things to come.

Mansell wanted to make a point about these times once I'd mentioned the word 'Schumacher'.

'Don't get me wrong about Schumacher. I admire him enormously, and for what he's done. You have to give him credit for his driving. And you have to appreciate how he's pushed Ferrari up to where they are today.'

You sensed a 'but' was coming along very shortly. 'But, timing is everything with Michael. I could sense the first shoots of recovery just when I left Ferrari in 1990. Michael's car has not broken down since 2001. If you have a car that is virtually guaranteed to complete every Grand Prix then it's almost "job done". If you then have the two best drivers in the world in your team, then the end result is a dead cert. It seems to me that Ferrari have all departments covered.

'I have two arguments against Michael being the best of the

best. The first is the competition. Or rather the lack of it. Look at the drivers on the grid for much of the time when I was around. Nelson Piquet, Senna, Prost, Jody Scheckter early on, Alan Jones too, Niki Lauda, Keke Rosberg, myself. All world champions. There were plenty of other great drivers, too.

'My point is that I liken that collection of drivers to the great days of heavyweight boxing in the 1970s when Ali, Frazier and Foreman were around. All those drivers were proven winners. All could win on their day. And all had been world champions. The competition was enormous, and it brought the best out of all of us. Okay, so there were plenty of rivalries, and we didn't all get on with each other, but there was plenty of respect. For Michael, apart from Mika Hakkinen, who has been and gone, there is no-one. I only hope Jenson Button can mount some kind of a challenge in 2005.'

His other point is the one made by Stirling Moss. 'It's unbelievable to think about the driving conditions the likes of Stirling and especially Fangio faced. No seatbelts. No helmets. One slip and it's most probably fatal. I think all us later drivers have to give the guys in the 1950s our complete respect.'

We had reached the seventh green now and Mansell's ball, as ever, was perched neatly within a couple of feet of the hole. All this talk of Schumacher and Fangio had made us forget about Mansell's year, 1992. It should have been the greatest time of his life. But it wasn't.

Clearly still bitter, he explained himself. 'I had just achieved a lifetime ambition and was then offered half my salary to stay at Williams. I was pushed out of the team for Prost, and then watched him win the 1993 world title. That was after winning twenty-eight Grands Prix for Williams.'

Despite this obvious hurt to his pride Mansell did not just slink away. That was not his style. Instead he joined up with the Newman-Haas (Newman as in Paul Newman) CART team in

America, winning the championship in his first year as a rookie. 'Four drivers in history have won both the F1 and Indycar championships,' he told me, clearly relishing this achievement so soon after his acrimonious split with Williams. 'Emerson Fittipaldi, Mario Andretti, Jacques Villeneuve and myself. But I'm the only one to have held both titles simultaneously.'

Thereafter his racing career petered out. From then on, save for the briefest of comebacks with McLaren and his heavy charity commitments (Mansell is President of UK Youth, for example, which works in areas such as drugs rehabilitation and helping teenage single mothers), life has been spent on the golf course.

Initially this was in Florida, latterly in Devon, where he bought and developed Woodbury Park, and now Jersey, where he and Roseanne live in tax exile. 'This,' he proclaimed, waving his golf putter around to show the surrounding environment, 'is my third world title. I've put £10 million into this place and turned it into a championship golf course. Golf is my love now, and I wish it had always been so.'

Meaning? 'Meaning that if I could live my life again I would have become a golfer. You can't have comebacks in motor racing. But you can in golf. It doesn't matter if you are a millionaire or not in golf, like it does in Formula One. All that matters is a few sticks and a ball. I think motor racing sucks now. It's far too political, and it's far too hard to make it these days.'

The final putt rattled into the ninth hole and I drove Mansell back to the clubhouse, with young Greg behind us in another buggy. Greg is named after his godfather, Greg Norman, who basked in the world number one status in golf at around the same time Mansell enjoyed his heyday. There is a Greg Norman suite at Woodbury Park, as well as a Colin Chapman suite. 'Two of my greatest friends and influences,' Mansell explained, as we sped past in the buggy.

I had been at Woodbury Park for over four hours. It was time for me to head back to London. Just as I was about to thank Mansell for his time he asked me about my motor-racing credentials.

'Well, you are looking at a bona fide racing driver,' I told him, on the basis of my ARDS licence.

'Yes,' he asked, clearly expecting more.

'I've driven an F1 car at Santa Pod. Raced Mini Coopers against Montoya. Taken on Markko Martin in the Ford World Rally Car. Plus lots and lots of other driving experiences.'

'And did you mention you wanted to take on Schumacher?'

I was feeling slightly awkward now. Over the past few months the word 'Schumacher' had loomed large and menacingly over me. Now, when posed the question by Mansell, it seemed a ridiculous and contemptible idea. There was still no sign of it actually happening. And, if it did, it would probably be a complete waste of the great man's time. 'Well, yes, as a matter of fact I do.'

'Just how do you think you're going to manage that, then?'

It was a good question, and still I possessed no answer.

Mansell shook my hand again, started to make his way back into the main foyer of Woodbury Park and turned round for one final comment.

'Well, good luck against Schumcher,' he added. 'But here's a tip for you. If you get it on, don't do it in a golf buggy because you've got no chance.'

Not in a golf buggy, not in a milk float, not in a racing car.

chapter nineteen

JENSON

It was still dark in the car park of the Valencia motor-racing circuit. Suddenly the door to a motor home blasted open, almost belting me in the process, and out from inside came a head, looking one way, then the next, followed by a big, cheesy grin.

'Morning, morning,' said Jenson Button.

Jules Kulpinski, his ever-present Australian facilitator, media manager, personal assistant and virtually you name it, cleared her throat and started her breathless Marilyn Monroe impersonation.

'Happy burthday, to yoooooo, happy burthday to yooooo, happy birthday Mr Button, happy burthday to yooooo.'

'Very nice, very sexy,' said the man who was supposed to be enjoying his twenty-fifth birthday in Milan with his then singer/songwriter girlfriend Louise Griffiths, but instead would be spending much of the day with me, instead, at a test track on the south-west coast of Spain.

That, I hasten to add, was not entirely my fault. The

BAR–Honda team should have been testing in Barcelona earlier in the week but upped their camp and moved down the coast after the newly resurfaced circuit proved far too slow. So, instead, Button and the rest of his team, plus the sleeping Louise in the motor home, found themselves in Valencia.

It was not all bad news, I reasoned with him, as I dug my hand into my overnight bag and pulled out a book. As a birthday present I thought I would present him with my last sporting participatory book. What a generous chap I can be! Unfortunately I pulled out of my bag first a paperback entitled *The Perfect Puppy*, a tome my wife was forcing me to read in readiness for the arrival of a young labrador at our home. Realising immediately what I had done I swiftly replaced it with my golf book.

'Actually, can I have the puppy book,' the birthday boy reacted. Oh yes. It was going to be one of those days. Jenson was a happy boy, on good form, and clearly up for some cheeky chappie banter.

I had been attempting to spend some time with Button for much of the past year. I believed that understanding what makes Britain's most exciting current driver tick, and a man whom many believe will win the world title sooner rather than later, was imperative to my own quest which was about to culminate in glory or abject failure.

The week before my trip to Valencia I had been told about an end of season event called the 'Race of Champions', a motor-sport extravaganza to be staged in the Stade de France in Paris, and featuring many of the world's leading racing drivers including, lo and behold, Michael Schumacher. I despatched a pleading email to the event's organiser. Maybe, just maybe, there was a glimmer of hope.

It was an indication of Button's standing in global sport, meanwhile, that it had taken this long to find a suitable slot in his packed diary, and even this was coinciding with an important day of testing. Sure, we had exchanged a few words in Shanghai, and nodded to each other inside Monaco's Amber Lounge, but this was the first time when we could share the best part of a day together.

What I had always liked about the man was his incessant jocularity. As I had discovered, most of the other F1 drivers were characters, too, but you had to dig a lot further and duck beneath the numerous barricades before unearthing this. With Button it was there right in front of you. There was something wonderfully unpolished about Jenson which, with luck, will remain the case. No soundbites or rehearsed, predictable statements. What you saw was what you got with this man.

I remembered five years before, when Button had just made it into F1, attending a Button family christening for a glossy magazine. I was supposed to be writing about it, but spent most of the day quaffing champagne on the Button family's insistence, sunbathing alongside Jenson by a pool, or observing his seaside postcard smile after he emerged from a room with a girlfriend. And this, don't forget, was at a family christening where elderly aunts and grandmothers were present.

We breakfasted in the makeshift BAR canteen pegged on to the side of a huge truck. Everyone who passed by from the BAR team wished him a happy birthday, which rather stymied the theory that, after Jenson's ill-fated attempt to leave BAR towards the end of the 2004 season for Williams, life might be difficult for him in 2005.

Jenson was brought up in Frome, Somerset (pronounced Froom – every time you say 'Frome' he is quick to point out your error), where, on his seventh birthday, his father, John, bought him a go-kart.

'It was the most fantastic present I've ever had,' he recalled, his eyes wild with excitement despite the early hour. 'I expected a football. Or maybe a dreadful hand-knitted jumper from one of my aunts.' He impersonated the reaction we have all been forced to produce at such moments. 'Hmmm, er, uhm, that's lovely, and look, it almost fits!'

John, now a regular sight on the F1 circuit as he follows his son around the world with the look of man who believed in his boy and came up trumps, used to race a little in rally cross. 'He also owned a Gulf which was the noisiest thing I've ever heard. I used to sneak into the garage and start the engine up. It almost blew my ears off.'

Before then he was, despite his name, a regular kid. Did he, for example, have posters on his bedroom wall of Mansell, or Senna, or Piquet?

'Did I hell,' he replied, rolling his eyes and stuffing his mouth full of fruit. 'I had Pamela Anderson and Bart Simpson on my wall.'

What, together?

'Oh yeah, of course. Wouldn't you like to know what they got up to.'

We've digressed, which isn't hard to do in conversation with Button, and something which would become a feature of the day. One moment we're talking about possible posters of motor-racing stars. The next we're conjuring up images of Mr and Mrs Bart and Pamela Simpson.

The go-kart proved to be the catalyst. He'd race it around kart tracks and, when unable to do this, he'd race it around the car park at his local pub. 'Only when it was shut, of course,' he added, lest one got the impression that he mowed down elderly couples gingerly making their way for Sunday lunch.

'I remember I'd done two or three races (which he'd won) when, at the age of eight, I'd be watching the likes of Senna and Prost and saying to my Dad: "Why are they making so many mistakes?" Then, at Suzuka, I remember they crashed. "Dad, why have they crashed? They shouldn't be doing that. They're professional."'

As he says this he mimicked the voice of an eight-year-old boy. Later he took a call from a local Somerset radio station and started making a strange, strangled whining noise down the telephone. 'That was the sound of an F1 car,' he announced, proudly, when I asked him what he thought he was doing.

Any particular car?

'Oh, probably an Arrows. I can do a Williams, if you like, or a McLaren!' He make a 'eeeoooowwww' noise to prove his point, although I reckoned it sounded more like a Renault. 'Ooops, sorry,' he apologised, raising his hand up in recognition of his guttural error.

Anyway, that was that. Every weekend from the age of eight Button raced karts. Early on in his 'career' he beat a bunch of twelve-year-olds. 'I would have been annoyed if I'd been twelve and just beaten by a scrawny eight-year-old.' His contemporaries at school thought he was bordering on the weird side. 'Well, I never saw them at weekends because I was always racing.'

All this changed one morning during school assembly with one of those seminal moments in life you never forget, despite your future achievements. 'The headmaster had me wheeled on to the stage in my go-kart,' Button revealed, his head in his hands now as he shook it from side to side. 'I'd just become British junior karting champion. I sat in the car with my helmet not saying a word while he went on about what a fantastic achievement it was, and that the rest of the kids could also achieve if they worked hard at school. Then I got wheeled off again. Before that moment everyone thought I was a bit different. You don't want to be seen as different when you're eleven. But after that day everyone thought I was cool.'

There is an additional line to this story, and one that Button is almost gagging to tell me. 'Do you want to know the name of my headmaster?' he asked.

Er, well yes, go on then.

'Master Bates,' came back the answer, coupled with a number of hearty bangs on the table. 'Head Master Bates.' There are almost tears in his eyes by now at this recollection. 'Can you believe that?'

This explained why surprisingly few teased him about being called Jenson Button. 'Let's face it, when your headmáster's called that, Jenson Button seems pretty normal in comparison,' he reasoned.

At this point he has to leave my company for a few minutes in order to sit in the car. 'Gotta make sure everything fits before I start testing,' he explained as he set off to the BAR garage.

We reconvened half an hour later, this time in his motor home. Jenson is stripped down to his underwear and lying, face down, on a masseur's table while his physio, Phil Young, is rubbing him down in readiness for what would prove to be a taxing day behind the wheel.

Phil used to be the team physio at Benetton, where Button spent years two and three of his F1 career, before moving across to BAR to stay in partnership together. Formally physio for the British cycling team, Phil explained to us how cyclists begin to lose their bodily powers during the last lap of a 1k sprint, the event in which Jason Queally won Olympic gold in Sydney, and Chris Hoy in Athens.

Jenson had to take a quick call on his mobile from his mother, wishing him a happy birthday. You might have thought his mobile would possess a trendy tune. Instead, it was a little Mexican ditty that went on and on and on. Any moment we were expecting the motor home door to blast open again and a man wearing a sombrero and bullet-studded belts criss-crossing his torso to enter. Throughout all this time Louise remained asleep in the back of the motor home.

At the age of fourteen Button decided he wanted to become a Formula One driver. Didn't everyone else think the same? That they were fantastically talented, and that they would make it?

'Maybe, but I had the results to prove it,' he explained, his face now sticking through the small hole at the top of the masseur's table.

Then came the true test of his resolve. From fifteen to seventeen he lived and worked in Belgium. 'I worked in my kart-team boss's workshop. I didn't enjoy it very much. I didn't know anyone, I mostly worked alone at his workshop or testing the karts out on the circuit, I couldn't speak any Flemish, and I often wondered what I was doing.'

This self-imposed exile seemed to do the trick, however. At seventeen, he explained, he became the European senior kart champion. I told him that I had done a fair bit of karting over the previous few months, but the conditions were always unfavourable, which is why I had failed to win any of the races.

'That's good,' Button replied, smirking. 'You're making excuses. That's the sign of a good motor-racing driver.'

From seventeen onwards Button's rise to F1 was both successful and meteoric. In 1998 he became British and world champion in Formula Ford, then followed this up with a third place in the Formula Three championship driving an unreliable car. By winning the Young Driver of the Year award part of his prize, as well as £50,000, was to get to test drive a McLaren F1 car at Silverstone.

'It remains one of the most amazing experiences of my life,' he recalled. 'I was so nervous about stalling it. I came out of the pits, accelerated and couldn't then stop screaming and laughing my head off. The whole garage could hear me over the radio but I didn't care. I'd been watching F1 for twelve years, I'd studied all the greats, and now I was driving a Formula One car.'

I leant over and told him that I, too, had driven a Formula One car, the Jaguar, at Santa Pod, and immediately felt like a fraud. 'Oh, well that's just great,' Button responded. 'So I spent twelve years karting all over Europe, missing out on all those weekends, driving Formula Fords and Formula Three's, just to get to this moment, and you just turn up at Santa Pod and get in one!'

Well, yes, that was more or less it. And, like Button, but not like Niki Lauda, I didn't stall it either. 'Bloody hell,' Jenson reacted. 'I may only be the second best racing driver in Britain, then.'

He should have completed twenty laps in that McLaren but, after twelve, he drove back to the garage. 'The tyres were getting old and I knew I couldn't go any quicker. I didn't want slower laps to spoil the moment.'

Within weeks, after constant badgering from his father and management team, Button was given another test, this time by Alain Prost, whose Prost F1 team would later go out of business. 'It was just to have a look at me with the future in mind. Jean Alesi (the experienced French Grand Prix driver) had tested the same car the day before but when I finished my session I discovered I had been two tenths of a second faster than Alesi.'

This had been just his second ever drive in an F1 car. Word quickly spread until one afternoon, drinking in a pub just before Christmas in 1999 with friends, he received a telephone call on his mobile.

'I was at the Vine Tree,' Button reminisced. If I were the landlord of the Vine Tree I would place a plaque on the wall to denote a moment which may go down in the history of motor sport.

'I didn't recognise the number and when I, amid the din of the pub, heard someone saying it was Frank Williams on the other end of the line I was far from convinced it wasn't a hoax.'

It was not. Reconvening the conversation in the relative quiet of the pub car park Button made a quite unbelievable error. 'Hello Jenson, I've heard a lot about you. Are you ready for Formula One?'

Button gave this question a couple of seconds thought and replied: 'No, I need more testing.'

He shook his head at this response. 'I thought it was the right thing to say. Anyway, how could I be ready? My team-mate would be Ralf Schumacher, and I'd be up against Michael Schumacher.'

What did Williams say? 'He said, "That's very honest of you, Jenson."' Button put on what he thought was a Frank Williams accent this time. It had been quite a morning when it came to impersonations. We'd had an eight-year-old boy, at least two different F1 cars, and now Williams.

At this point, tantalisingly, Button had to begin testing. We walked together over to the BAR garage, where I was presented with a set of headphones and watched Button clamber into his car. 'It's an exciting point in the story to take a break, isn't it?' he said, just before placing his helmet over his head.

I noticed that while David Coulthard proudly wore his Scottish Saltire on his helmet, the Union Jack was resplendent on Button's helmet and boots. 'We're mainly data-logging in the morning session,' Button had explained. 'Just making sure everything's working before this afternoon.'

For the next couple of hours he lapped the Valencia circuit, sometimes alone, and sometimes accompanied by other teams all taking an early look at what to expect for the 2005 season. It was an important time because, that afternoon, he would be simulating a full Grand Prix.

In the meantime I took a stroll around the Valencia circuit. Button has his own group of loyal supporters known as Jenson's Barmy Army, a gaggle of petrol-heads who follow just about his every move. On this special day one group had parked their people carrier right next to Button's motor home, and decked out their car with 'Happy Birthday Jenson' banners, normally accompanied by Union Jacks.

Midway through the session he took a quick toilet break. 'Bet you're wondering what happened after I told Frank I wasn't ready, aren't you?' he said, with a grin.

An hour later we were both sitting in his motor home again,

ploughing through a pasta dish that his physio, Phil, referred to as a 'power lunch', and joined by Louise, who had woken from her slumbers.

'Er, so where we were?' Button asked, as he covered his pasta in parmesan. 'Ah yes. I'm outside the pub. As soon as the line had gone dead I thought, "Why the hell did I say that?" I told my Dad and he nearly had a fit. "You're fucking joking," I think was his response.

'Anyway, he and my management persuaded Frank to meet me. I went along to the Williams headquarters very nervous, and in a suit. I told Frank that, actually, on second thoughts, I was ready for F1. He replied, "Well, Jenson, I have lists of people who think they can drive for me and can test for me, and you're not on either of them.'

'I sat there and thought, "Er, so why am I here?" Frank told me it was nice to meet me in any case and then, a couple of days later, called to invite me to test.'

It turned out to be a straightforward shoot-out between Button and the more experienced Giancarla Bruni. 'I convinced myself I wouldn't get it. Frank and Patrick Head were old school, they weren't risk takers, I was less experienced than Bruni, and he had far more technical knowledge.'

After two days of testing in Barcelona Button was summoned to the Williams office. Not surprisingly, Button can remember every second of the meeting. '"Hello Jenson, come in," Frank began,' Jenson recalled, again reverting to his Williams impersonation. '"How are you?"

'I said, "Fine, thank you," but I was thinking, "Just bloody tell me the verdict." Frank bowed his head for a second, then looked me straight in the eye. "Jenson we've decided to choose you to drive the Williams car. You'll be alongside Ralf for this year."

'As I stood there gobsmacked, in walked Ralf. He started to shout at Frank about not having a car to take him to the circuit.

"The next time that happens I won't come testing," Button declaimed, now putting on a German accent. I was beginning to feel as if I were in the company of Rory Bremner.

'"Calm down, Ralf, calm down," Frank said. "I've chosen Jenson for the drive." Ralf gave me a quick glance and said, "Oh, I know that, Frank. I knew Jenson was going to get it." With that he walked out.

'Outside the door my dad was waiting. I said to him, "Dad, I'm going to be a Formula One driver." And then we both burst into tears.' At the time Jenson Button was still only nineteen years old.

Louise is listening to all this and gives her boyfriend a squeeze of the hand at this point. 'It's great hearing all this,' she says, with the first signs of a tear in her eye.

The next five years would prove to be a fascinating time for Button. In year one, with Williams, he would score twelve championship points in the days when, remember, points were awarded only down to sixth place in a race.

His arrival was met with a mixed reception. Michael Schumacher, for example, was welcoming. '"Good luck," Michael told me. "It should be a great experience for you."' Others weren't quite so accommodating. 'Because I was so young and inexperienced I hadn't actually completed enough testing to earn a super-licence which was required to drive in F1. Jacques Villeneuve and Mika Salo both argued that I shouldn't be given it, but we asked Bernie Ecclestone nicely and he granted the licence.'

There is an irony to this story. We were sitting in the motor home once owned by Villeneuve, who sold it on to Salo, who then sold it to Button. 'Makes me enjoy spending time in here even more,' Button explained, with a broad grin.

By the end of that first season the data proved that not only had Button made fewer errors than anyone else on the grid, despite his obvious lack of experience, but that he was also out-qualifying his team-mate, Ralf Schumacher. Yet Williams had been pursuing

Montoya for a number of years and, when they had the chance to capture his signature, Button was leased out to Benetton.

Thus started the worst year of his short career in F1. Handed a poor car he managed to score just two points and, worse still, was heavily criticised for what was perceived to be the speed in which he had adopted a 'playboy' lifestyle. It came to a head at Monaco when his boat, *Little Missy*, was parked right beside the paddock.

'I wouldn't have got negative press if I'd been winning,' he pointed out. 'But I guess it was a mistake to park it in that particular berth. It was not a good idea to have a boat, but only because it gave people ammunition. I didn't enjoy the year at the time but, looking back, it put me in good stead. Up until then everything had come easily to me. This was just about my first experience of failure. I realised then I couldn't simply rely on my talent.'

The following year he worked much harder in the garage. He learnt the importance of driver input, created a better working atmosphere and, in assembling fourteen points, out-scored his teammate, Jarno Trulli.

At this point he decided not to take the easy option. Although offered drives with Jaguar, Jordan and Toyota, he went for BAR, and this meant teaming up with the notorious Villeneuve. 'Yeah, I like it easy, don't I?' Button laughed at this juncture in his story. 'Everyone in the paddock knew that Jacques liked to destroy his team-mate.'

Sure enough, at the launch day of the new 2003 BAR F1 car, Villeneuve likened Button to a 'member of a boy band who won't do any good'.

'I was already gaining a great deal of support from the team. They wanted Jacques to do well, of course, but they knew what he was like and told me to look after myself. When I heard Jacques' comments it only served to motivate me that much more.' Motivate him enough to score seventeen points and see off Villeneuve who quit in ignominy before the end of the season.

It would prove to be the launchpad for the 2004 season in which Button not only scored eighty-five points and finished third behind the two Ferrari drivers, but helped BAR to second in the constructors' championship, and secured his first-ever podium place with a third place in Malaysia at only the second GP of the year. He would go on to secure ten podium finishes in a remarkably consistent year, including eight second places.

It was not all plain sailing, though. Towards the end of the season he became embroiled in a controversy that saw him attempt to leave BAR for Williams for the 2005 season. From afar it did not appear that Button had been best advised on this matter, and when the Contract Recognition Board decided in BAR's favour, it put an end to the issue. 'It was an uncomfortable time for me and I wish it hadn't happened,' he reflected, his face losing its hitherto permanent smile for a second or two.

'I'm happy that's all over. I received some bad press. Some of it I deserved.' Really? 'Yes, I did, not for wanting to move to Williams, but for not speaking to [previous BAR head] Dave Richards. As you can see, it's not a problem with the team any more. We're all working really well together.'

Apart from this hiccup the season, on the track, delivered most of Button's childhood aspirations. 'Absolutely awesome,' was Button's own description of his best ever year in F1. 'Getting that first podium had been a massive goal for me to achieve but, funnily enough, once I'd done it a couple of times, I immediately set my sights higher. After all, I was still looking up at the bloke in red on top of the podium.' Meaning, of course, Michael Schumacher.

'Do you know, this is my sixth year in Formula One now. Every season so far Schumacher's become world champion. I don't know of anything else. I can't make any excuses from now on. I'm no longer the promising youngster. I see myself as a senior pro in the sport now.

'I am absolutely convinced that I will become world champion, providing I'm given the car to do so. It's not about the money. It's never been about the money. I earn a good enough salary and wouldn't go to another team just to make more like some of the other drivers. It's because I want to be the best in my field. I'm not yet, but I aim to be.'

It was time for the afternoon's testing session. 'Seventy-five laps. Not so much fun as in a race because I'm not up against anyone, but it's crucial for the car and for the tyres. By the time we begin the season proper in Australia we'll know exactly what this car can do.'

After thirty laps, however, the engine blew, mainly because Button had been instructed to push the car to its absolute limits. His testing would end an hour earlier, although he still faced post-mortems later with both the engineers and tyre specialists.

The sun was rapidly descending on the Spanish horizon and the moon had appeared, surrounded by a darkening blue sky. Back in the motor home Louise was talking of her hopes in breaking through in the music industry. Button, on inspecting a dirty patch on my jeans, was telling me to sue my dry cleaner. And, having twice tripped over his motor home steps, citing large feet as the problem, both Jenson and Louise said in unison: 'You know what they say about large feet? Large shoes!'

It had been that type of day. I had one final subject to talk about. Taking on Schumacher. 'Er, just give it your best, don't hold back, and hope he makes a mistake,' was the advice Button delivered.

I looked across at a young, smiling man, sitting inside his fabulously expensive motor home, with his beautiful girlfriend. Button had flipped open his laptop lid and started gazing at private jets, one of which he was about to hire for 20,000 euros to fly him to Vienna. I thought about suggesting Air Niki. Then I remembered my day in the cockpit with Lauda and thought better of it.

All those lost weekends as a kid, the embarrassment of being wheeled on to the school stage, the lonely years in Belgium. It all appeared well worth it to me. But if I had been given a kart at the age of eight, and raced it all my formative years, I still would not have found myself sitting in a similar position today.

Why, then, was Jenson Button a better racing driver than me?

'I take your point,' he replied. 'Of course there's been a lot of hours, a lot of dedication, and probably some raw talent obtained from my dad and granddad, both of whom raced a little. But ultimately, I don't really have a clue.'

He shrugged his shoulders to underline his cluelessness, then followed it up with an 'Aha. On second thoughts I do. It's all down to your arse.'

I'm sorry? 'It's down to feel, much of it from your arse. It's something I have, and maybe you don't.'

Button really had to dash now to make his first post-mortem. So what was his point?

'It's simple, Ian,' he concluded. 'I have a better arse than you.'

And with that he and his better arse were gone.

chapter twenty

KERPEN: WHERE THE STORY BEGINS

Alexander, the taxi driver, was keen to talk about Michael Schumacher. 'He is the best, ja, the best in the world,' he said. 'There will never be another like him. We are proud of him. Very proud of Michael.'

He said 'we' not only because we were in Germany, but also due to the fact that we were driving along Michael Schumacher Strasse at the time, heading towards the Michael Schumacher Kart Centre in the hamlet of Kerpen-Sindorf, a twenty-five-minute journey from Cologne.

I had come to the home of the legend to see for myself how it all began, and his legacy on an area of Nordrhein-Westfalen known throughout the world as the place where Schumi grew up honing his driving skills. I was in Schumacher territory, and it was immediately clear to the senses.

There was another reason, though. But I had also come to pit my questionable driving skills against the man. Schumacher wasn't actually there, of course, but I wanted to get to know my now increasingly possible opponent. My excitement had grown considerably a few days before arranging this trip to Kerpen after receiving an email back from the chief of the Race of Champions in Paris. 'Maybe, and I'm only saying maybe, we can put you in the same car as Michael will be driving, record your fastest lap, and then ask him to see if he can beat it,' wrote back Fredrik Johnsson.

If this could happen not only would I achieve my ultimate quest, but I would escape possible death and probable humiliation on the ski slopes of northern Italy. I read that last line of Johnsson's email again. I rather appreciated the fact that he referred to 'seeing' if Schumacher could beat me. There was, it appeared, a possible room for doubt.

If it were to happen – and there still remained a big 'if' – then I wanted first to pit my questionable skills against the man by driving a kart on his own circuit. Schumacher was not there, of course, but I wanted to get to know my now increasingly possible opponent using every tool at my disposal.

The people of Kerpen have every right to be proud of their first son. Once a year – or seemingly, bearing in mind how many times Schumacher has been world champion – the townsfolk gather to watch their own win the world title. If it is early in the morning, as it was in 2001 when Schumi's Ferrari took both the Japanese GP and the title in Suzuka, it meant breakfast, beer and a local disc jockey revving up the party atmosphere. In Kerpen they have New Year's Eve and F1 World Driver's Title Day.

Bidding Alexander farewell I entered the main reception of the kart centre and immediately observed Schumacher's 1996 Ferrari – the first Ferrari he drove since leaving Benetton – stuck to the wall like a spider. Beside this stood a waxwork model of Schumacher, complete in driver overalls.

Inside the centre a huge, indoor kart track can be found, complete with a massive Schumacher helmet in the centre of the circuit and walls adorned by posters and pictures of the German on various winners' podiums. Built seven years ago and opened by the man himself it also sports a Schumacher shop and a restaurant. 'Michael likes Italian food best of all,' explained the centre's manager. 'So that's why we have this.' He pointed to 'La Piazza', the centre's Italian restaurant.

The shop is devoted wholly to Michael Schumacher, save for a tiny corner in which various bits of brother Ralf Schumacher's merchandise can be bought. Elsewhere you can buy Michael towels, dressing gowns, baby grows, all kinds of posters and pictures and even Michael dolls. Making out that it was a present for my daughter I bought one of these. 'You want a Michael Barbie?' asked the shop assistant. I handed over my forty-five euros wondering why exactly I had decided to do this. I was, after all, a bit old for dolls, let alone the wrong sex, even if the slightly smiling Michael had more of the look of an action man. There he was, complete with red driver overalls, booties and holding his helmet in his hands.

Then I remembered I did exactly the same thing a couple of years before when, finding myself in Japan whilst writing a golf book which climaxed with a meeting with Tiger Woods, I bought a smiling, and indeed nodding, Tiger Woods doll. Michael and Tiger could adorn the window-sill of my study, I decided, when I returned home.

There is also a Michael Schumacher Museum at the kart centre. A Herr Rolf Bieler escorted me kindly around the premises, pausing at every exhibit for me to digest the history. At every turn there is film footage of a young Michael. One depicts images of him driving his first car, a small, red Fiat, at the age of just eleven, in a field. The Fiat now stands in the museum. Another shows him as a baby pushing a toy car around. A third made me stand and stare for quite a while as a feeling of foreboding increased.

There, amid the winter white of a heavy snowfall, was young Michael, aged ten years old, on skis and looking like Franz Klammer. Down he swept amid a mild snowstorm, bobble hat flapping in the wind, looking as if he had been born wearing skis. 'Ja, that's beside the Nurburgring,' Rolf explained, when he saw me staring at this particular film. 'Michael's always been very good at skiing.'

That, as I realised my first ever skiing lesson had not even been arranged, was precisely what I did not want to hear. I hoped to God Fredrik Johnsson could make it work for me in Paris. Moving quickly on I came across a room full of F1 cars. 'After every championship Michael likes to buy them and then place them in here,' Rolf added. There, gleaming under the museum's spotlights, were the 1994 Benetton, the car that gave Schumacher his first world title, plus the 1999, 2000, 2001 and 2002 red Ferraris, the latter three more world championship-winning cars. Enclosed behind numerous trophy cabinets were also a few examples of his winning cups, plates, shields and trophies, ranging from the Monaco GP in 1995 to the Australian GP in 1997, the Canadian GP in 2001 and the Spanish GP in 2002.

I was still gazing at all this silverware when Rolf beckoned me over in a rather animated fashion. 'Look what I have here,' he exclaimed. He held up a rather gaudy red, tinsel wig. I recognised it at once as the red wig Schumacher wore on the winner's podium at Sepang having won the Malaysian GP and his first world title for Ferrari in 2000. The rest of the Ferrari team, including Rubens Barrichello and Ross Brawn, who joined Schumacher on the podium, also wore the red wigs in celebration. There is a large picture of this hanging on the factory wall at Maranello.

'Put it on,' Rolf said. It was meant to be a suggestion but, in his forceful, Germanic way, it sounded more like an order. Whatever it was, it was a tone that begged for no debate. Feeling rather self-conscious, I placed it on my head while Rolf snapped away on a camera. 'Now you are like Michael,' he announced, rather pleased with the whole affair.

Actually, I was beginning to feel like a stalker. Here I was in Schumacher's home town photographed wearing his wig. What next, I wondered? Maybe I could go through his drawers, leave his pet rabbit boiling in a pot, appear at the foot of his bed?

Instead I thanked Rolf for his time and caught a cab. Apart from the main town of Kerpen there are five surrounding hamlets, including Kerpen-Sindorf, where the kart centre is, and Kerpen-Manheim, five miles away, where the most popular outdoor kart track in Germany can be found, and where a young Schumacher was discovered.

I had come to this track for two reasons: to race on the same circuit Schumacher returns each year to relive his childhood, and to meet those who had nurtured an incredible young talent twenty-five years previously. Peter Kaiser, the circuit manager, was there in welcoming mood when my taxi dropped me off in a large bowl of a valley surrounded by a thick set of trees.

The Schumacher family once lived no more than 100 yards from the 1100-metre kart track. Father Rolf used to manage the smaller hire-kart track next door. Schumacher's late mother, Elisabeth, rented and ran the pub-cum-restaurant which is dripping in her son's memorabilia.

It was here that Peter took me for a morning coffee and the chance to be introduced to Gerhard Noack, owner of the shop that sells the kart parts, and the man, more than anyone else, who set Schumacher on to the road of fulfilled dreams.

I explained to Gerhard, a fifty-two-year-old, chain-smoking, moustache-wearing man, that my German was *nicht so gut*. 'Ach, no problem,' he said, sounding as if he was about to suggest we spoke in English. 'Your German will be fine.'

This was not a good idea. My German, at the best of times, is very average, and then only after three or four days of acclimatisation in Germany. But on the first morning of my time in Germany, and after a very early start from England, I found smatterings of French creeping into my conversation. It wasn't helped by the fact that the restaurant owner and his friend, a retired airman, sat around the table too, half-listening and, when not eating or drinking their coffees, joining in. After five minutes of this Gerhard waved his hand nonchalantly and suggested he, myself and Peter retired to his office overlooking the track where we would be able to converse more quietly and, thanks to Peter's interpretation, more clearly.

Noack's office was full of yet more Michael artifacts, from trophies from way back to his early karting triumphs, to the engine from Schumacher's first Ferrari in 1996, plus a couple of dozen photographs of his former protégé.

'So, begin,' Gerhard announced, lighting up the first of many cigarettes and letting out a long and rather exaggerated puff. It turned out that his story began when the Schumacher family bought a kart off him in Kerpen. Within six months they were back knocking on Noack's door.

'They could not afford to keep on running the kart and wanted to sell it back to me. I had a better idea, though. I said you can keep the kart, but I get Michael.'

By this he did not mean literally. The Schumachers did not sell their son to Noack, merely loaned him. Observing my confused face Gerhard explained. 'You see, I'd already watched this young boy Michael Schumacher kart on an old circuit nearby and I could see he was good. So, my proposition to the Schumacher family was that I'd take him under my wing to make him a better racing driver. I had no children at the time, so I saw him as a son of mine.'

Every day after school Schumacher would report at the Kerpen-Manheim kart club. 'I sponsored him, his kart, even his overalls,' Noach continued. 'We raced every weekend and I was his manager and mechanic.'

And so began their journey, from eight-year-old boy to teenage star. 'Outside the kart he was like any other eight-year-old German boy. He liked his football, and he was rather quiet. Rather shy. But the person changed when he was in the kart and ready to race. You see, there were two Michaels. The one inside the kart knew he could beat anyone. And he did. All over Germany.' Two Michaels. Thank goodness he did not need to catch a taxi in Shanghai!

After seven Formula One world championships Schumacher is recognised to be the leader in driver fitness, in driver input into the mechanics of the car, and in pure driver intelligence in terms of handling a race. Gerhard explained that all these attributes were apparent even in the eight-year-old boy.

'Ah yes, he did lots of fitness when he was eight and nine. Can you believe that? Eight years old and he was already working out and concentrating on his physical fitness. He was by far the fittest boy I've ever come across.'

That wasn't all. 'You look at Michael now when he's racing and he always knows about the guy in front, and the guy behind. Normal juniors either crashed or just went off the track. That never happened to Michael. He's always been a clever driver. Others try and overtake as soon as possible, but Michael always picked his moments. Today it is just the same. He understands the whole race better than the others.'

I should have known. What possessed me even to think that with a little training I could make a good account of myself in the world of motor racing? Schumacher was the best through no accident. He merged his God-given talent with an incredible dedication and work ethic at an age when I was playing conkers in the school playground.

Peter Kaiser had been translating up to this point but now wanted to add his own observations on a man he also knew well. 'When Michael decides to do something he has to win. It doesn't matter if it's football, cards or skiing.' I flinched at the mention of skiing, thought about explaining my predicament to Peter, and then thought better of it.

'One of the many reasons why Michael has been world champion so many times is that he never thinks about world titles, only the next race. That's where all his focus centres on. His aim is to win the next race. If you keep on winning the next race then world titles take care of themselves.'

Kaiser laughed, muttered something in German to Noack, and then beckoned me to come a bit closer, as if he was about to convey a secret. 'Let me tell you a story that tells you everything you need to know about Michael,' he began.

'Last year he decided to enter the Winter Cup here at Kerpen-Manheim. [The Winter Cup is a low-key, annual competition for European karters held at Kerpen.] During the Saturday practice we both felt the kart was not fast enough. We worked on it throughout the rest of the day in order to improve it. That night we went to a friend's house to eat dinner. It must have been eleven o'clock when we sat down. Our friend and I talked about the weather, our children and all the usual conversations. Michael did not say a word. He just sat there, playing with his food and deep in thought.

'Then, after half an hour, he spoke. 'I think we need to move the seat further in front,' he said. So here we had a guy who had just won his sixth world Formula One title, and all he could think about was improving his chances in a karting event in Kerpen. Michael and I started work at seven o'clock the following morning, doing exactly what Michael suggested. That Sunday afternoon he won the final.' Kaiser and Noack both laughed at this and shook their heads. 'So, that year Michael wins not only the

Formula One World Championships, but also the Kerpen Winter Cup.'

Gerhard lit up another cigarette and took over the story again, with the aid of Peter's interpretation. 'That's Michael,' he said. 'Everything he does has to be approached with 100 per cent professionalism. Not only by himself, but by all those who work with him; 95 per cent will not do.'

Extraordinarily, the Kerpen-Manheim kart club has also seen brother Ralf Schumacher, as well as other F1 stars Heinz-Harald Frentzen and Nick Heidfeld, nurture their talents as junior karters. 'They were all exceptionally good drivers, make no mistake,' Gerhard pointed out. 'But none of them were like Michael. You could see it then and, of course, you can see it now.'

In the twenty years since Schumacher left Kerpen Noack has only come across one talent who reminds him of Michael. He is currently karting in Europe and making a very big name for himself. 'His name is Sebastian Vettel and I urge you to look out for him,' Gerhard advised. 'He reminds me so much of Michael. The same hunger, the same will to win, the same professionalism.'

At fifteen Schumacher took up a mechanics' apprenticeship at a Kerpen garage and started to drift away from Noack. Managed by Willie Weber he would venture into single-seater racing around Europe before realising his dream with a first drive of an F1 car at the Belgian Grand Prix at Spa in a Jordan car.

'I felt sad when he went his own way at first,' Gerhard admitted. 'But fledglings must fly from the nest. We're all very proud of Michael. And when he comes to see us he is the same person. Sure, he has changed a little because he is in his mid-thirties now. He's no longer a boy. We all change. But he is more or less the same. He speaks to the president of the kart club who was the same president when he was a boy. And he always sees me to tell his stories.'

He laughed at this point, let out a wheezy cough and slapped his thigh. 'The other year we went on a pub crawl. At midnight, after we had drunk a few beers, we decided to have a race here at the track. There are no lights so it was pitch black. Ralf spun off. So did I. In fact everyone did. Except Michael, of course. He won because he was the only man who could drive his kart on the track in the dark.'

Talking of which Gerhard and Peter had kindly arranged for me to sample the circuit for myself. It was still relatively early and the cold, winter chill, coupled with some overnight rain, had made the track treacherous in certain areas, notably the two corners shadowed by the nearby trees which kept the morning sun at bay later than anywhere else on the circuit.

Changing into my red, Maranello overalls, Peter leant me a helmet, asked one of his mechanics to lead me out to the garage and pointed towards a kart. 'That, my friend, is yours for an hour.'

It was a big enough challenge slotting into the seat. Like a foot shoe-horned into a boot, it took a little time and some far from gentle persuasion but, once I was in, there was absolutely no danger of my ever falling out of the seat. As the mechanic pushed me towards the track I was acutely aware of both Peter and Gerhard standing close by, their arms folded and their expressions revealing a weird interest in how this Englishman would fare.

I had not bragged about my driving prowess to them. How could I? Yet somehow I sensed they were expecting to be impressed. By the second corner they would have a pretty good idea. This was the first of the two slippery corners and it proved far too hard for the like of me. Round I span, punching the wheel in frustration and embarrassment, before continuing on my way, retracing the route Schumacher knew blindfolded. The rest of the first lap went okay until the second to last corner which, like the first, shaded area, resembled an ice rink. For the second time in the very first lap I span, ending up pointing in completely the wrong direction to the way I intended to drive.

Slowly, as I completed more laps, I picked up speed. There was a boy also karting on the track that morning. With large glasses behind his helmet he looked like Joe 90. I overtook him at one point, a feat that absurdly provided me with enormous pleasure. I looked across triumphantly at the boy as I sped past him in he straight, and my expression, half-masked by my helmet, said this: 'This may have been Michael's patch but now it's mine.' Ludicrously my confidence soared.

I still managed to spin on at least one in every fourth lap but, after completing forty of them, I pulled in to the pits happy that I had conquered Kerpen. 'So, you wanna know your best time?' Peter asked.

'Yes please,' I replied, as if Peter had just offered me a bag of sweets.

'55.6 seconds,' Kaiser said. 'Now do you wanna know Michael's best time here?'

'Why not?' I replied, my previous excitement replaced with foreboding.

'43.7 seconds, and that was in easier conditions than you when the track was completely dry and the weather was warmer.'

On the face of it, then, I was less than twelve seconds slower than Schumacher. Knock another, say, four seconds off because of the conditions, and I was down to within eight seconds of the maestro.

'What do you think, then, Gerhard?' I asked, my face beaming under the delusion that I had just excelled. 'Maybe you have discovered another driving superstar?'

Noack laughed so much he ended up suffering a major coughing fit. Eventually he spoke. 'You know, even if we give you eight seconds, that's eight seconds a lap, and the lap takes only forty-three seconds. So Michael is 20 per cent quicker than you. He would take just five laps to lap you. In a twenty-lap kart race you would be lapped four times. In a forty-lap race eight times. In a . . .'

I got the picture. Maybe I had come to Kerpen a little too late, say by around thirty-two years. Maybe if Gerhard had seen me as an eight-year-old, then maybe he would have said Michael Schumacher would be the next Ian Stafford?

Now both Peter and Gerhard were laughing as the taxi arrived to take me back to Cologne Airport. 'You are crazy,' Noack concluded, slapping me on the back. 'And you can kart a little. But you are no Michael Schumacher.'

My face dropped. Seeing this, Noack added a final statement.

'I'll tell you what. If it makes you happier I will leave you with this. Michael Schumacher is no Ian Stafford, either.'

It wasn't quite what I wanted to hear but, with the chance of challenging Schumacher looming fast, it still managed to sound profound.

chapter twenty one

HEAD TO HEAD WITH MICHAEL SCHUMACHER – 2

'Let me put it this way, Fredrik,' I reasoned down the end of a telephone line to a beleaguered Swede in Paris. 'If you can let me get a lap time, and persuade Michael to compare mine with his, not only is my quest achieved, but you will probably save my life.'

I am sounding increasingly desperate and becoming more dramatic by the second. I told the organiser of the event, Fredrik Johnsson, of my snap answer in Shanghai to Ferrari's suggestion, and the predicament I was potentially going to find myself in on the icy, danger-ridden slopes of the Italian Alps. 'This could be life or death, Fredrik,' I concluded.

Faced with such impassioned pleas Johnsson caved in just enough to present me with an opening. 'Okay, Ian, you come over and we will see what we can do,' he answered. 'But I'm not making any promises.'

If I had been on the Starship Enterprise, working with one of Niki Lauda's spangly-dressed stewardesses, I would have transferred myself immediately to the Stade de France. Instead I threw my racing overalls and Barrichello-signed helmet into a bag and headed off to catch the Eurostar. 'I'm going to whup Schumi's ass,' I declared to my sceptical wife as I bade her farewell.

She had been regretting ever mentioning the name Michael Schumacher to me for some time now. Together with my two children she watched from the kitchen window as I drove out of our drive and headed for the railway station, an expression of incredulity etched all over her face. As for the kids, well they had been here before. I had hugged them goodbye and gone off to get beaten up by Roy Jones junior, bouncered by the Australian cricket team, mauled by the Springboks and birdied by Tiger Woods. This, to them, was almost an everyday happening. Where's Dad? Oh, he's just gone to embarrass himself in front of Michael Schumacher.

Well, we would see. We would see.

The Race of Champions had been running for seventeen years. Initially conceived to be a shoot-out between the best rally stars in the world in Paris, it soon changed its venue to the Canary Islands, attracting many of the world's top racing stars from other disciplines. Past competitors in this 'Superstars' style event included the MotoGP world champion, Valentino Rossi, six-times Le Mans 24 Hours winner Tom Kristensen and four-times Nascar champ Jeff Gordon. This year, when the event would be staged for the first time at the Stade de France back in Paris, F1 stars David Coulthard, Jean Alesi, Felippe Massa and Schumacher would all attempt to wrestle away the domination of this event by rally drivers.

They would be up against the likes of the current world rally champion, Sebastian Loeb, the twice former champion Marcus Gronholm, from Finland, Britain's Colin McRae, the 1995 world rally champ, the two-times Nascar runner-up Jimmie Johnson, the 1998 IRL champion in America, Kenny Brack, who also won the prestigious 500-mile Indianapolis the following year, Tony Kanaan, the 2004 IRL champ, plus a few other top drivers from touring cars numbering sixteen in total. They would have a series of one-on-one shoot-outs in knockout stages before deciding who was the best rally driver on the night, and who was the best non-rally driver. The winners of each would then conclude the Saturday evening's entertainment, played out in front of 75,000 fans packed inside the venue of the 1998 World Cup football final, with a winner-takes-all climax.

On arriving at the stadium I collected my pass and, whilst waiting to meet Fredrik Johnsson and hear my fate, ventured out into the arena. Just five days previously the New Zealand All Blacks had trounced the French Les Bleues in a rugby international. Although some of the rugby markings were still visible, most of the paint had now been covered by an asphalt, figure-of-eight circuit laid across the turf, with a bridge in the middle for cars to speed over and under. It was, for someone quite used to witnessing football and rugby internationals here, a bizarre scene.

A man who rather resembled Bjorn Borg in his heyday walked up to me. 'You must be Ian,' he said. 'I'm Fredrik Johnsson.' I shook his hand so hard and for so long that the Swede almost had to wrench it away from my grasp before placing his shoulders back in their sockets. 'I have some good news for you,' he announced. 'You will be a co-driver in tomorrow's Race of Champions with Kenny Brack. That means that you will sit with him when he competes in the Nations Cup.'

Well, that was a welcome dessert, but what about the main course? Would he allow me on the track to record a lap time? 'I'm still working on that, Ian. I don't want you to die on the slopes, so

I'm just seeing what can be organised.' I felt tantalisingly close to taking on THE man now. So near, and yet still so far.

In the meantime I could at least find out more about Kenny Brack. 'Ah Kenny,' Fredrik said, with a smile. 'Great guy. Great enthusiasm. This, and hard work, got him to where he is. He had no support in Sweden, where he is from, so he went over to the States and made his name. You are very privileged to be sitting in the same car as him in a race. Not many will have done that with an Indy 500 winner.'

There was a 'but', though. 'I'm not sure how he's going to be. In the last race of last year he was involved in a huge crash. He hurt himself real bad and was in intensive care for five days. We were all so worried for him. No one thought he would survive. Then, a week later, my mobile rang. "Fredrik, it's Kenny,"' Johnson said, in a pained whisper as he imitated a stricken Brack. '"I don't think I can come this year to the Race of Champions." This phone call was about a fortnight before the event. We all thought he was going to die, and he was more worried about letting us down. He's quite a guy.'

Did Fredrik have any tips for me as Kenny's co-driver? 'Don't throw up over him.' Er, any more? 'Motivate him while he's driving, and look out in case the opponent touches a wall during a race. That's an immediate ten-second penalty and then Kenny can afford to slow down a little.'

He headed back to his temporary office deep in the bowels of the stadium to see if he could swing a lap or two my way that evening, while I went off to meet some of the drivers who were just arriving at the Stade de France.

David Coulthard saw me enter the room, waved and ambled over. 'How are your shoulders and biceps,' he asked, his wide grin revealing that he was teasing. DC was in high spirits, even if his time at McLaren was now down to its last couple of weeks. He could not officially make an announcement there and then, but he was confident he would be driving for Red Bull Racing, the Austrian outfit who bought out Jaguar a fortnight earlier, for the next season. After the individual 'Race of Champions' event he would be partnering Colin McRae and competing for Scotland in the Nations Cup. 'I'm going to rely on Colin to hold us up,' he said, winking at McRae who had joined us.

'We've got a problem, then,' McRae answered. 'I was rather banking on you holding me up.'

The Red Bull acquisition of Jaguar was good news for many. Much of Jaguar's workforce would be saved, the number of teams for the 2005 F1 season had not been reduced, and DC was not lost to the sport. A week after the Race of Champions his seat with Red Bull Racing was confirmed. Dave Pitchforth and Tony Purnell, with whom I had shared a lift in Shanghai, oversaw the changeover from Jaguar and Red Bull, and then were promptly sacked. Nav Sidhu, meanwhile, left to set up his own company. Why provide the likes of George Clooney and Brad Pitt while in the employment of an F1 team, he reasoned, when he can do it off his own back?

Back in Paris, meanwhile, I was introduced to Kenny Brack. 'It's going to be very challenging,' he explained. 'It will be down to the guy who doesn't make mistakes. He's got to be on the limit, but not over it. I usually do well in these events. That's because I was brought up driving old Saabs on icy roads in Swedish winters. The problem is I'm a bit rusty. I've not driven for a year, save for one outing in a Porsche race a few weeks ago.'

The year is down to his accident. What did he break? 'It's easier to say what I didn't?' he answered, with a wry grin. 'I broke everything except my right arm and left leg. The rest was in pieces. It's been a long road since.'

Could he recall the crash? He shook his head vigorously. 'Uh-uh. All I know is that it was a collision with Tomas Scheckter.'

Tomas Scheckter. As in the son of Jody. I thought about

recounting my day on the farm story for Kenny's interest, then thought against it.

'Our cars touched, I went airborne and smashed into a post. Once you're up in the air in a racing car you know you're in trouble. I got knocked out and was in a coma for five days.'

There is a footnote to this painful anecdote. Kenny's wife was about to give birth to their first child. While Kenny lay in bed on the ninth floor, with a broken back, both legs and arms sticking up in the air in plaster, and tubes inserted into most of his orifices, his baby daughter was born in the same hospital six floors below him. 'It's a week I'm never likely to forget,' he added.

Of course, this is a blip – albeit a major blip – on an otherwise successful career. How did a little-known Swede end up not only racing in America, but winning the Indy 500? 'I was a successful Formula 3000 driver. I well remember racing against David Coulthard, for example, when we were both in our early days, but I had no money and no sponsors. After all, it's hard to get someone to sponsor me £4 million so that I could drive a poor car, finish well down the field and disappear off the face of the earth. I went to America and got paid straight away. Lots of young drivers thought F1 was the only thing to do, me included. But Indycar and Nascar and, to a lesser extent, Champ Car is very fast, very exciting and very competitive. And they pay you. That's how it should be. It shouldn't be where you, the driver, have to bring $10 million to the party. Anyway, I've done okay racing in America, and I managed to win the biggest race in the world.'

Back in Sweden Brack is now a household name as a result of his American feats. 'That's one of the strange things about Sweden. If you go abroad and do well then you are seen as a God. If you stay at home and achieve then they kick you. Sweden is the land of average. Everybody thinks it is a wonderful place to live, but that's people who don't actually live there.'

Brack was being ushered out of the room but, before he left for the night, he had some words of advice for his co-driver. 'Make sure you have a good crap before you get in the car, Ian,' he advised. 'We need to be as light as possible.' Er, right, I'll see what I can do on that score, Kenny. 'Also, if you're going to puke, puke either before or after our race, but not during, and definitely not all over me.' Okay. 'Oh, and bring a CD to play while we're racing. Bring some Motörhead. You can be in charge of that.'

Right. It wasn't looking too likely that Kenny, in his rusty, recovering state, was going to win the Race of Champions, but it looked like it was going to be a lot of fun attempting to do so.

In the corner of my eye I could see Fredrik Johnsson waving his hands at me. 'You're in luck,' he shouted, with a beaming smile. 'In a moment of madness I've managed to get you a ROC car. You've got to get changed into your overalls right now, get down to trackside and get on with it.'

Waiting for me by the start was the 'Fast and Speed' racing car team from the Netherlands. They were responsible for the ROC buggies, of which there just four in the world. They would, in part, be used during the following night's racing, and can be best described as a dune buggy. Although a Ferrari 360 Modena Challenge, a Citroen Xsara WRC and a Peugeot 307 WRC would also be used during the event the demands of the circuit, with its tight bends and bridge that demanded a super-strong suspension, the 4 cylinder, 170 HP, 1100 CC buggy was the fastest vehicle of the lot.

'This,' said Jonny Hakvoort, in the kind of Euro-pop accent Dutch people tend to have, 'is the car Michael Schumacher will be racing in tomorrow. So, guess what. Please do not crash it, yes? Otherwise we are all in big shit.'

Fair enough. I'd been here before, of course, what with the F1 Jaguar and the Ford World Rally Car. This time, though, was even more pressurised. This time I was driving Schumacher's car, inside a now pretty dark Stade de France. Moreover the weather had turned bitterly cold, so cold in fact that a drizzle of rain was turning to sleet.

I placed my Barrichello helmet on my head and looked at the buggy as its engine was revved up for my benefit. The Stade's lights were now blazing brightly as the last remnant of daylight disappeared. Johnsson appeared to watch the forthcoming laps. He looked nervous. That made me feel nervous. Maybe I had oversold my driving ability to him? Maybe? Definitely!

Fast and Speed's Fritz Duizendstar, a three-times European Auto-cross champion, put his hand on my shoulder for a final briefing. 'You've got to be careful out there,' he warned. 'There's some dust on the track, it's new tarmac so there'll be no grip. It's freezing conditions now and that rain is turning to sleet. It looks like ice is appearing. Oh, and it's a small, tight track, so you can't see too far ahead and plan your corners.'

Great! Apart from that it should be a piece of cake. Or *tarte*, as they say in these parts. The windchill meant that the temperature was well below freezing now as the Red Helmet climbed into the ROC buggy, pressed his foot down on the gas to rev up the engine, and gave Jonny, Fritz and Fredrik the thumbs up.

I had been warned that the conditions were slippery, but not like an ice rink. Oversteer was the order of the night. Every time I reached a corner the back end of the buggy was sliding round at twice the speed of the front. At first I manoeuvred the car gingerly around the circuit. The gently falling sleet had now transformed into a driving sheet of ice. My hands, gripping the wheel, were turning numb with the cold air blasting through the open grill that acted as a non-existent windscreen.

Gradually, I began to speed up. This was bad in terms of the icy winds buffeting my hands, my body and, once I had opened my visor to prevent it steaming up, my face, but it was good news if I wanted to lay down any kind of marker for Schumacher. That's if he turned up, of course. My initial lap times were recorded around the one minute, twenty second mark, but slowly this time decreased.

Twice my buggy caressed a wall of tyres, which would have been an immediate ten-second penalty during the race, and once I slid on to a grassy patch when the buggy refused to turn a corner, but after a dozen laps I was beginning to get the hang of it.

Round and round I went, down the home straight in which you could accelerate up to 70 mph, tightly around corners when sometimes your speed nose-dived to 20 mph, and over the bridge when, if you were driving fast enough, your car temporarily left the surface and enjoyed the briefest of flights.

After twenty-five laps everyone started to wave me in. Apart from those couple of minor prangs I had managed to deliver the ROC buggy, indeed Schumacher's buggy, in one piece. The relief, I can assure you, was as much as it was the day I safely returned the Jaguar F1 car to its rightful owners.

'One minute, six seconds,' Jonny announced. 'That's your fastest time and, in these conditions, that's not bad. I think Schumacher's got a big problem on his hands.'

I decided I liked Jonny. He was friendly, he was helpful and, best of all, he could bullshit with the best.

I received a call from Fredrik Johnsson the following morning just as I was arriving at the Stade de France. 'Now we're in big trouble,' he told me. 'They've been working on Schumacher's buggy all night trying to repair it after you had a go in it.'

'What? But I hardly touched the walls!'

'Well, Jonny and the crew have had no sleep at all. It's touch and go if the car will be ready. And we'll be expecting Michael any minute now.'

I scampered down to trackside and went underneath the stands where the temporary pits and garages were. 'Hi champ,' a beaming Jonny greeted me. I told him Johnsson's story. 'Ah no, he's having a joke with you,' Jonny laughed. I cursed Fredrik and then realised how grateful I was that it had been, after all, just a joke.

Out on the track Kenny Brack was walking the circuit. I felt, as his co-driver in the Nations Cup, that I should be doing the walk with him. 'Have you been yet, like I told you to do before we drive tonight?' he asked, as an opening gambit.

It is probably the first time in my life that someone I had met for the first time the day before was already enquiring about my bodily movements. 'Oh, and where's that Motörhead CD?'

Was Kenny feeling good? 'Not bad, but those rally guys will be tough to beat. I think they came out of their mothers' wombs sideways when they were born.' Then he made an important decision. 'I am officially appointing you as my Chief Motivational Officer. That okay with you?' Sure, Kenny. We were going to kick ass that night.

It was at that point Schumacher appeared, surveyed the circuit, and headed off to take a few practice laps before the night's main event.

My opportunity to talk to the man had finally arrived. I had not tried too hard to do so before during my year of spills and thrills but now, somehow, seemed to be the perfect moment. Having just flown in from America he had left it all a little tight and, in the briefest of conferences later, did not sound too confident. 'It's not been the best preparation for me, and I'm sure the rally drivers will beat me up on this type of circuit, but it will be fun and I shall try my hardest to win.'

There was no time to explain all my adventures, the long road I had taken to reaching this point, and the various drives and cars that had come my way in the process. But there was time to see the real Michael Schumacher. The man behind the cold, Teutonic image who sets out to win and destroys everything in his path.

'Well, people don't know me, do they?' he reasoned, in flawless

English. 'My family at home know me. My family at Ferrari know me. But the public can only go on how I'm portrayed in the media. You see, right now you are in the company of a big kid. You have to be when you are driving. You have to get the thrill out of it, otherwise what's life all about? At the same time it is also a serious sport that gives me enormous satisfaction. Racing is the only thing I know I'm good at, at least to the level I have reached.'

Who, then, is the real Michael Schumacher? 'The real Michael Schumacher is just like your neighbour,' he replied, with a shrug of his slender shoulders. 'I'd be a very boring person to write about if I didn't happen to drive racing cars. People are constantly looking for something special but I'm an ordinary husband and father, with the same values as anyone else. My perfect day is to play with my kids in the morning, have a game of soccer after lunch, maybe go horse-riding, spend some time with my dogs, chickens and rabbits, and have a barbecue with my family in the evening.' He smiled, an almost apologetic smile. 'That's me.'

Sounded pretty idyllic to me, although I bet he has the fastest animals in Switzerland, where he lives. Imagine keeping a Schumacher chicken? You could forget about eating it because you would never catch it in the first place.

His ordinariness, he argues, helps to make him the champion he is. 'I think my major attribute as a driver, apart from the thirty years I've been racing, is that I'm naturally calm and balanced, and much of this can be put down to the life I lead away from F1. The support of my family is crucial. At home I recharge my battery so that I can return to work refocused. It may seem odd after all these years but whereas I'm built for racing cars I'm still not comfortable in the spotlight. The real me is either at home or sitting in the cockpit of my Ferrari.

'Driving is the most natural thing in the world to me. It's like walking, or breathing. Anyone can become a good racing driver, but to become an F1 driver it has to be that natural. When I fly a helicopter I often try to get it to hover a couple of metres above the ground. I fail to achieve this because I am not a natural helicopter pilot. But in a car I can do anything.'

Oh yeah? Well, let's see if he can beat one minute and eight seconds, then. Actually, I didn't quite put it like that. In fact I didn't put it at all. As he was competing in the Race of Champions I figured he'd be trying his best to record the fastest lap possible in any case. I felt it only right not to place a heavy slice of extra pressure on the man an hour before the start of the competition.

The Stade de France was filling up fast, now. The predominantly French crowd were coming in their thousands to see the showdown of showdowns: Schumacher, the F1 world champion, against Loeb, the world rally champion. They got their way when, in a special head-to-head, Schumacher defeated Loeb 2–1 in a best of three contest. Loeb was consoled by the fact that at least he had won the rally drivers' section.

Schumacher, in contrast, was beaten in the racing drivers' final by a little-known Finn named Heikki Kovalainen, who boasted beforehand the smallest profile out of all sixteen contestants in the Race of Champions. He was a champion in the 2004 World Series by Nissan but this, compared to Schumi and Loeb, was small fry. When he beat Schumacher he celebrated by enacting a small dance on top of his car. When he then beat Loeb in the rally versus racing final, he reproduced the jig again. Along the way he had seen off David Coulthard, Jean Alesi, Schumacher and Loeb. Not a bad quartet of scalps on one night.

My man Kenny Brack lost out in the first round to the 2004 Champ Car champion, Sebastian Bourdais. 'I crashed that bloody buggy,' he told me. 'One mistake in this and you're out.' I considered advising him about the ROC buggy but thought better of it, especially as I would soon be sitting alongside him in the Nations

Cup.

I had worked out that if 'we' – that was Kenny and myself, plus 2004 DTM champion Mattias Ekstrom and his co-driver – could beat the Finns in the first round, we would most probably be facing the Scottish team of Coulthard and McRae in the second. That was something I would have dearly loved to experience, especially if we could get the better of DC. A few comments afterwards would have repaid him for his obvious glee in my painful reaction to working out with him in Monaco.

There was one, minor problem, however. First we had to beat a Finnish team of Kovalainen, the man of the moment, and twice former world rally champion, Marcus Gronholm. Ekstrom lost to Gronholm in the first heat, which meant that Brack and I had to see off the Race of Champions individual champion in the second heat, this time driving the Ferrari 360 Modena Challenge.

I was forced to sign a waiver. At least, I thought, as I scrawled a nervous signature on the paper, this would be the last waiver I would be completing for a while, certainly in a motor sport context. Kenny came up to me and grabbed my shoulders. 'Give me some advice, partner,' he said.

I wasn't sure whether he was joking or not, but I responded, in a fashion. 'Er, well Kenny, keep it smooth and keep it steady. Don't, repeat don't, touch the walls. If we are nice and careful we will win.' I didn't feel this was Churchillian enough, so added, 'I want you to do this for your country, and for your family, Kenny. But, most of all, I want you to do it for yourself. You owe it to yourself to go out and kick his butt.' I raised my voice to pronounce those last three words. '*Kick his butt*.' Kenny blinked a few times and looked aghast. I'm sure he was convinced he would be spending the next few minutes with a madman.

Matters got worse once we had made our way out into the open area. As we revved our engines up on the starting line, and Kenny's hands began to grip the steering wheel, a multitude of flashlights dotted around the stadium began to blind us. I looked across and saw the Finn, Kovalainen, exchanging glances. 'Don't mess with the big boys.' That was the message I tried to convey as he caught my stare. 'Well, okay then, don't mess with Kenny.'

The starting lights flashed and we were off. Finding ourselves slightly behind after the first of two laps in the race I was about to shout some unwanted advice when something utterly stupid happened. I had completely forgotten to leave my mobile phone behind in the co-drivers' dressing room. It was now nestling in my pocket. Worse still, it had been left on.

Of all the times in the world for someone to choose to ring me, this was most definitely not one of them. We were hurtling around a Stade de France circuit in front of 75,000 fans in the middle of a heated race which we were on the way to losing. And now my mobile phone was blasting out its high-pitched tune.

Kenny, despite the situation he found himself in, looked across at me and the phone. 'Aren't you gonna answer it, then?' he said.

'Er, thanks Kenny, but I'll leave it until after the race.' Can you just imagine it? 'Hello. Hello. Sorry, can't really talk right this second. Bit busy. What? Oh, well I'm in a racing car inside the Stade de France competing in the Nations Cup for Sweden against Finland, there's 75,000 in the stands, millions of television viewers, and I'm distracting my driver.'

We lost to Mr Golden Bollocks from Finland! I was concerned that Kenny might have been a tad irritated by my untimely phone call. 'That's the first time that's ever happened to me,' he said as we clambered out of the car. 'And we never played Motörhead, did we?' He was laughing as he said all this. For Kenny Brack, after spending five days in a coma less than a year before, was just happy to be back behind the wheel of a racing car.

Jonny and Fredrik were standing in the drivers' tunnel, the latter clasping a piece of paper in his hand. 'Okay, Ian,' Fredrik said.

'Here is the big result. Ian Stafford: Fastest lap: one minute, sixseconds. Michael Schumacher: fastest lap: fifty-two seconds. I hereby declare Michael Schumacher the winner. But I also congratulate Ian for making sure he does not now have to break both legs on the ski slopes.'

I'd forgotten about my forthcoming winter sports nightmare in the heat of the battle and was very, very grateful to have found a way round what would have been an unmitigated disaster.

Jonny, meanwhile, was shaking his head at all this. 'Maybe, but Ian's conditions were far more taxing than Michael's,' he argued. 'Tonight there was plenty of grip on the track, and no dust, and it was a lot warmer, too. There was no ice, no sleet, and much better driving conditions in general.'

So what was he saying? 'I'm saying that we should knock five seconds off your time because of the lack of grip, three because of the dust, another three because the air temperature was a lot warmer and another three because there was no sleet and no ice. What does that make?'

Fourteen, I answered. Hey! Hold on a minute! Knock fourteen seconds off my time and that means Michael and I have drawn!

Jonny hadn't finished. 'And as you improved your lap time from one minute twenty to one minute six, you win the most improved driver at the Race of Champions award.'

Fredrik started to laugh. Jonny and I followed suit. Then I saw Schumacher again, this time watching recordings of the finals on a TV monitor.

'Congratulations,' I said to him, as we shook hands. 'Well done for beating Loeb. But I have to tell you that you and I drew in our head-to-head.'

He didn't actually know about 'our' head-to-head, but when I told him the times, and how we had deducted fourteen seconds off mine, he refused to accept this.

'Uh-uh,' said the greatest motor-racing driver of all time. 'The records show that I was faster than you. If you had worse driving conditions that's tough. It's your bad luck, and I'm sorry for that, but I won by fourteen seconds.'

And with that he was off, smiling at me, enjoying the moment's joust, and seemingly grateful to add the prized scalp of the Red Helmet to his many other less notable achievements.

Can you believe it? Controversy had struck right at the very end of my journey. Could Schumacher really take the victory? Didn't I have a strong case? I looked around for some support, but the other drivers were already packing their bags and heading off into the night. 'What about a rematch?' I shouted, as the red back of Schumacher turned the corner and disappeared.

I sat down on a bench in the co-driver's dressing room, alone and sweating in my overalls. My forehead was drenched, my hair wildly misplaced. All in all it had been a bizarre night, what with mobile phones ringing and world champions claiming a win over the forty-year-old English bloke who suddenly recalled how all this had begun now that I had reached my journey's end.

A year earlier my wife had accused me of being Michael Schumacher. I had set out to prove not only man's superiority, but my superiority on the roads. It had taken me to some far-flung places, with some far-flung people, but if there was one common denominator it was, save for my defeat of the elder, Kiwi version of Michael Schumacher, this: that I had been beaten by everybody in every type of racing car; that I had been humiliated and criticised by all sorts of people, both male and, yes, female; and that being a top-class racing driver required a degree of skill and talent far, far beyond my reach. There! I've said it.

And yet. Right at the end, when reality and fact appeared to have merged with fantasy and fiction, I deluded myself into believing that I had a case to say I had matched the greatest racing driver in the world.

Then the cold air of the Paris night hit me square in the face. Matched Michael Schumacher! Now that's really silly. I couldn't even match karters at Buckmore Park. I concerned Juan Pablo Montoya so much with my driving he turned abusive. I couldn't even get close to Markko Martin.

It was now obvious to me. My wife had uttered the first correct thing ever in our car with me at the wheel. I quite clearly was not Michael Schumacher, and it had taken me a whole year to prove a point she had made twelve months previously.

Well, I consoled myself, as I traipsed away from the Stade de France and along a St Denis pavement on a now miserable, cold night.

At least I was still the best driver in my house!

EPILOGUE

It was the week before Christmas. Some snow had already fallen in west Kent, and there was a cold, winter chill in the air. A CD of Christmas carols was playing on the car's music system and as we made the short journey to a nursery to purchase a tree the whole family hummed along to the annual selection of seasonal tunes.

I felt happy with my lot. The past year had been a blast. I had got to do things I had never dreamt of doing. I had driven the most unbelievable cars, raced with some of the world's most unbelievable drivers, and visited some of the most unbelievable corners of the world.

Best of all, better than all the other experiences put together, I had found a way of pitting my skills against Michael Schumacher at one of the great stadiums in one of the great cities.

The funny thing was, now that it was all over, I wasn't missing any of it. I wasn't missing the nerves that consumed my body every time I sat in a racing car. I wasn't missing the possibility that I could actually kill myself, the very thought that appeared to light a racing driver's fuse. I wasn't missing the competitiveness, and this was coming from a competitive person. I wasn't even bothered about being forty any more.

Right then, I couldn't think of a better thing to be doing than collecting a Christmas tree with my family a week before Christmas.

The car in front came to a sudden halt for no apparent reason, causing me to press my feet down furiously on to my brakes. We stopped a few inches away from piling into the back of the other car. I let out a sigh of relief.

'That's what happens when you're driving too fast,' my wife suggested.

We pulled into the nursery, parked the car and got out.

'Come on,' I said, with a smile and an arm around her. 'Let's go and get us a tree.'

ACKNOWLEDGEMENTS

A big thank you to the following, without whose help none of what you have read would have taken place. The list is in chronological, not preferential order.

Bill and Tom Sisley at Buckmore Park; Ken Bowes, and everyone at the Silverstone Drive School; Sonia Irvine at the Amber Lounge; Grand Prix Racewear at Silverstone; Greg Billings and Sandy Myhre in Auckland; Chris and Tish Amon in Taupo; Michael and Jill Schumacher in Auckland; Robert Lee at Karting Direct, Penrose, Auckland; Sir Jack Brabham; Peter and Beverley Brock in Nutfield; Ron Walker in Melbourne; Jaguar Racing; Martin Brundle; Aled Rees at Vodafone; Patrick Gosling; Mark Thompson from Getty Images; David Coulthard; David Cawthorne; Alex Wooff at Formula One Management; Bernie Ecclestone; Budweiser; Juan Pablo Montoya; Niki Lauda; Mark Wilford, Malcolm Wilson and everyone at the Ford World Rally Team; Peter Philips, Clare Williams and everyone else at the BMW Williams F1 team; Markko Martin; Jody Scheckter and everyone at Laverstoke Park; Sir Stirling Moss; Nigel Mansell and everyone at Woodbury Park; Jenson Button; Jules Kulpinski; Gerhard Noack and Peter Kaiser in Kerpen; Fredrik Johnsson, the Fast and Speed team and everyone connected to the Race of Champions; Kenny Brack; Cecile Simon; Michael Schumacher.

A special thanks to the *Mail on Sunday* and its Sports Editor, Malcolm Vallerius, who allowed me time and gave me opportunities to research this book. Also to the country's leading motor sport journalists – especially Ray Matts, Kevin Garside,

Stan Piecha, Byron Young, Richard Williams, Bob McKenzie – and others for their support.

Special thanks also go to Nav Sidhu for producing so many miracles; to Robert Kirby, my agent; and to my editor, Hannah MacDonald, who forced me to complete many more laps in search of the chequered flag, and everyone else at Ebury Press involved in this project.

Finally, to my wife, Karen, and my children, Charlotte and Harry, who allowed the man in the house to act like a man! (Read what you may into that.) Although their scepticism drove me on, their patience, understanding and tolerance were the true reasons why I was able, once again, to pretend to be someone else. Without them, none of this would have been possible, nor worthwhile.